Detroit
Reprints
in
Music

Frederick Freedman, General Editor
Case Western Reserve University

BARTÓK STUDIES

COMPILED
AND
EDITED
BY
TODD CROW

Detroit Reprints in Music
INFORMATION COORDINATORS
1976

To Linda, Evelyn, and Daniel

CONTENTS

INTRODUCTION

Béla Bartók would have been astounded to know that only ten to fifteen years after his death, he, with Stravinsky, would be the only composers of this century to claim a significant number of works in the standard repertory of orchestras, soloists, and chamber groups. And as his musical works came to be more widely performed, a concurrent stream of research into his life and works produced an unusually large body of scholarly material. Our present knowledge of Bartók is in no small measure due to the exhaustive efforts of a number of Hungarian musicologists who have dedicated themselves to the legacy of their country's most venerated musician. The reverence accorded to Bartók by contemporary Hungarian scholars is a reflection of the composer's present day stature, a position which places him in the line of Hungary's greatest historical figures—Rákóczi, Széchenyi, Petőfi, Kossuth, Ady.

Hungarian musicology began with the scientific methodology used by Bartók and Zoltán Kodály for their collecting of native folk music during the early years of the twentieth century. Since the time of their discoveries Hungarian students of music have been schooled in the traditions of Hungarian folk music with the same emphasis as that imparted to the study of Western art music. As stated by many commentators, Bartók typifies the synthesis of Western art music and fundamentally Eastern folk music. The resultant intellectual and spiritual affinity for this duality, which Hungarian scholars are uniquely qualified to discuss, give to their research a validity that comes only from years of contact with this musical heritage. Only in recent years has the English-speaking public been able to partake of this vast reservoir of Hungarian Bartók scholarship. It is the editor's contention that the present volume constitutes an important contribution to furthering the dissemination of Hungarian research, much of which has not been published in English previously. Many of the authors of the essays in this volume were at one time students at the Royal Ferenc Liszt Academy of Music in Budapest and were either under the influence of Bartók himself or his tradition. The knowledge they provide must necessarily assume special significance.

Much of the current research is conducted at the two Bartók Archives located in New York and Budapest. From the source material available at these two archives, investigators have uncovered many facts about the composer and his music including some of the documents, letters, and biographical information in this volume. In addition, the two archives have provided sources for the publication of Bartók's ethnomusicological writings, most of which were never printed during his lifetime. Except for one short period in his youth and another in the earlier years of his career (before attending the Academy of Music in Budapest), Bartók's life has been considerably documented. The copious work done by the dedicated Bartók scholar, János Demény, is expected to result in a full scale documentary biography in the near future.

The articles of the present volume are gathered from *The New Hungarian Quarterly* with the object of presenting a wide cross-section of, primarily, Hungarian thought on Bartók with viewpoints of both scholars and artists represented.

The New Hungarian Quarterly is essentially a continuation of its English-language predecessor, *The Hungarian Quarterly*, which was first published in the spring of 1936. As is stated on the inside cover of each issue of *The Hungarian Quarterly*, the object of the periodical was "to spread knowledge of Danubian and Central European affairs and to foster cultural relations between Hungary and the Anglo-Saxon world." The journal continued to appear through 1942 when wartime circumstances forced its cessation. Publication of *The New Hungarian Quarterly* began in September, 1960, and has continued uninterrupted since that time. A principle objective of the journal is to present a diverse picture of contemporary Hungarian thought from prominent specialists in literature, the arts, and the social sciences. Although occasional articles are by British and American authors, the contributors are primarily Hungarian. A great majority of the articles appear for the first time in English in *The New Hungarian Quarterly*.

The Editorial Board of the journal consists of an impressive list of Hungary's most distinguished men of letters. The musical representative on the Board until his death in January, 1973, was Professor Bence Szabolcsi, an internationally known scholar and dean of Hungarian musicologists. Several of his articles appear in the present volume.

The articles selected offer a many-sided view of Bartók. All but one of the authors are of Hungarian birth and all have distinguished themselves in their respective fields. Those who have written essays on the history and theory of Bartók's music enjoy widespread reputations not only in the field of Bartók scholarship but in other areas of musical research as well. In addition to the various documents, letters, remembrances, assessments, and theoretical discussions, contributions by two of Hungary's leading poets are included.

The articles republished here are from the period 1961-1973 and are arranged into six groups. The first group, on Bartók's musical style, contains four essays. The three by Professor Szabolcsi include a brief discussion of Bartók's compositional methods, an analysis of *The Miraculous Mandarin* (one of the most penetrating of Szabolcsi's writings), and an equally important essay on Bartók and natural philosophy. The latter two articles vividly detail the various "elemental forces" which tend to underlie all of Bartók's compositions.

The essay by Lendvai, perhaps Hungary's most brilliant Bartók theorist, is an introduction to his "Golden Section" theory which has become a landmark in Bartók scholarship. The theory relates Bartók's choice of scales, chordal structures, and harmonic and formal procedures to the principle of the Golden Section, which is described as a ratio which divides a given distance into two parts whereby the proportion of the whole length to the larger part equals the proportion of the larger to the smaller part. The author contends that most of Bartók's music after 1926 (and some earlier works as well) exhibit Golden Section characteristics. Lendvai's use of the Golden Section principle in the analysis of Bartók's music has been the source of much controversy. Bartók himself never wrote or verbalized any detailed theories of composition (with the exception of specific uses of folk music). Therefore, Lendvai's systematization of Bartók's formal and harmonic structures must be recognized as only an ingenious product of the theorist and not based upon a prescription by the composer. Nevertheless, the approach is intriguing and one profits by the close examination of Lendvai's methods for insights not only into Bartók's music but into earlier music, especially music of the Classic Era and sonata form in particular.

The second group of articles discusses Bartók in relation to his precursors and contemporaries. Kecskeméti comments upon Bartók's reverence for Liszt and specifically upon two influential aspects of Liszt's art: the less well-known later works that have begun to receive attention only within the past twenty years, and the Faust legend from which many parallels can be drawn between the two masters. Bónis' article describes Wagner's influence on the young Bartók and the recurrence of Wagnerian traits in such later works as *The Wooden Prince* and *The Miraculous Mandarin*. Kárpáti explores the relation of Bartók to Stravinsky and Schönberg, and assesses Bartók's position in the context of twentieth-century music. Although the influence of Bach, Beethoven, Debussy, Strauss, and Kodály is not discussed at length by the authors in this group, various other articles in this volume touch on facets of their relationship to Bartók, and assist in completing a picture of those most influential in determining the course of Bartók's musical maturation.

The third group contains, for the first time in English, the libretti for two of Bartók's dramatic works, *The Wooden Prince* and *The Miraculous Mandarin*.

The fourth section includes Bartók's famous 1911 essay on Liszt, followed by a selection of letters from friends, many of whom are among the most famous musicians of the twentieth century: Darius Milhaud, Francis Poulenc, Joseph Szigeti, Wilhelm Furtwängler, Eugene Ormandy, Yehudi Menuhin, and others. Liebner's study is in two parts, the first offering insights into a recently disclosed fifth movement to the *Suite*, Op. 14, and the second part containing texts of Bartók's last American radio interviews. The section closes with Ruffy's discussion of Bartók's will and of the problems relating to the Bartók estate. Although only the Hungarian viewpoint is expounded here, equally valid arguments expressing the American position have been articulated by officials of the New York Bartók Archives. Needless to say, it is hoped that the two sides will soon reach an accord.

The fifth group contains aspects of a more personal nature, including remembrances by Bartók's elder son, Béla, and by a former piano student, Lajos Hernádi. Hernádi's article is especially illuminating in that it is the only one in this volume dealing with Bartók as a pianist and pedagogue. For nearly thirty years Bartók taught piano at the Royal Ferenc Liszt Academy of Music where he trained a great number of musicians, some of whom became professors at the Academy, and many of whom distinguished themselves as pianists. It is even possible that Bartók's greatest influence today is not as a composer but rather as a piano pedagogue. Not since Bach has any composer systematized keyboard technique and provided a textbook of compositional procedures so well as Bartók presents in the six volumes of *Mikrokosmos*.

The fifth group continues with Gerald Abraham's review of Bartók's contact with English musicians in a discussion of the composer's trips to England in 1904, 1922, 1934, and 1938. The following three articles consider the events surrounding Bartók's participation in the League of Nations' *Comité de Coopération Intellectuelle* which sat in Geneva in the summer of 1931. At the time of his election to the *Comité* Bartók immediately voiced scepticism, noting the futility of "lofty notions" when not coupled with practical methods for solving the world's problems.[1] Bartók's prediction came true as the committee wallowed primarily in procedural matters.[2] However, as a result of his participation, Bartók was able to renew his acquaintance with Thomas Mann. As demonstrated in the recollections of Yolan Hatvany and Mann himself, the mutual admiration between Mann and Bartók ran very deep. The two men met occasionally at subsequent meetings of the *Comité* during the next five years. Of special interest in the Hatvany article is a rare display of Bartókian extroversion as shown in his willingness to play the piano for three hours in response to Mann's seemingly insatiable musical appetite.

The final article of the fifth group contains the text of an interview which originally appeared in the May 1932 issue of *Nouvelle Revue de Hongrie*. For Bartók to grant an interview was rare, and one learns much of his character, interests, and mode of thinking from this important and, until recently, unavailable (to English-speaking readers) source. The sincerity and integrity with which he speaks of his love for folk music and its relation to art music reveals the dedication he gave to all facets of his musical life. Included in this interview are some of Bartók's comments on aspects of contemporary music and thoughts on the art of composition. "It is not so much the theme which matters but rather what the artist can make of it . . . Let us recall how many formulae Johann Sebastian Bach . . . borrowed from his contemporaries and predecessors. The big test of a real talent will be the form he lends to this loan." Indeed, in his own music, the penchant for variation, for full development of ideas and scorn for mere repetition, the urgent need to explore all possibilities, is indicative of the standard Bartók set for himself and proposed for others.

The final group of articles explores Bartók's position today and includes an essay on past and present reactions to his music, a Marxist-humanist discourse on Bartók's significance in Hungarian history by Hungary's greatest Marxist philosopher, the late György Lukács, and a survey of Bartók scholarship through 1961. Bartók has been the source of inspiration for many Hungarian poets, and it is fitting that poems by Illyés and Nagy are included in this section. The group also contains a short tribute to Bartók by István Láng, one of Hungary's more important younger composers. Láng's sympathetic appreciation is indicative of the admiration that Bartók commands from

---

1 *Béla Bartók Letters*, ed, János Demény (London: Faber & Faber; NY: St. Martin's Press, 1971), 221. [Letter to János Buşiţia.]

2 Ibid., 211-16. [Letter to his Mother.]

the younger generation of Hungarian composers. Since Bartók adamantly refused to accept pupils in composition, he left no direct disciples. Therefore, his influence on the younger generation is predominantly as a spiritual father rather than as a creator of more direct or tangible musical models. His music, so cosmopolitan and individual, despite its inevitable relationship to the folk idiom, defies imitation. Láng notes that contemporary Hungarian music has, and always will, retain a special national character. Even though many of the composers have turned their eyes to the West, to the music of Webern and his disciples, and more recently, to the progressive experiments occurring in Warsaw, Darmstadt, and other European musical centers of the avant-garde, a sense of tradition links them to Bartók.

Many of the articles of the present volume originally appeared in Hungarian journals, or other foreign language journals. In addition to identifying the articles as they appear in *The New Hungarian Quarterly*, the Source Notes document earlier or later versions of the articles, and additional information of special interest. A section of Biographies of Authors, a Bartók Bibliography covering recent research, and two indexes have been included.

Permissions were granted by Gerald Abraham to reprint his article, "Bartók and England"; Bayreuther Festspiele to reprint "Bartók and Wagner"; Frau Thomas Mann to reprint a letter of her husband's in "Thomas Mann and Bartók"; and Yehudi Menuhin and Eugene Ormandy to reprint their letters from "Documenta Bartókiana."

The editor wishes to express his gratitude to the following whose assistance has been greatly appreciated: The Vassar College Library; The Vassar College Committee on Research; Professors Janet Knapp and Edward R. Reilly (Vassar College); Philip Winters (New York); Professor László Somfai (Budapest); and Frederick Freedman (Case Western Reserve University). The tragic news of the unexpected death of Fred Freedman, shortly before this volume went to press, came as a shock to all who knew him. His enduring support and tireless editorial efforts were invaluable to the editor during the preparation of this book, and his counsel and friendship will be sorely missed.

TODD CROW

Vassar College
Poughkeepsie, New York
October 1975

STUDIES IN MUSICAL STYLE

BARTÓK'S PRINCIPLES
OF COMPOSITION

by

BENCE SZABOLCSI

In 1937, at the zenith of his career, at the peak of his creative energies, at the time he wrote Music for String Instruments, Percussion, and Celesta, Sonata for two Pianos, and Concerto for Violin, Béla Bartók talked to his first important biographer, the Belgian music scholar, Denijs Dille, in Brussels. Among other things he said:

"The 'absolute' musical forms serve as a basis for freer musical formulae even if these formulae involve characteristic melodic and rhythmic types. It is clear, however, that folk melodies are not really suited to be used in forms of 'pure' music, for they, especially in their original shapes, do not really yield to the elaboration which is usual in these forms. The melodic world of my string quartets does not really differ from that of folk songs: it is only their setting that is stricter. It has probably been observed that I place much of the emphasis on the work of technical elaboration, that I do not like to repeat a musical thought unchanged, and I never repeat a detail unchanged. This practice of mine arises from my inclination for variation and for transforming themes. I am not merely playing when, at the end of my second Concerto for Piano, I reverse the theme. The extreme variety that characterizes our folk music is, at the same time, a manifestation of my own nature."

Later, he went on to add that those who know folk music at any depth cannot fail to recognize the small distance between the string quartets and folk tunes, with the reservation that "in my string quartets an extreme concentration prevails."

What is most conspicuous in this statement is that Bartók talks about a particularized opposition of forces: the impulse which follows the trend of folk music on the one hand, and the impulse counterbalancing those trends on the other, which are both manifested in his art. An inclination to variation, an aspiration related to the ever-changing, shaping nature of folk music that creates something new from what it finds, and derives its creative force precisely from leaving nothing untouched. And the strict framework, the tendency for concentration, for uniting and distilling, which rules out precisely such elements as are temporary and loosely burgeoning, is therefore a counterweight to folk variation and the unconscious growth of folk improvisation. These forces have naturally been at work not only in Bartók's art; what we have here are almost geological, primordial forces which are centuries, thousands of years old. But how characteristic it is that Bartók met them in his most introspective, most personal work and had to face them as Madách's Ádám had to face the Spirit of the Earth. What we have here are two aspirations fighting and complementing each other: the vegetative force of folk music, the foremost manifestation of which is variation, and the creative composing force of the conscious artist: his concentration, restraining and shaping that other force, binding it into form and enclosing it into a framework.

There had been significant musicians in the past too whose artistic evolution took place in terms of such historical oppositions. Dufay and Josquin grew into greatness in a transition from song and twining forms into musical composition. Monteverdi could feel behind him the tension of the Old and the New Practice, the Prima and Seconda Practica. Bach lived simultaneously in the melodiousness of his countrymen and in the fantastic vaultings of counterpoint. One of Mozart's recent critics (Alfred Einstein) has aptly said that all his work wears the stamp of the constantly changing, yet polarized contrast of the *galant* and the *gelehrt*; and Beethoven, when mentioning "the polemics of the mind and the heart" did, in effect, express the same opposition, the contest between the styles of intellectual intricacy and emotional overflow. We are forced to say: there have been few great artists who were not standing, from this point of view, on "the boundary of periods", at a meeting-point of opposed forces, who did not have "to choose," or step from one realm into the other, and who did not contribute to the birth of a new realm themselves.

What Bartók says in his remarkable statement not only places him along the old masters, but also places him on a special footing. There are always ideologies lurking behind styles. The two kinds of style mentioned by Bartók express not only ideologies, but represent the decisive phases, "world phases" as it were, of musical culture. An artist is speaking here, who consciously stands on the boundary of two worlds, at home in both. But when he wishes to unite in his art the forces of those two worlds, the burgeoning of folk music and the concentration of the creative individual, the unconscious and the consciousness, he, at the same time, steps consciously from one world to the other, dissolving the one with the other, creating the one from the other. "I want to raise folk music to the status of written music," the young Bartók announced in a letter, when he was about to start out on his work of collecting folk songs, hardly suspecting as yet the true richness of folk music. But his programme is already "final" and this programme is not only his. "In Eastern Europe folk music is becoming written music almost visibly," said Zoltán Kodály in one of his lectures, pointing to the most vital process of the musical history of our century.

The historical position of Bartók and Kodály, therefore, does not so much remind one of the position of the composers we cited as of that of Leoninus and Perotinus, the two great Parisian masters, who around 1200 could well regard the world of homophonic Western melodies as their natural home, but who nonetheless took the decisive step, never to be revoked, into the artistic world of polyphonic composition, moving from the impersonal and general into the personal and individual, from the world of improvised and varying melodies into that of fixed and closed musical creation. What Bartók modestly said about himself is today the decisive phase of Eastern European and Asian musical development, and in a wider sense, the decisive coming-of-age of all musical culture; the growth of unconscious music into conscious texts, the forms of constructed and built-up musical art, "composition." Bartók's modesty prevented him from pronouncing this truth, but today his very words remind us of the fact that his art has been the seismograph and the timepiece of a historical turning-point for the whole of mankind.

BARTÓK'S MIRACULOUS MANDARIN

by

BENCE SZABOLCSI

I

From October, 1918, to May, 1919, Béla Bartók worked in Budapest, chiefly in the suburb Rákoskeresztúr, on the music of his pantomime, The Miraculous Mandarin. The libretto had been written by Menyhért Lengyel during the First World War and published in the 1917 volume of *Nyugat* ("West").* As regards the form of the work, in the later arrangement for four hands as well as in the score it was called a pantomime in one act. Bartók himself said of it: "My pantomime, The Miraculous Mandarin—who knows when it can be performed?" in a letter written in the summer of 1919; at the same time his wife wrote: "The new pantomime is finished, Béla is now doing the orchestration."**

Recent research has revealed that Bartók finished the orchestration of the work only five years later, in the autumn of 1924 (which may provide an explanation for the strikingly novel orchestral tone of the Mandarin, novel even as compared to his style of 1919). Moreover, in 1931 he composed a new *finale* for the pantomime; this version is to be found in the manuscript score of the Budapest Opera House and closely resembles the conclusion in the new edition of the arrangement for four hands.

As indicated by Bartók's remark quoted above, it was predictable that the work would not be performed for a long time. The experimental and

---

* See p. 111.
** Béla Bartók, *Levelek, fényképek, kéziratok, kották* (Letters, photographs, manuscripts, music). Collected and arranged by János Demény, 1948, Budapest, pp. 82 and 90. Menyhért Lengyel's story is said to have been originally intended for the Diaghilev Ballet and was inspired by that ensemble. Bartók came to know Menyhért Lengyel's work only in 1918, through István Thomán. (Information supplied by Béla Bartók, Jun.) Concerning manuscript variants, see the study of O. A. Nirschy (Studia Musicologica, Budapest, 1962.) and J. Vinton: *The Miraculous Mandarin* (The Musical Quarterly, New York, 1964.)

often eccentric avant-guarde spirit of the "Weimar period" might have aroused livelier interest in it on western stages, but the difficulties presented by the music and the choreography constituted a grave obstacle even where "moral concern" was not decisive.

In 1923 a fragment of two pages from the arrangement for four hands appeared in the issue of *Nyugat* published for the anniversary of Ernő Osváth. Two years later the complete arrangement for four hands appeared (as op. 19) in the Vienna Universal Edition; again two years later what is called the *Suite* containing the first part of the composition (*Musik aus der gleichnamigen Pantomime*) was published by the same house. (The two-page fragment in *Nyugat* was headed "Copyright 1923 by Universal Edition.") In the four-hand arrangement for piano the work was broadcast over the Budapest Radio in the spring of 1926 by the composer and György Kósa. The first stage performance—in a strongly expressionistic style—took place in November 1926, at Cologne. To the best of our knowledge Bartók was among those present. The première, conducted by Jenő Szenkár, ended in a scandal and a demonstration, followed by protests from the Church and the authorities, while the conductor nearly lost his post.*

The *Suite*, when given its first performance before a Budapest audience in 1928, was conducted by Ernő Dohnányi. At the same time the Budapest Opera House also began to show interest in the composition. Later, in 1931, and still later, in 1941, preparations were made for its staging, but as described in the memoirs of Gyula Harangozó.** "...the pantomime was banned in both cases immediately before the première." In fact the first performance did not take place here until after Bartók's death in December 1945, when the pantomime was presented in an "adequately purged" form with an arbitrarily changed background scene. Finally it was staged in its authentic and complete form first at the National Theatre of Szeged (in 1949), and then at the Budapest Opera House (in 1956).

There are no records to the effect that the composer actually saw his work performed anywhere besides Cologne; however, the Frankfurt revival in 1954 was claimed to have been staged in the spirit of his one-time

---

* Letters, I, 115. Musikblätter—des Anbruch 1926, No. 10, p. 445.—Prokofiev's pantomime, "The Love of Three Oranges," presented not long before at Köln, had a similar fate.—On the first night in Prague (1927) see the communication of János Demény in *Zenetudományi Tanulmányok* (Musicological Studies), Budapest 1962, October, pp. 201–205.

** *Táncművészet* (Ballet Art), Budapest, 1955, February, p. 53.—As far as I know, at the sight of a rehearsal at the Opera House where the Mandarin was to be "tamed" by a change of scene, Bartók himself prohibited the performance of his work in Budapest. Concerning the vicissitudes of the Budapest first night, see János Demény (*Zenetudományi Tanulmányok*, 1959, Vol. III, pp. 413–416, and 1962, Vol. X, pp. 394–396), furthermore György Kroó, *Bartók színpadi művei* ("Bartók's Works for the Stage"), Budapest, 1962, pp. 187–196.

personal instructions, based on his experiences at Cologne. In Bartók's life-time The Miraculous Mandarin was thus regarded as a failure, though, as set forth in the memoirs of Harangozó, "...The Mandarin must have been one of his favourite works, for talking about it could dispel even his sad thoughts" (just before his emigration, in the autumn of 1940, five years before his death).

What was it that made this work so inaccessible, and what is it that still stirs up debate about it?

It is not difficult to answer these questions. The Miraculous Mandarin marked a turning-point in Bartók's development indicating the composer's entrance upon a novel, steep path. Moreover, this new start coincided with a significant crisis in the musical life of Europe, at a time when the fever curve of music was at its peak in every part of the world. Bartók's third and last work for the stage signified the most dazzling encounter with this crisis and, at the same time, a show-down with and a turning away from it.

The story of the pantomime, which was mentioned with such abhorrence by musical moralists both in Hungary and other countries, is as follows: In a metropolis, somewhere in the Old or in the New World, in a gangsters' den, three bandits bully a girl into beckoning to passers-by from their attic window and enticing them to come up. A shabby old gallant and then a shy, awkward youngster seize their chance and climb up the stairs to the attic; but having no money, both are thrown out mercilessly. The third is a strange and formidable guest, a Chinese mandarin on a visit to the metropolis, with whom the frightened girl hardly knows how to deal. Her seductive dance gradually arouses the awe-inspiring visitor's passion and he begins to pursue the girl with ever increasing ferocity. The gangsters attack and rob him and then kill him three times, first by suffocating, later by stabbing and finally by hanging him, but to no avail. The victim cannot die until he has received from the girl the kiss he so deeply desires.

What did this libretto convey to Bartók, and how did it come to attract his attention? Why did he say of it in spring 1919 in a press interview* that it was... "wonderfully beautiful"? What chord did this ancient motive of oriental tales, the Undying Lover—alter ego of the Undying Hero— strike in his soul?

In his other two works for the stage, presented at the Budapest Opera House in 1917 and 1918 respectively, long before The Miraculous Mandarin, in the Wooden Prince and Bluebeard's Castle, the problem of love was approached from different angles. Bluebeard's Castle, of earlier origin

---

* Bartók Béla válogatott írásai ("Selected Writings of Béla Bartók"). Collected and arranged for the press by András Szőllősy. Budapest, 1956. p. 339.

but presented later, emphasized the hopelessness of a truly close relationship between man and woman; in The Wooden Prince, subsequently composed but performed ahead of Bluebeard's Castle, the symbolical trials of the lovers and the final happiness of their finding each other took place in the optimistic atmosphere of a folk tale. In the Wooden Prince the lovers—-the prince and the princess—triumphantly overcome the hostile forces of the surrounding world which stood in the way of their happiness.

In The Miraculous Mandarin this picture became more sombre than in either of the others. Here love is killed by the hostile environment, itself becomes sullied from the very first; here we are faced with the meeting of a prostitute and an exotic spectre, not of the innocent lovers of a folk tale. But who is responsible for this sullied love and for its inevitably horrible end? There can be no doubt about the answer: the predatory world that has condemned men and women to such love, exploits and distorts their whole being and finally flings them into the pit. In The Miraculous Mandarin the environment and the colouring of the outer world turned to darkness, and human passion changed into almost pathological torment. Whereas in the Wooden Prince the obstacles to human happiness were transient, fabulous trials and afflictions that were soon relieved, the milieu of The Miraculous Mandarin was transformed into an inhuman, murderous world, into an enemy that destroyed every form of life.

Bartók hated this enemy; his hatred was incandescent, elementary, and more frantic at this stage than ever before or after.

To conceive such a hatred he had to encounter the object of his hatred; he had to live through a turning point of history that revealed to him the infernal and destructive inhuman forces of life in all their depth.

2

The discontent of the intelligentsia of Europe developed slowly, even after the outbreak of the First World War, but from 1916 onwards it became increasingly aggressive. At the beginning of the war there were those on both sides who cherished the illusion that the war was fought for a "true cause." The socialist and the radical bourgeois was the first to reject this illusion; yet even these strata were long at a loss as to the instruments, the ways and means for starting a struggle against the war. In the letters of Zsigmond Móricz and Béla Bartók it was chiefly from 1916 that the voice of protest against the war became noticeable, and those of our contemporaries who lived through the First World War may still remember that at the same time anti-war propaganda grew steadily stronger in the literature, press and theatres of Hungary.

Musical life reflected the same change, with the difference that under the rather backward Hungarian conditions these characteristic movements, which in the West ever more openly expressed the increasing anger and despondency of the intelligentsia, were less conspicuous in Hungary. Anger and despondency—the two were not reflected in equal measure, but almost everywhere both were to be found and their proportion lent a positive or negative emphasis to these movements. Here we have in mind those trends that branched off from futurism into expressionism and dadaism, which assumed an important role in the western cities, at least in the domains of literature and art, and other disruptive tendencies that with growing insistence called for the annihilation of traditional art forms and, directly or indirectly, of the social system that maintained them.

On the whole these artistic, literary, and musical movements had common slogans and certainly employed similar instruments. They agreed that the immediate past was to be abandoned and replaced by something radically new; they branded the world of bourgeois morality as false and obsolete; they also agreed on using a whole series of novel, hitherto unknown or formerly somewhat ignored artistic means for giving vent to their hatred and protest. Some of them aggressively accentuated distortion and ugliness, in order to reveal and expose the hideousness and wickedness of the existing order; others emphasized the decomposition of forms with a view to proclaiming anarchy as the only way out; a third group elaborated new, speculative systems to stress the necessity of evolving a new way of thinking, a new world order. In all cases, preoccupation with machines and masses was intended to draw attention to the novel experiences of proletarian life and of the big cities.

All these instruments appeared together, often overlapping and inter-penetrating; all were fed by moral, aesthetic, social and political aspirations, and all of them entered into European musical life.

The year 1918 was an important milestone in the history of European music. It was in this year that the greatest French composer of the era, Claude Debussy, died in Paris while the Germans were shelling the town. In the same year the Group of the Six was founded in Paris for the purpose of introducing a new and harsher, "everyday" note into music. That very year witnessed the first scandals and demonstrations provoked by dadaist and expressionist movements in France, Germany and Austria. In the autumn of 1918 The Soldier's Tale was given its first performance on a small Swiss stage, marking the entry of Stravinsky into the musical life of post-war Western Europe. It was in 1918 that the debates around Schönberg became more and more acrimonious in Germany and the vogue of American jazz appeared in the West.

October 1918 was the time of the bourgeois revolution in Hungary, while the proletarian dictatorship was proclaimed in the spring of 1919. In Hungarian literature 1918 saw the appearance of Zsigmond Móricz's novel "Torch" (Fáklya) and the last volume of poetry published by Endre Ady, "At the Head of the Dead" (Halottak élén). Both books contained powerful visions of death and rebirth. Móricz was the first to pass judgment on a foundering world, and Ady dealt with the fate of the nation in a kind of danse macabre.

It was in October 1918 that Béla Bartók began to compose his danse macabre music to The Miraculous Mandarin. By the time he finished it in spring 1919, the Hungarian revolutionary government was engaged in a defensive war for its very existence against the onslaught of superior numbers from every side. All around there was war and revolution, confusion and disaster, visions of threatening death and extermination. There were also visions of a past that could not be continued in the old way—of good and evil, locked in mortal combat, of violence and will to survive, of humanity and inhumanity, of West and East, of chaotic metropolises and rebellious peasants, of civilization and primitive forces.

It was in this period, at the height of this clash of forces, that the Hungarian composer created the music of The Miraculous Mandarin.

3

Until the end of the First World War the music of Bartók and Kodály was rarely played in the West and remained practically unknown to wider circles. Beginning with 1910 some of their pieces for piano or chamber music were occasionally played in French, Swiss and American towns, but they could not become more generally known and new works could not be taken out of the country on account of the war. In 1918 Bartók found a publisher for his works in Vienna (the Universal Edition), and from that time on his compositions reached the West more easily, more quickly and in larger numbers. On his earlier concert tours, from 1904 on, Bartók had been to English, French, German and Spanish towns; but at the time he was known as a pianist and hardly, or not at all, as a composer. Now, he entered European musical life as a composer "published in Vienna" and again as a piano performer from 1919–1920 on. As a composer he was introduced into it by the year of the revolution, as a pianist he was exiled into it by the counterrevolution.

The world that faced Bartók here was absolutely alien to him, confused and in many respects repellent. He did not retreat from it, but observed it with distrust and even anger. He was shocked by the turmoil, the noise and the elbowing in the western capitals, and revolted by the savage ruthlessness with which the weak were swept aside and trampled down in the world of apparently free competition. He was angered by the advertising drive, by the "all-for-sale" market.

It was not long before Bartók turned away from this world and recalled the touching memories of his old tours through the villages, the dreamed-of virginal purity and human depth of peasant life in Eastern Europe. A contributory factor was post-war confusion: the anarchy of social life undergoing reorganization in the large cities, where the morass of war profiteering had suddenly increased to an incredible degree and implicated immense areas; the breathless rush that dominated not only the bourgeois life of these societies but their entire spiritual life as well; the good or evil slogans of the "new art" taking shape in various centres, under various slogans, and proclaiming alternately cubism, atonality, mechanical music, choral speaking or the chaotic language of dadaism as the leading principle.

Bartók was simultaneously attracted and repelled by these movements. Attracted, because he could pick out from them what aroused his instinctive curiosity, what was likely to enrich his own developing language and means of expression, and perhaps still more because with every one of his nerves he sensed this labyrinth, this confused undulation, this all-embracing crisis. He was already a universal artist, sensitive to the manifestations of every nerve of the universe and to its entire nervous system. He may have failed to notice what had happened during the war to that old, ideal world which he carried in his memory; for the (apparent) harmony of the lovely Hungarian, Rumanian, Slovak, and Ukranian villages had been broken as a result of the terrible storm of the war. It was the crisis and the confusion itself that first clamoured for expression in him; but from the very beginning there was also a desire for elucidation, for weighing, for reckoning, accompanied by immeasurable indignation over the corrupt hooliganism of the cities, capable of any infamy.

Bartók's encounter with the metropolis and his conflict with the new forms of life came about in the period after The Miraculous Mandarin; but a premonition was induced by the war, and it was The Miraculous Mandarin which made it evident that within him the "reckoning" had already begun. A man for whom Nature was the principal criterion and the ethics of Nature the highest moral standard may at all events have wondered what would happen if real jungle law were introduced one day in this monstrous human jungle.

More than half a century earlier a great Hungarian poet was seized with a kindred passion, a similar wish for a reckoning, and was roused to similar anger by the inexorable drive of the capitalist metropolis. In Madách's "Tragedy of Man" (*Az ember tragédiája*) the London fair makes Adam exclaim:

> What competition, if one, sword in hand,
> Confront another rival weaponless?
> What independence, if a hundred starve,
> If they will not submit to one man's yoke?

The significant question receives an equally significant reply:

> Deemest thou there is never harmony,
> No system in the workshop of this life?
> Gaze, then, a while with spiritual eyes,
> And mark the work they bring to plenitude.

At the same moment the whole London fair is transformed into a single scene of *danse macabre* where everyone utters his last word, setting forth the single meaning of his life before jumping into the common grave.

In truth, those who posed the question with such moral stress and such sharpness had ever since the Middle Ages been attracted to the *danse macabre*. "Let me go to my death!" were the words the writers of medieval chronicles put into the mouths of their heroes, because it was in the light of death that they could show most clearly the true meaning and lesson of life. Not in vain did the *danses macabres* of Orcagna and Holbein inspire so many writers and artists. When the composers of the nineteenth century, Berlioz, Liszt, Verdi and Mussorgsky, apparently returned to Orcagna and Holbein in their own compositions on death, they were in fact creating the great *danse macabre* of their own age, calling for analysis, decision and judgment.

Béla Bartók's own vision of the *danse macabre* followed in their steps. He passed judgment on his age in an appalling pantomime, the libretto of which could have been no more than a hair-raising, sensual Grand Guignol for anybody else; he recognized in it an appropriate framework for his own merciless sentence. That is why and how he undertook to compose music to Menyhért Lengyel's pantomime at a time when almost every critical issue of his age had become intolerably acute in his eyes.

4

The forces and impulses of the period come on the stage in all their starkness and bareness, simplified in terms of allegory as in a mediaeval morality play. Oppressed and Venal Love (the girl) appears as the forced ally of Murderous Villainy, and the Elemental Impulse of Vitality (the mandarin) steps in; the episodic figures of the conflict are Helpless Youth and Helpless Old Age (the youth and the old gallant). These "simple" allegories acquire an extraordinary emotional and moral impact as, charged with dynamic power, they combine or clash. Characteristically, the figures are in steady dramatic motion and shift their positions in such a way that Bartók's attitude towards them clearly emerges.

The musical atmosphere of the opening is metropolitan, only later is it revealed to be that of the murderers, of Villainy; as such it gives unity to the composition as one of its fundamental themes. The other most significant basic theme—as will be seen—is that of the mandarin; it is remarkable that the third theme, that of the girl, standing between the two, gradually approaches the second, to which it actually corresponds (minor thirds or augmented seconds) and with which it finally joins forces against the first, thus unfolding with it and in it the girl's own denied and sullied affections. However, this attachment gains strength only in the shadow of death.

As pointed out before, the love that unfolds in this pantomime—in a situation and form that is "beyond morality and society"—is branded as distorted, suffocated, crippled, abnormal love. This applies to the young visitor's helplessness and shy desires no less than to the girl's sensuous flirtation and the mandarin's sudden blaze of passion. Love and death —fatal love and fatal death—are, nevertheless, the essence of this work. It is the inhuman world in which the action takes place that has made a mockery of love and death, has maimed and poisoned it.

Love and death: here neither is timely, neither can exercise its power naturally, elementally, but inevitably errs into by-paths; both only serve to cast a still deeper shadow on a sombre and deprived life. Yet, breaking through all this debasement, rising above "the flowers of evil" and thrusting them aside, true love and true death emerge as the decisive laws of life. The victory of this elemental, positive law is, however, due to Bartók's music and not to the libretto.

The musical concept of the work counterposes crass extremes: the civilized confusion of a European metropolis and the "primitiveness" of Asia; corrupt calculation and elemental desire; violence and emotion; life and death. In creating these tremendous tensions, these decisive antinomies, the composer declares his own attitude. Had Bartók written this work in his youth, under the influence of Wagner's Tristan, he would most likely have emphasized that infinite longing can be appeased only by death. In this case death would have been a veritable relief and an escape to a happier world. But here the situation is very different. Even in death the mandarin's desire is a protest, and in satisfying it he triumphs over his murderers, for he has overcome and survived murder itself and been allotted a tragic death of a superior order signifying victory, the supreme victory of life.

In the end it is not the mandarin who is conquered but his murderers. Thus there is no trace of Tristan ecstasy, no escape, no nirvana: desire defies and annihilates murder, derides it and bursts forth in death as triumphant vitality. There is something of this in Tristan too, despite Wagner; at all events this deed of Wagner's, this self-refuting idea, was further developed by Bartók in The Miraculous Mandarin.

It is as if this fundamental idea was expressed by the relentlessly strict symmetry of the work as follows.

INTRODUCTION: METROPOLIS, THE GANGSTERS' DEN

I Thrice-repeated gestures of seduction (Two episodes, two minor characters)

III Mandarin's dance

II Mandarin's appearance Amorous play

IV Thrice-repeated murder

V The Girl's kiss. Death

Thus it is the Mandarin's dance, this fierce burst of passion, this "allegro barbaro" more awe-inspiring than any other of Bartók's compositions, which is in the centre of the work. What precedes it is the presentation of the hostile world; what follows it is the struggle of vital force and of passion against this world, its tragic end—a deathless death that brings victory and exaltation. Before the Mandarin's dance the might of a hostile world is represented by thrice-repeated gestures of seduction, after the dance by a thrice-repeated murder—this is the ordeal the envoy of a remote world has to face. If he can assert himself he will triumph and receive the kiss without which he cannot die and after which he may die. In accord-

ance with the rules of classical tragedy the moment of his downfall fills
him with a strength exceeding that of his adversaries. With his entrance
greatness appears in this base world and passes from it with his death.

The musical structure emphasizes the same idea. Here the three
gangsters are a single amorphous group represented by rhythm and motion
rather than tune; the rhythm, as pointed out before, is that of the metropolis.
A large city, violence, crime and murder all have the same meaning for
Bartók at this turning-point in his life. (His hatred and indignation were
to find similar expression much later in his Concerto.)

(N. B. This was the motive of the hero's despair in the Wooden Prince.)

The musical world of the girl is far more human and at the same time
more sensuous, though more erratic and indeterminate. These tunes follow
the pattern of the princess' movements in the Wooden Prince, but instead
of being playful and childish, they are of serpentine intricacy, suffocated
and suffocating; they emerge from obscurity and return into obscurity. The
domain of instincts here is not serene, but tormenting and tormented and
shackled by grim memories.

(Note the triple step accompanying the mandarin's figure.)

The libretto surrounds the figure of the mandarin with a mysterious
atmosphere. While for Bartók too it is mysterious, it is, nevertheless as
physical as an elemental phenomenon of nature, as the whole of the human
world, if we take into account its great motive forces, great conflicts and
great destinies. Its impulses are recognized impulses, but, having become
overcharged and uncontrollable, they break the bounds of civilization and
step into a sphere that this civilization finds mystical and superhuman. The

"folk music" that flashes and re-echoes in the composition is represented by the Mandarin's music with its Asian flavour, its "untuned pentatony" whose exotic yet steely brilliance and stubborn progression announces the irresistible will and passion of the hero.

(Rhythmically and partly also melodically these "Chinese" tunes appear to be echoes of well known Chinese pieces of music.)

"The vital force of Asia opposed to the corruption of Europe" was the comment on this figure made by appreciative critics, who saw in this the essence of Bartók's message. Those who subscribed to this view profoundly misunderstood the all-embracing humanism of Bartók, who proclaimed the greatness and beauty of human advance, the heroism and loftiness of the fight against dark and blind fate in every manifestation of naive purity and of popular strength, in the sparkle and thunder of every "allegro barbaro." The object of his enthusiasm was not barbarity, but man maintaining harmony with the great forces of nature in an epoch of distortion, unnaturalness and inhumanity. Béla Bartók, a professed pantheist as early as 1907, a dozen years later dared to stage primeval nature itself as a protest, in Asian disguise, against the free-for-all Europe of 1919 which brought dishonour to the continent.

Only heroes with intense passions can suffer as immeasurably and death-defiantly as does the heroic figure of the mandarin. The theme of his agony and unquenchable desire, reminiscent of a sigh and a moan, already hinted at when he enters the stage, is heard throughout the second part of the pantomime, becoming a chorus of wordless wailing behind the scenes in the most horrible moments; it then declines with the life of the mandarin and flickers out in the orchestra after a last burst of resistance.

(The sobbing of the violas, then violas and violins rising above the chorus tune represents the first trace of the stifled chromatic dirge that was to come into its own twenty years later in the second movement of the Divertimento.)

In general, an outstanding role is assigned in the music of the pantomime to tunes or fragments of tunes that remind one of sighs, cries and gestures. The appearance of such gesticulating, sometimes feverishly projecting and loose melodic lines that virtually beat the air, may be followed in Bartók's music since the Second String Quartet, especially since 1915/17, i.e., approximately from the time when melody based on fourths began to play an important part in his musical language. This kind of theme predominated till about 1923, up to the elaboration of the Dance Suite, and then waned. The music of The Miraculous Mandarin stands in the centre of this creative period, as the most powerful summary of the composer's achievements in this period, i.e., the years around 1920. Only two earlier works approach it in importance—The Wooden Prince and the Second String Quartet.

Here a few words have to be said about some other peculiarities of the Mandarin's music. For a fairly long time the work was held to be atonal. This attitude seemed to be justified by the circumstance that it is not easy to define the central key of the composition and that the tonal functions are in most places blurred by a structure resting on chords by fourths. However, Bartók's later words: "...at one time I approached a kind of twelve-tone music, but even my compositions of that period are unmistakably constructed on a firm tonal basis," apply also to The Miraculous Mandarin.* As a matter of fact it contains scenes with a clearly recognizable tonal centre, and the whole pantomime is built up around such loosened centres, from the first seduction, through the great central dance, to the scene of death. (Thus the three seductions are in A, C and E, respectively, the great scene of the mandarin's persecution is in A, while the murders are in C sharp and B, and the end is in F.)

* _Bartók Béla válogatott zenei írásai_ ("Béla Bartók's Selected Writings on Music"), Budapest, 1948, p. 17.

As has been mentioned before, the use of fourths played an outstanding part in loosening these centres. Chords by fourths appeared also in the last compositions of Liszt, while Skriabin evolved a whole system based on fourths. However, at this time, it was not their example that encouraged Bartók to apply chords by fourths. Later Bartók declared that . . . "the accumulation of peculiar fourth steps in their old tunes provided the initiative to build chords by fourths."* In this connection one may also think of the influence exerted by Schönberg's compositions.

Apart from these chords by fourths there are many more novel features in the music of The Miraculous Mandarin. Mention has already been made of the "untuned pentatony" which in the scenes of the Mandarin furnished a basis for the most singular combinations; to this we may add the Arabic or Javanese scale which had enriched some movements of Bartók's works from the Suite for Piano (op. 14), to reappear not only nearly twenty years later in the Mikrokosmos (On Bali Island) but also in the first movement of his posthumous Concerto for Viola. Equally striking is Bartók's dramatic chromaticism, which easily leads to the growth of a tissue woven of second and seventh dissonances; his dramatic rhythm, which instinctively avails itself of asymmetrical "Bulgarian rhythms"; his treatment of the orchestra, which in this work completely abandons the school of Strauss and shows a link, if any, with Stravinsky alone; the staggering and disquieting effect of the wordlessly wailing chorus, which had to be dropped from the Suite, the orchestral adoptation of the work. It may be stated in general that in the first period of his activity up to 1920, and even much later, right up to the Cantata Profana, Bartók did not compose any symphonic work that equalled The Miraculous Mandarin in power, courage and dramatic truth.

5

The years that followed The Miraculous Mandarin brought a change in the problems that aroused Bartók's concern. The issues of love, instinct, desire and fate receded, to give place to much sharper contrasts, like man and nature, and the duality of civilization and freedom. The free man, the figure of Homo Naturalis, who engrossed Bartók's fancy in this period, sometimes simply bore the name of Peasant, another time he appeared as a mandarin or a mythical stag, hinting at the atmosphere of the Hungarian Great Plains or Rumanian forests or Chinese mountains. Meantime, not only did the principal figure assume another shape, but behind it also

* ibid. p. 23.

the mountains, the forest, the lowland farms in the background, indeed Bartók's whole natural and human world.

At the time of The Miraculous Mandarin Bartók entered the lists as a warrior in the chaotic struggle designed to rescue the human dignity of European art: the defence of humanity against violence, barbarity and inhumanity. Eleven years later, under a menacingly overcast horizon, when Bartók again raised the disquieting question of "saving humanity," his reply did not issue from such close-at-hand wrestling, but from a more removed height, and therefore more triumphantly. The great work we have in mind is the Cantata Profana and was composed in 1930, at a time when Bartók had set himself the clearly defined target of helping to create "a brotherhood of the peoples." The letter in which he described his creed was addressed to a Rumanian acquaintance. His friendly relations with Rumanians and his passionate inquiry into Rumanian folk music ten years later caused official Hungary to bring against him the ridiculous accusation of high treason. The virtually unprecedented renewal of his musical language at this time was promoted by the abundant treasures of Rumanian folk poetry. The words of the Cantata Profana, also derived from Rumanian folk poetry, were intended to be the opening item of a series of major cantatas linking several nations.

Of the planned series only one was completed, the "profane cantata" on the mythical stags, protesting more convincingly than any explanatory words could have done and sounding a warning alarm against the approaching horrors. Bartók saw only one way to avert the underground, insidious movements setting peoples and nations against one another: away from the lowly cottages, back to nature, reject all the old lies! He who has returned to nature, who stands on the mountain top and again holds up his head freely may again become master of his fate and keep clear of base contagion. That is how the mythical stags of the Cantata Profana stop on the summit of an imaginary mountain, the mountain of freedom, calling on humanity longing for liberty to follow them.

The battle to be fought was fought by Bartók from this mountain top alone, from a great altitude and distance. His anger did not burn so fiercely or so closely as in The Miraculous Mandarin. In the Cantata a surprisingly big role was assigned to narration, to depicting the situation, to epic elements, to reminiscences. In his review of the première of the Cantata Profana in Hungary, Aladár Tóth wrote on November 9, 1936 "...Here the composer relates... how he was transferred in his dreams to a vast, fabulous, legendary, trackless forest, where he found a new life without any limitation or compromise. He describes... the demoniac relief he felt when, his heart filled with youthful, bold and boundless love of freedom, he broke through the virgin wilderness"; "... he tells about the revolt of the young against their fathers"; he, "...the most daring of the warring young generation, describes the terrible pain caused by breaking away for ever from the happiness and comfort of home life that he who leaves and those who remain behind experience with equal vehemence. Having vowed to live for freedom, he will drink no more from a glass, but only from a pure spring..."

This passionate declaration, though following logically from Bartók's former development, was nevertheless an entirely new feature. Equally new was his rejection of all compromise, of any "parleying"—even of the direct contact involved in fighting, wrestling and meeting the enemy. With a single prohibitive gesture he swept aside for his heroes and for his own liberated self all possibility of coming to terms with the old world that was clamouring for his return home. This is not a contest between generations, but between slavery and freedom, between those born to be slaves and modern man born to be free. Bartók's disillusionment, his breaking away from the "world of cottages" was so consistent and incisive that his austerity, his boundless adoration of nature tend to make him appear almost inhuman. Discerning contemporaries, however, recognized that it was not man as such whom Bartók hated, but the coward who has degraded himself to servility and denies the great truths of life.

"This titanic music is the Song of Wolves in an age of servility," wrote Aladár Tóth. "At the same time it is an excruciatingly painful message that grips us to the depths of our souls by its warm humanity; it is the message of a poet whose eagle soul has broken out of our everyday life into eternal freedom—into solitude... Yet perhaps it is really he who speaks the truth of our time and of all times as he boldly and sublimely utters the secret and suppressed truth of our souls. Listen to the rumbling applause of the young thronging the gallery! Who would dare to say that the proclamation of human freedom elicits no response in our century?"

By now we know that Bartók did not stop at committing himself to breaking out of prison (and society), to this detachment, but went still further, another step higher. For, obviously, the next step was that of peopling his pure and superhuman Nature, the primeval wilderness of the Cantata Profana, this crystalline vehicle of freedom, so that it should one day become humane and human. This great step was taken in Bartók's last works, another fifteen years after the Cantata Profana, most likely as a result of the composer's last ordeals. His return into mankind's midst had actually begun long before; the Music for Strings and Percussion (1936), the Divertimento (1939) and the Concerto for Orchestra (1943), with their finales recalling folk festivals, can hardly be imagined otherwise.

This return characteristically coincides in the works themselves with the tormenting visions of the Second World War. Such extreme poles as deepest mourning and loudest rejoicing, despair and certainty, were already present in them; only the last, reconciling unity and the final summary beyond contradiction were still missing. They were realized in Bartók's last masterpieces.

As in the last works of Beethoven, the austerity of the suffering composer was mitigated by love of mankind, sympathy, confidence and humanity at the highest and most glorious level. The humanity of Béla Bartók's art is embodied in the warmth of his last great compositions. The sylvan hymn of the Third Concerto for Piano transformed the grim natural world of the Cantata Profana into the happy summer wood of our childhood. The homecoming wanderer enters eternal silence in a happy reverie, like one who at the end of his struggles lies down peacefully at the threshold of his birthplace.

DUALITY AND SYNTHESIS
IN THE MUSIC OF BÉLA BARTÓK

by

ERNŐ LENDVAI

There are many persons to whom it gives pleasure to behold a cathedral, who are delighted with pictures and poems," wrote Bartók, "but who will never take the trouble to find out who was the architect or the author of the work. Naturally—or at least it should be so—interest is shown for the works and not for the names of authors and details of their lives. One may well wonder whether it would not be better to play compositions without mentioning the names of composers." This statement would seem to lend itself readily for a motto, to which I should like to add Schweitzer's remark on Bach to the effect that his works would be the same even though his life had followed a radically different course. Characteristically, Bartók said nothing or very little about his own compositions (though he liked to emphasize the relations of his music to folklore, chiefly with the intention of propagating folk music). "Let my music speak for itself; I lay no claim to any explanation of my works"—with these words he meant to avert curiosity, for there was nothing more abhorrent to him than any prying into his private life or the possibility of infringement on the independence of his personal feelings. In everything he laid stress on what bound him to humanity in general, the element common to everybody. His music aspired toward the medium of universal laws. I would like to add a few strokes to this aspect of Bartók's portrait.

*

In the line of Bartók's works, his opera entitled "Bluebeard's Castle" (1911) is perhaps the first to present his music in full maturity. Bartók's style took shape suddenly, virtually between one day and the next—it burst forth, to put it more accurately. About the time he composed his "First String Quartet" (1908) he produced a final style which, in regard to essential features, continued unchanged to his latest works. His later style does not display a single significant element that was lacking when he composed "Bluebeard's Castle." With him, unity of personality implied that of style, as well as of his musical mother tongue. It was by no means accidental that the moment when Bartók found himself, and the magic of Strauss and Reger vanished, coincided with the discovery and study of peasant music. On one occasion Denys Dille addressed the following question to Bartók: "Is there any difference of technique or trend between the famous string quartets, piano concertos, and the three stage works and the compositions based on original Hungarian tunes or melodies of your own invention, such as the 'Dance Suite' and the two rhapsodies for violin and orchestra?" "This difference is only apparent," Bartók replied. "The melodic world of my string quartets does not differ essentially from that of folk songs, except in so far as the setting of the former is more severe. Folk songs should be known as we know them, and then the existing distance will be undeniably diminished. In the string quartets I go in for excessive concentration." An astonishing result of my studies on Bartók relates to the unity of style in his music, which is at least as organic as that of, say, Bach or Mozart: "Bluebeard's Castle," "Music for Strings, Percussion and Celesta," and the "Concerto for Orchestra" permit analysis by the same means. This is the characteristic that distinguishes Bartók from most of his contemporaries (Stravinsky, primarily); his life-work is void of arbitrary turns, for he always remained constant to his principles.

Any attempt to explore the strata underlying this style and the meaning of what is known of Bartók's world of form and harmony calls for inquiry into the relationship of Bartók's idiom to (1) folk music, (2) functional harmony, (3) impressionism, and (4) atonal trends.

I

The words of Bartók's musical language stem from the deepest layer of folk music. He himself strongly believed that every folk music of the world can finally be traced to a few primeval sources; in creating his musical idiom he was demonstrably inspired by the possibility of such a "primeval" music. Now, what is to be denoted hereafter as the "golden-section system" is simply an integration of pentatonic primeval motions and primitive affinities into a system. Bartók's most characteristic chords can be traced to simple pentatonic basic steps. Moreover, from stylistic analysis of Bartók's music I have been able to conclude that the chief feature of his chromatic technique is obedience to the laws of golden section in every element.

Golden section *(sectio aurea)* simply means division of a distance in such a way that the proportion of the full distance to the larger part should correspond geometrically to the proportion of the larger to the smaller part (that is, the larger part should be the *geometric mean* of the full distance and the smaller section). As shown by computation, when full distance constitutes the unit, the value of the larger section amounts to 0.618 and that of the smaller section to 0.381.[1] Golden section is a no less significant constituent element in Bartók's creation of form, melody and harmony than overtone harmonization and construction in periods embracing eight or four bars in the Viennese classical style.

For example, in an earlier study ("Bartók's Style," Zeneműkiadó [Music Publishing House], Budapest, 1955) I demonstrated that every unit of the "Sonata for Two Pianos and Percussion," from the whole of the work to the tiniest cells, is divided according to the rule of golden section. I performed nearly a thousand geometrically satisfactory measurements. Thus, golden section of the first movement indicates the centre of gravity in the movement: the beginning of the recapitulation. (Since the movement consists of 443 bars, and $443 \times 0.618 = 274$, recapitulation sets in precisely in the 274th bar!) Golden section may be observed to touch, in every case, the most important turning-point of form in the analysed unit. For instance, the principal theme of the finale shows the following articulation: $A_1 + A_2 + B$. The main section naturally determines the place of the member "B" ($43.5 \times 0.618 = 27$), while the two members "A" are adjusted to each other with golden section ($27.5 \times 0.618 = 17$).

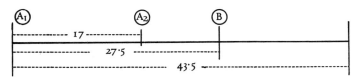

Golden section may be further observed to follow one of two courses, according to whether the longer or the shorter section comes first. Let us call one of the possibilities *positive* (long section followed by the short one), the other *negative* (short section followed by the long one). The best example is offered by the fugue movement (first movement) of "Music for Strings, Percussion and Celesta." From pianissimo the movement reaches the boil-

[1] Accordingly, the larger portion of any distance divided by golden section may be expressed by the product of the figure reflecting distance and the proportionality factor 0.618.

ing point by a gradual rise to forte-fortissimo, then gradually recedes to piano-pianissimo. The 89 bars of the movement are divided into parts of 55 and 34 bars by the pyramid-like peak of the movement. From the points of view of colour and dynamic architecture, the form is proportioned within these units, by cancellation of the sordino (in the 34th bar) and its repeated use (from the 69th bar), with the part leading up to the culmination showing a relationship of 34 + 21 and that from the culmination onward, 13 + 21. Thus, in the rising member the longer section comes first (34 + 21) and in the falling member the shorter section (13 + 21). The points of junction condense around the culmination. Positive and negative sections embrace each other like the rising and sinking of a single wave.

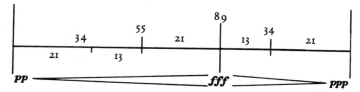

(It is no accident that the exposition ends with the 21st bar and that the 21 bars concluding the movement are divided into parts of 13 + 8.) We shall shortly return to the series of numbers that figure here (8, 13, 21, 34, 55, 89).

The measurements can be continued all the way down to the smallest units. As a final example the golden-section scheme of the introductory part of the "Sonata for Two Pianos and Percussion" may be cited (first movement, 2 to 17; for detailed analysis see the Corvina Bartók Album).*

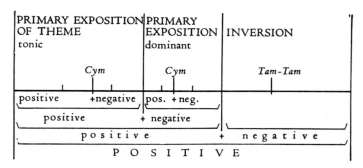

As may be seen, in form units of both higher and lower orders the positive and negative sections are associated as if reflected in a mirror, so that ultimately the details merge in a large positive section. Therefore the process

---

* See the author's article in the volume, *Bartók. Sa vie et son œuvre*. Edited by Bence Szabolcsi. Corvina Publishing House, Budapest, 1956, 320 pp. (also in German).

is coupled with a powerful dynamic increase (from *pp* to *fff*). Analytical studies permit the conclusion that the positive section is accompanied by enhancement, dynamic rise and intensification or condensation of the material, while the negative section is marked by sinking and ebbing.

These studies lead directly to the questions presented by melody and harmony formation. Bartók's chromaticism, as mentioned, follows the laws of the golden section, more particularly of Fibonacci's numerical series. This series is characterized by the fact that each expression is the sum of the two preceding numbers and, further, by containing the simplest golden-section series expressible in whole numbers:

2, 3, 5, 8, 13, 21, 34, 55, 89 . . .

(For instance, the golden section of 89 is 55 and that of 55 is 34). Compare this series of numbers with the proportions of "Music for Strings, Percussion and Celesta," analysed before. (Calculated in semitones, 2 means a major second, 3 a minor third, 5 a fourth, 8 a minor sixth, 13 an augmented octave, and so on. For the present the musical tissue may be imagined to be built up of cells, 2, 3, 5, 8, and 13 in size, with cell division following the pattern provided by the proportions of the above series. Thus, the 8 may be broken up only into 5 + 3. The supplement below shows the themes in the first movement of the "Sonata for Two Pianos and Percussion." The opening of the leitmotif includes 8 semitones, divided by the fundamental note c into 5 + 3 (see below). The principal theme comprises 13 semitones, divided by the fundamental note c into 5 + 8. The first phase of the secondary theme embraces 13 semitones, the second phase 21 semitones. Hence the various themes develop in golden-section order.

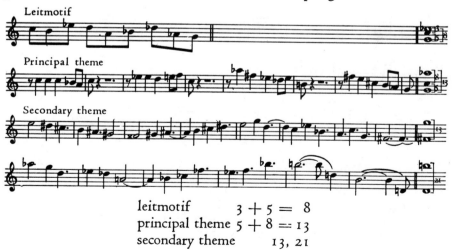

Leitmotif

Principal theme

Secondary theme

leitmotif   3 + 5 =   8
principal theme 5 + 8 = 13
secondary theme   13, 21

From the point of view of harmonic architecture, this exposition also bears witness to a systematic arrangement. The principal theme gains its characteristic tone from a pentatonic harmony (scheme "a" prevails also in melody: bars 37, 39); the formula might be 2 + 3 + 2. Toward the middle of the principal theme a unit built on 3 + 5 + 3 is added (scheme "b" from bar 41), while the fourth, e flat—a flat, is divided by an f sharp into 3 + 2. Parallel fourths (5) and minor sixths (8) join the secondary theme (scheme "c," which grows more clearly discernible in the recapitulation, from bar 292); finally, the closing theme is accompanied all along by parallel minor sixths: 8 (scheme "d," from bar 134 to 160). Thus each new harmony rises one golden-section step higher.

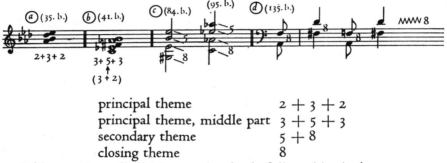

principal theme	2 + 3 + 2
principal theme, middle part	3 + 5 + 3
secondary theme	5 + 8
closing theme	8

Golden-section cell division can be clearly followed in the last movement of the "Divertimento." The principal theme appears in the following variations (the quotations have been grouped according to size and typical division has been denoted in connection with every variation):

Since the fifth line is the continuation of the fourth, in bar 4 the melody rises not by a minor third (3), as in the preceding line, but by a fourth (5)—in conformity with the augmentation.

The same correlation of motifs is encountered in the mime-play "The Miraculous Mandarin":

The harmony type shown below occurs in Bartók's music perhaps even more frequently than did sevenths in 19th-century music:

Now these are marked chiefly by being built up exclusively of golden-section intervals (2, 3, 5, 8).

minor thirds (3)　　major seconds (2)　　fourths (5)　　minor sixths (8)

It is typical that whenever Bartók used a triad in a chromatic movement he placed the minor third over the fundamental note and the major third below it, tuning the chord to acquire the proportions 8 : 5 : 3.

major   minor   chord typical
3+5 = 8   5+3 = 8   of Bartók!
« major-minor »

That golden section is not an exogenous restriction but one of the intrinsic laws of music is evidenced most convincingly by *pentatony*, perhaps the most ancient human sound system, which may be regarded as the purest musical conception of the principle of golden section. Pentatony, particularly the more ancient form of minor pentatony, rests on a pattern reflected by the melody steps of major second (2), minor third (3), and fourth (5).

From this aspect, golden-section architecture is extremely interesting in the "Dance Suite," which appropriately has been given the name of "Eastern European Symphony." Construction of the golden-section system can here be followed virtually step by step, for this work actually demonstrates this technique in its genesis; starting from the elements, the world of multifarious tones rooted in pentatony is developed before our very eyes:

At first it may seem astonishing that with Bartók pentatony is so closely tied to chromaticism. This relationship is, however, natural; where the element of stress has access to chromaticism, animated tension is expressed by golden section, and an atmosphere of a more "humane" world is created. A great value of Bartók's music, as perhaps most nicely phrased by László Németh, lies in its exploration of "sub-European geology," in his having discovered and drawn into his art the laws governing depths of the human soul which have not been touched by civilization. The place of popular romanticism was taken by a deepening of the prehistoric memory of man, with a sort of excavation of the soul and an attempt to find beneath the deposit of modern times the sound and desirable basis of a new civilization, the "common human element" alive in everyone.

It has been said that the more recent a style the farther it goes back into the past: "Early romanticism to the Middle Ages, Wagner to Germanic polytheism, Stravinsky to totemism," writes an eminent commentator of modern Western music. In a figurative sense this applies also to Bartók. In the course of my investigations, I have come to the conclusion that Bartók's art represents a logical continuation and, in a certain sense, a conclusion of the development of European music; the circles of harmonic development are fused into a single, coherent, closed unit in Bartók's sound system: the "axis system" (to be discussed later). This circle is, however, closed in the opposite direction as well; Bartók's art goes back to the remotest past of music, and it can be said to penetrate to the core of music, to the most elemental interrelations. The most intricate has been traced to the most primitive; the "excessively concentrated" string quartets were enriched by simple folk songs. This was the break-through for which the majority of his contemporaries longed in vain.

2

Another clear feature of Bartók's music is its wide European horizon. "Every art has the right to stem from a previous art; it not only has the right to but it must so stem," declared Bartók. His sound system grew out of functional music; from the beginnings of functional music through the harmonies of Viennese classicism and the tone world of romanticism a line proceeds without a break to the development of the axis system. By this system Bartók set down the final results of European harmonic thinking. As revealed by analysis of his compositions, this axis system can be traced to the peculiarities of classical harmonies: a) functional affinities of the fourth and fifth, b) the intimate relationship of parallel major and minor keys, c) relationship of overtones, and d) the role of leading tones. Here I should like to sum up briefly a few characteristic traits of this system:

First, in classical harmonies (in the case of C-major tonality) the circle of fifths F—C—G—D—A—E corresponds to the functional series S—T—D—S—T—D. When this periodicity is extended over the entire circle of fifths, the scheme of the axis system may be clearly recognized.

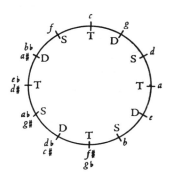

Chords resting on fundamental c, e flat = d sharp, f sharp = g flat, or a possess a tonic function; those based on e, g, b flat = a sharp, or c sharp = d flat have a dominant function, and chords built on d, f, a flat = g sharp or b have a subdominant function.

Second, Bartók is generally known to have shown a preference for the use of so-called major-minor chords (with neutral third), for instance, the following form in c tonality:

Function remains unchanged when the C-major mode comprised by the above chord is replaced by the parallel a minor or when the c-minor tonality comprised by the chord is replaced by the parallel E-flat major; this process occurs at every step in Bartók's music:

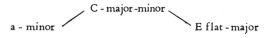

These substitution chords may also be employed in major-minor form, which brings the system to a close, because the parallel of A major, f-sharp minor and that of e-flat minor, G flat major arrive at an enharmonic meeting (f sharp = g flat):

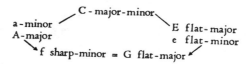

C - major-minor

a - minor   E flat - major
A - major   e flat - minor

f sharp-minor = G flat-major

Thus the axis extends the use of parallels over the whole system. (Naturally only major and minor keys of equal signature may be regarded as parallel, *e.g.*, C major and a minor, or c minor and E-flat major.) Application of these parallel connections to dominant and subdominant function leads to the scheme of the axis system.

Third, the acoustic precondition of arriving from the dominant to the tonic is to reach the fundamental tone from an overtone (this results in the affinity of various cadences). Accordingly, the dominant of c is not only g but also the near overtones e and b flat (therefore the circle of tonic-dominant relationships is expanded to include e—c and b flat—c). Since the D—T relationship corresponds relatively to the T—S and S—D relationships, overtone-to-fundamental-tone attraction prevails between the T—S and the S—D. When these conditions are applied to the circle of fifths, the results agree completely with the axis system.

Fourth, in the simplest cadence—in the affinity of the fifth-degree-seventh and the first degree—the chief role is played by the so-called sensitive sounds: the leading tone strives to reach the first and the seventh the third degree of the tonic—that is, the leading tone b is resolved by c and the seventh, f, by e or e flat. These two characteristically sensitive tones, however, stand in a tritonic relationship to each other, the tritone being distinguished by the characteristic that it persists when its tones have been exchanged. Thus, if the b—f relationship is converted into an f—b relationship—as is frequently done by Bartók—as a result the f (e sharp) assumes the role of the leading tone (striving towards f-sharp instead of e), while the seventh, b, strives towards a sharp (or a) instead of c; thus, instead of the expected tonic C major, the "counterpole" but equally tonic F sharp major (or minor) steps in.

Music, fourth movement

(cf. also 73-74, 98-99, 243-244, 275-276. bars)

G⁷ ——→ f-sharp

So far I have published some ten sorts of deductions from this system.

A survey of the past and of the development of harmonic thinking is bound to convince us that elaboration of the axis system was a historical necessity. As compared to the past, the advance consisted mainly of Bartók's having extended these affinities uniformly to the entire twelve-tone system. Moreover, his axis system represents not only a development of European functional music but also its consummation and even its conclusion, because by extending functional correlations to the homogeneous twelve-tone series he put the coping-stone on further development.

3

Among the influences that affected Bartók in his youth that of the French impressionistic school, particularly of Debussy, was decisive. What is today referred to as the "acoustic" system in Bartók's compositions drew chiefly on the colouristic chords of French impressionism. Bartók himself liked to allude to the wealth of inspiration he owed to modern French music. Without this factor the characteristic duality of his harmonic thinking could never have taken shape. From such evidence as has been given here it becomes clear that Bartók contrived to melt material that appeared to be incompatible into a comprehensive style, and it was this incongruous material that produced the most striking feature of his music: the dualism shown in his technique of polarization, or, in other words, the peculiar visual system which consistently permits things to be seen from two aspects and which with Bartók grew into a veritable philosophical standard, as if contrast were the only means to justify the existence of things. Bluebeard's night would be inconceivable without the luminous chord of the fifth door, the f sharp without the c, the Inferno without the Paradiso.

One may well wonder about the source of this tendency to polarize. Sometimes it would seem to flow from the attitude in Bartók of the scientist who knows that no existence can be imagined without positive and negative poles. Sometimes the impression is thereby created of harsh judgment, as with Dante; on other occasions it appears as a crystallized philosophical system. For the most part, however, it serves to mirror life: the unfathomable depths when from the world of light it plunges us into darkness or (as in the "Music for Strings, Percussion and Celesta" and the "Sonata for Two Pianos and Percussion") when from the night it leads us into daylight, pointing the way to solution, to joy.

In my analytical studies I have used the terms "bartokean chromaticism" and "bartokean diatony" to denote Bartók's dual world of harmonies. On the basis of their most characteristic traits, I have named the former the golden-section system and the latter the acoustic (overtone) system. Let us take a look at the properties that ensure the unity and polar division of the two systems. On this occasion we shall have to be content with a few main correlations.

First of all, it is common knowledge that Bartók's most markedly diatonic melodies constitute an acoustic or overtone scale. In the finale of the "Sonata for Two Pianos and Percussion," for example, the acoustic scale of c—d—e—f sharp—g—a—b flat—c hovers over the c—e—g (C major) chord. This scale is dominated by the major third, perfect fifth, natural seventh, and, further, the augmented fourth and the major sixth, in contrast to the minor third—perfect fourth—minor sixth (3 : 5 : 8, c—e flat—f—a flat) milieu of the golden-section system.[2] These two worlds of harmony complete each other to such measure that the chromatic scale can be separated into golden-section and acoustic scales.[3] Separately each is merely a part of the whole, and neither can exist without the other.

In the second place, the two systems are in a relationship of inversion, reflecting each other. By the inversion of the golden-section intervals acoustic intervals are obtained—from a major second (2) a natural seventh, from a minor third (3) a major sixth (with Bartók, the "pastoral sixth"), from a fourth (5) a fifth, from a minor sixth (8) a major third—and at that the most characteristic acoustic intervals. Systematically, therefore, they become related by organically complementing and reflecting each other. Their unity rests on mutual interdependence. The opening and closing of the "Cantata Profana" offers a beautiful illustration: two scales mirror each other tone for tone—a golden-section scale (intervals 2, 3, 5, 8, with a diminished fifth) and a pure acoustic scale:

[2] Compare, in "Sonata for Two Pianos and Percussion," the principal theme of the chromatic first movement with that of the diatonic third movement:

[3] Golden-section scale:

		3	5		8	
Golden-section scale:	C	E flat	F		A flat	
Acoustic scale:	C D		E	F sharp G		A B flat
	2		4	6 7		9 10

Third, although the features cited seem to concern external factors, this is no longer the case when it is shown that the acoustic system can admit only consonant intervals (because of overtone harmony), whereas the intervals of the golden-section system are tense and "dissonant" (this, by the way, shows forth the contrast between the western "acoustic" and eastern "pentatonic" attitudes).

An equally deep secret of Bartók's music (perhaps the most profound) is that the "closed" world of the golden-section system is counterbalanced by the "open" sphere of the acoustic system. The former is inevitably associated with the presence of the complete system (its configurations being representable only in the closed circle of fifths); the latter was moulded by Bartók from a single tone derived from the overtone series of a single fundamental note. The former does not respond to the requirements of "up" and "down," and its material is permanently in process of concentric augmentation and diminution. (The above-cited themes of the "Sonata for Two Pianos and Percussion" are, for instance, subjected to incessant increase, the principal theme being augmented from bar to bar and the tone series of the second theme expanding similarly from step to step until it attains a broad sixth; "cornet-shaped processions," "scissor-like" movement of voices, and sequences proceeding by augmented steps are frequent, and even these processes follow a planned course, every detail of the movement showing augmentation up to the geometric centre of the movement, after which every step is systematically diminished.)

Bartók's mode of acoustic writing is, on the other hand, marked by permanence; his harmonies radiate their energy for prolonged periods of time with motionless, unwavering constancy. For the closed world the emblem of the "circle" and for the open system that of the "straight line" automatically present themselves (chromatic configurations being bound to the circle—the circle of fifths—as opposed to the overtone system, where the component tones strive upward in a straight line). There is an obvious reference here to Dante, the emblem of his Inferno being the circle, the ring, and that of his Paradiso the straight line, the arrow, the ray. The rings of the Inferno undergo concentric diminution to "Cocitus" whereas those of his Paradiso are widened into the infinite "Empyreum." With Bartók, the themes follow the same pattern: chromaticism is associated with the circle and diatony most naturally with straight lines of melody.

» circle « (beginning)   » straight « (end)

Thus the two systems form unity and contrast; they require and preclude, affirm and deny each other. They constitute each other's negative impression in the twelve-tone system, each being capable of disclosing only one aspect of life. In Bartók's music, ideological unity and a complete picture of the world can be achieved by chromaticism only together with diatony and by diatony only together with chromaticism. It may be interpreted as a poetic symbol that in the diatonic system harmonic overtones develop above and in the chromatic system below the fundamental tone.

C[7]   C[7]
(acoustic)   (golden section)

In some of his works Bartók went so far in the polarization and simplification of the material that material and content, emblem and program, means and expression, were amalgamated to the point of inseparability.

4

So far, this investigation has sought to establish the ties between Bartók's music and that of the remote and recent past—folk song, functional music and French impressionism. The question naturally arises now of whether any correlations can be discovered between Bartók's art and the aspirations of the atonal school ("Zwölfton-Musik," as he liked to call it).

These days we may witness a curious phenomenon: formerly, even one or two decades ago, Bartók was attacked by his enemies for "aggressiveness" and "Asiatic gruesomeness"; today his music must be defended from attacks launched from the opposite side. The adherents of the twelve-tone system accuse Bartók of conservatism, compromise and "convenience" (in a dictionary of music recently published in western Europe "Bluebeard's Castle," for instance, was relegated into a class of compositions "intolerably superannuated"). Is it possible that Bartók, whom his contemporaries stigmatized as a barbarous shatterer of form, when regarded from a certain distance should suddenly turn out to have been no revolutionary but the heir and bearer of classical ideals? "In art there is only slow or rapid progress, implying in essence evolution and not revolution," Bartók said in an American interview in 1941.

It is certain that the peculiarities of Bartók's idiom tended gradually to disappear, as they grew more familiar and natural, while firmness of classical form, balance and proportion, simplicity and clarity of expression came more and more to command admiration. In "Music for Strings, Percussion and Celesta" we are held no longer by peculiar effects of colour but by the brilliant and unique grandeur that communicates a deeply human message, taking the listener from the resounding chaos of the first movement, through the biting humour of the second and the nature-bound spell of the third, to the joyous round dance of the fourth and the tones of fraternal love that crown the composition. To ears trained to atonality this music may really sound as if "softened by humanity." It is, however, worth-while to examine more closely the accusations thrown at Bartók. Extremists like to reproach Bartók for two things in particular: first, for his construction, with the claim that in the organization of material he fell far behind Schönberg and Webern, and second for his failure to attain the perfect "indifference" of the twelve tones and to give up the principle of tonality and achieve independence from harmonies. (According to one critic, "he did not recognize the possibility of culmination beyond harmony.")

In this controversy the material analysis of Bartók's works has produced a most unexpected turn; from the point of view of construction his works have been found to rank by no means behind those of Schönberg or Webern. On the contrary, with highly superior and much stricter organization his compositions actually surpass the works of the above-mentioned composers. If, on analysis of Schönberg's music, Adorno could declare, "There are no more free notes!" this statement can apply to the "Sonata for Two Pianos and Percussion," among other works. Here organization is really extended to everything, to form and proportions no less than to rhythm and harmony and even to dynamics, colour and register. But this constraint did not flow from a speculative tendency, as in the case of the atonal test tube; Bartók's solutions are always and everywhere musical and perceptible and are due to his having been able to reduce music to something extraordinarily elemental, ancient and fundamental. This is apt to appear with such straightforward bareness as to assume outwardly the form of mathematical formulas or symbols, yet they do not create the impression of abstraction. Rather, this simplification to symbols intensifies their elemental power.

Before proceeding further along this line, let us make a short detour. No one would think of asserting that the *la-so-mi* figures of the oldest nursery songs resulted from deliberate construction, though the notes of the melody are tuned after the "geometric mean," *i.e.*, after golden section. Hardly anyone remembers, when listening to music, that the consonance of the simple major triad results from the harmony of the nearest natural overtones; the perfect fifth and the major third bring to our ears the simplest process of vibrations. Now let us turn again to the "Sonata for Two Pianos and Percussion." The melody and sound system of the first movement may be traced to the most primitive pentatonic turns; in the principal theme of the finale, the melody simply spreads out the natural overtone scale above a C-major chord. Yet this major triad, appearing here, comes as a true revelation. How can a simple major triad be invested with such explosive content?

To approach the issue from the other side: may the contemporary composer avail himself at all of the services of the "major triad," the once vital significance of which has worn off until it has become an empty husk? Actually, the elemental effect of Bartók's music lies for the most part in apparently casual presentation, with plain connections, of the strongest means of expression. The major triad may be in itself a worn-out cliché, but when it is brought into polar-dual relationship with another system—as it was by Bartók—it may promptly regain its original and deep significance. Let us set up the formula of the work and add immediately the explanation: the golden section (geometric mean) between two poles always cuts into the most tense point, whereas symmetry creates balance (the overtone series is void of tension, because its notes are integer multiples of the fundamental tone's vibrations):

Dynamic proportion = golden section = pentatony = opening movement
Static proportion = symmetry = overtone scale = closing movement

In this connection *la-so-mi* and the major triad are not only representative of purest music but also elements of form and organization in construction, which are given the role of restoring to these apparently defervescent forms the fire that they may have possessed only when they came into being. What I should like to denote as the elemental rebirth of music is this reconstruction of musical means. Every element of music has been regenerated in a similar manner by the touch of Bartók; the most ancient element he recreated on the loftiest plane, so that beginning and end form an inseparable unity. There is no reason to question the authenticity of the thought attributed to Bartók in A. Fassett's book to the effect that he believed the very new could be borne only of the very ancient and that he had by-passed all the intervening and unnecessary complications separating the present from its origin.

It is inconceivable that Bartók, who applied thorough scientific methods in analysing, classifying, and systematizing folk songs, should have been naively uncritical when it came to his own compositions. I have no wish to prove that he aspired to an arithmetic or geometric system; he did, however, by going back to the roots of music, discover fundamental laws and "root" correlations which may be expressed by formula-like, mathematical symbols. In the last analysis, the whole technique of his music was based on these fundamental laws, and, with a consistency comparable only to that of the greatest masters of form, he expanded the system of laws derived from popular as well as art music over the whole of music, proceeding from the simple to the complex.

It was shown above that in the "Sonata for Two Pianos and Percussion" (as in numerous other compositions) every unit is divided after the rule of the golden section, from the whole of the work to the smallest cells. In these phenomena a much greater role must be ascribed to instinct and musical sensitivity—just as it was unnecessary for Mozart to count bars in order to compose periods of $4 + 4$, $8 + 8$, or $16 + 16$. That Bartók was not inspired by formalistic tendencies emerges from the fact that he treated the secrets of his forms as real "secrets" and never evinced any desire to explain his music. His high-tension message, however, stood in need of guarantees. With him, architectonic bonds implied recognition of the possibilities inherent in the material and of natural attractions; form did not represent a mere "façade" for composition. In the history of music, every truly great composition is imbued with the longing for full possession of the material, for completeness. With Bartók it also involves the triumph of man over unbridled instincts. Indeed, does the word "art" not intimate discipline over formless, chaotic material, thus giving expression to man's longing for order, to the healing power of art?

In Bartók's case, however, we have to repulse attacks on two fronts. Let me present a typical instance to those who reproach Bartók for having omitted the "total and radical reorganization of the material." In form the "Sonata for Two Pianos and Percussion" follows the pattern of "slow—fast+slow—fast"; the golden section may therefore be expected to come in at the beginning of the second slow movement. The result fulfils our expectations with astonishing accuracy: the time value of the complete work is 6,432 eighth notes and that of golden section, 3,975 eighths.

Those who speak of Bartók as a romantic retrograde bent on seeking asylum in folklore must have failed to grasp the exceptional coherence of his thought-processes and his all-embracing spiritual vigour. In architecture, his compositions are in no way looser than those of his contemporaries. Bartók's new adversaries are misled chiefly by the fact that these features escape notice, because with him geometry never appears as a sign of outward restriction but flows from the nature of his music, following the natural motion of the musical material. "We follow nature in composition," wrote Bartók, who proclaimed peasant music to be a "natural phenomenon."

Let us return to the second accusation, namely, that he failed to obey the demands made by the twelve-tone system on 20th century composers. This issue is answered most convincingly by Bartók's sound system. This system possesses the peculiar, dialectic trait of being approachable from the points of view of both functional and twelve-tone music, since in the axis system the principles of tonality and distance are equally realized—the latter to a degree that could not be surpassed by the use of purely logical methods. In Bartók's chromatic world, functional chief tones step into relationships of the augmented triad (cutting the system into equal thirds); hence with c as the tonic, the chief note of the dominant is represented by e and that of the subdominant by a flat; each of these permits substitution by the tritonic "counterpoles" (dividing the system into symmetric halves), while the poles of single functions rest on the basis of a diminished fourth (corresponding to equal quartering of the system). Thus the axis system can be built up also of mere distance formulas[4], which from the historical angle is an organic continuation of the age-old struggle between the principles of tonality and distance, with the gradual ascendency of the latter, which finally made it possible for the twelve notes of the chromatic scale to be subjected to equal, free treatment (with introduction of the tempered sound system in the centre of development; in some of Liszt's and Mussorgsky's attempts the distance principle was made to prevail faultlessly). Bartók's greatness lies precisely in his having realized his ideas while maintaining tonality and even function, because he was familiar with the surfaces of contact by whose aid these two arch-enemies could be

[4] The axis system may be defined also as follows: given the twelve-tone system and the three functions, it is the only system that can be realized with distance division.

reconciled. (He traces the minor-third circles of various "axes" to the minor-third relationship of parallel major and minor modes; for models of the augmented-triad correlations linking the three functions, Bartók may have drawn on such examples as are offered, for instance, by romantic harmonies.)

*

Particular significance may be attributed to the fact that pentatony is the most characteristic form of Bartók's chromaticism (golden-section system) and overtone chords, of his diatony. This duality would seem to give expression to the two perhaps most ancient endeavours of music. Clearly, the physiological apparatus of our ears (with the logarithmic structure of the cochlea) is such as to make *so-la-so-mi* (2, 3, 5) congenial at the earliest stage, of which the primitive levels of folk music and the simplest nursery songs provide unequivocal evidence. In such primitive melody cultures, the sense for major tonality and functional attraction are completely unknown. Harmonic thinking arises from a quite different source, from the overtone system, which could have come into its own exclusively with instrumental music (it cannot be considered as accidental that functional thinking is no more than a few centuries old). Pentatony may be deduced from the sound system of Pythagoras, harmonic music from the overtone system.

One wonders if pentatonic (golden-section) and harmonic (acoustic) thinking—these two points of departure for every kind of music—had a double root. If so, Bartók actually seems to have seized music at the very root. On one side is "inner" hearing—based on the build of the ear—and on the other the "external" hearing, so to speak, or physical harmony. The former is more ardent, expressive, and emotionally charged and the latter more radiant and luminous, richer in sensuous elements.

The above considerations agree with the scientific observation that golden section is associated only with *organic* substances (Fibonacci himself discovered it in connection with an investigation of natural phenomena). Without the contribution of man's emotional world, pentatony, with its tension, would never have come into existence. The acoustic system, on the other hand, may develop independently of the phenomena of human life (a pipe-like column of air or motion of a string-like material will suffice to bring it about).

Pentatonic and acoustic endeavours follow demonstrably contradictory courses. Physiological efforts organize and create tension, while physical efforts disorganize by striving to abolish tension. Here the thesis may be formulated that the golden-section system creates a *closed* world, heavy with inner tension, while the acoustic system is *open* and strives to dispel tension by overtone consonance.

It may be added that this closed-in form is an organic feature of golden section—quite apart from Bartók's sound system. Closure and golden section are related phenomena (the capacity of golden section to organize is due to this property). As an illustration of the correlations between the two; golden section can easily be brought about with the aid of a simple "knot" on a strip of paper*; every proportion of this knot—without exception—will display geometric golden-section.[5]

$$d:c = c:b = b:a = 1:0·618$$

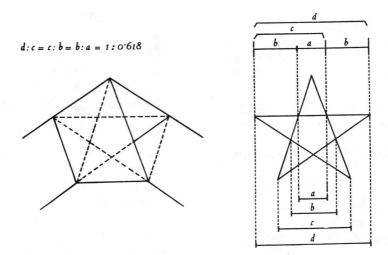

It is this property of the pentagram closed form thus obtained that Goethe alludes to in Faust, Part I:

* See Otto Schubert: *Gesetz der Baukunst* (Seemann, 1954, Leipzig).

[5] The correlations of the closed form and golden section became clearly discernible in Bartók's axis system. The following example presents the most characteristic axis turns and their golden-section construction:

Meph.: Let me admit; a tiny obstacle
Forbids my walking out of here:
It is the druid's foot upon your threshold.
Faust: The pentagram distresses you?
But tell me, then, you son of hell,
If this impedes you, how did you come in?
How can your kind of spirit be deceived?
Meph.: Observe! The lines are poorly drawn;
That one, the angle pointing outward,
Is, you see, a little open.

*

I would like to attempt here an interpretation of Bartók's dual world, his "yang-yin" technique, in terms of an equation, contrasting some special elements encountered at every step in Bartók's compositions. This interpretation is particularly applicable to the construction and content of the "Sonata for Two Pianos and Percussion."

First, "Inferno" movement	Third, "Paradiso" movement
chromaticism	diatony
golden-section system	acoustic system
closed world	open world
circular pattern of melody	straight pattern of melody
presence of central tone	presence of fundamental tone
rhythm with strong ending	rhythm with weak ending
uneven metre	even metre
asymmetries	periodicity
f-sharp minor beginning	C-major end
demoniac world	serene world, festive and playful
instinctive existence	intellectual existence
organic	logic
love—hatred	perfect understanding—irony
tension	freedom from tension
emotional nature	sensuous nature
inspiration	thought
experience	knowledge, solution

feminine symbols	masculine symbols
dependency on fate	law, order, form
permanent change	validity at all times
augmentation—diminution	stabilized forms
occurrence	existence
process in time	extension over space
origin—development—conclusion	division
finite: circular motion	infinite
geometric nature	mathematical nature
(key figure to golden	(key figures to overtone
section: irrational figure)	system: integrals)

It is interesting to note that Bartók presumably intended—as supported by the date of its composition, 1937—the "Sonata for Two Pianos and Percussion" as the crowning of the "Microcosmos" (1926—1937): the "Macrocosmos."

While the important questions of symbolism of keys and the role of rhythm cannot here be dealt with at great length, a few outstanding features may be pointed out. Bartók's rhythm is also governed by strict laws. The circular course of the first movement of the "Sonata for Two Pianos and Percussion Instruments" is in no slight degree brought about by the "absolute" uneven measure (three times three eighths), while the third movement owes its static character to its "absolute" even measure (twice two eighths); in the second movement, even and uneven bars are intentionally made to alternate between the two. Bartók was greatly interested in the idea of even and uneven metres ("Second Piano Concerto," "Concerto for Violin and Orchestra," second movement of "Music for Strings, Percussion and Celesta," "Microcosmos" No. 137—with these, themes presented in even measure recur in uneven rhythm, and vice versa). In addition, the rhythms with a "strong" ending in the first movement have counterparts with "weak" endings in the third movement[6]:

conclusion of theme

[6] Consequently, the themes of the first movement acquire a closed and those of the third movement an open form. The most interesting circumstance is that the dimensions of the complete work were not accidental—to quote only the final results, the time value of the composition (the above-mentioned 6,432 eighths = 804 whole tones) may also be traced to the symbol of the circle: $2^8 \pi = 4^4 \pi = 16^2 \pi = 804$.

Let us finally take up the role of Bartók's art in the music of our century. Bartók's golden-section system was rooted in eastern popular music and pentatonic conception; his acoustic system he owed to western harmonic thinking. His greatest achievement was the integration of these two ways of thinking. Hence those who respect Bartók as the epitomist of the music of the peoples of Eastern Europe are no less mistaken than those who would like to monopolize him on behalf of extremist efforts and condone his relations to folk music as a "regrettable pastime." He himself liked to refer to popular music and the French impressionistic school as the sources of the most decisive influences that shaped his art. Through his compositions we can extend the dimensions of this idea: what Bartók achieved in his art amounts to a synthesis of East and West, where folklore meets the counterpoint of Bach, the forms achieved by Mozart and Beethoven, and western harmonic thinking. Bartók is a classic master because he aspired to completeness. If his art and his position in the history of music could be summed up in a single sentence it would run as follows: Bartók achieved something that few others have been able to realize: a symbolic handshake of East and West, a union of the Orient and the Occident.

MAN AND NATURE
IN BARTÓK'S WORLD

by

BENCE SZABOLCSI

Beginning with the first fruits of his art, the compositions of Béla Bartók have aroused lively attention, commentaries and debates in both Hungarian and foreign musical criticism and musicology. We allude above all to the writings of his great contemporary, Zoltán Kodály, and to the reviews, tantamount to studies, of Antal Molnár, Béla Reinitz, Sándor Jemnitz, Cecil Gray, and Michel Dimitri Calvocoressi. However, the first presentation, as a systematic, comprehensive and coherent view of the world, of Bartók's ideas expressed in his music and writing was probably given by Aladár Tóth as early as the 1920's. In 1927, for instance, he wrote: "To Bartók the people means perpetual freedom, the road into the domain of unaffected primeval instincts. Here the people becomes the threshold to nature..." These words constitute the first summary statement of the four fundamental concepts, the four axes of Bartók's universe, with a clear recognition of their interrelation. They are: the people, freedom, the world of instincts, and nature. The few lines quoted above represent the first endeavour to clarify the position of man and nature in Béla Bartók's intricate world.

In attemptig to trace these postulates, our investigations have to go back to the beginning by acquiring an elemental knowledge of Bartók's world. The first problem that arises, namely, Bartók's relations to nature, will also point the path to the solution.

That Béla Bartók was, from his early childhood, bound to nature by the very closest ties, that he responded with highly susceptible nerves to the innumerable shades of landscapes, of the seasons and of the day, of form and of motion, may be clear even to those who have never heard any of his compositions or read a line of his writings; the perusal of a list of his works will suffice. It is not necessary to know that his "Night's Music" was inspired by the mumbling of bullfrogs in a pool on the Plains, the overture of the "Wooden Prince" by a forest of the Székely country, the nocturno of "Music" by the sighing of the wind; it is enough just to glance through the titles. The first childhood work of any considerable length was "The Danube"; the orchestral compositions include "Flowering" and "Village Dance," and in the late version of the Second Suite the "Puszta Scene." Among the pieces for piano the reader's eye may run over a multitude of the most colourful visions, from "Dawn" to the "Island of Bali"; among the songs his attention may be arrested by the striking series of poems on autumn, like "Autumn Breeze," "Autumn Tears," "Autumn Sounds," and the strange elegy beginning with the line "Autumn is killing down here in the valley." Should the reader be interested in anecdotes of a personal nature, he may learn from Agatha Fassett's book* how the composer relied for orientation in foreign regions, among men and animals, on an instinct and scent like those of a forest beast of prey; and he may muse over Bartók's remark to Endre Gertler during a performance of his "Music," written for grand orchestra: "Do you hear? This is the sea!"

All this is repeatedly confirmed, acquiring concrete substantiation and biographical authenticity, if the interested reader begins to peruse documents that have a personal bearing on Bartók's life, his letters, articles, studies, and the reminiscences of those who lived near him. The figure of a ceaselessly scrutinizing artist stands revealed, who from his earliest childhood was a passionate collector and student of the living, moving universe: butterflies, beetles, silk-worms, birds, trees and flowers he found no less absorbing than the mountains, oceans, and the movements of the stars, and he even cherished a desire to know the fauna and flora of remote continents. Wherever he went, his eye was caught by nature. His letters and studies are all relevant; here it must be borne in mind that with Bartók's laconically objective, invariably reticent style, the very fact that he mentions these phenomena is significant. Here, for instance, is the picture he gave of the Parc Monceau in Paris in the summer of 1905: "Sauntering aimlessly along the avenues of Paris, I suddenly came upon a tiny paradise. The entire little garden is perhaps twice as large as Erzsébet Square in Budapest. But only the French are gifted with the ingenuity to exploit nature and art in magically turning such a small place into so fairy-like a spot. The lovely trees, flowers and bushes harbour enough statues for a minor spring show... A tiny little lake nestles in the cool shade of the trees, with a row of crumbling, tottering Greek pillars along its shore as though the ruins of some ancient edifice had found their way here. Some of the columns are overrun

* "Béla Bartók's American Years—The Naked Face of a Genius" (1960, 320 pp.)

by creepers... In the Jardin des Plantes I walked beneath cedars of Lebanon..."*

In 1908 he wrote: "Travelling via Lyon, Vienne, Valence and Avignon, at last I attained the peak of my desires, the sea. Only the small Mediterranean, but, nevertheless, the sea... This is where first I bathed in the sea... and first beheld—a mirage!"** In the autumn of 1908 he wrote from Torockó: "Yesterday I walked along the mountain-gorge of Torda, today I am enjoying myself in Torockó, at the foot of Mount Székelykő... Of the Hungarian villages I have seen so far, this one definitely lies in the most picturesque region. And in addition, the yellow-red forests..." (*ibid.* 86). Early in 1911 he wrote from Topánfalva: "The surrounding country is of miraculous beauty; even if I had to leave empty-handed, I would not mind. Among pines, gigantic snow-capped mountains, rapid streams, on carriage, sledge or on foot. All this is so new to me, I have never been to wild woodlands in winter before..." (*ibid.* 92). From the vicinity of Besztercebánya, in 1915: "One gets a view of Liptó County where rocky mountains of rather phantastic shape are to be seen..." (Letters I, 86). From the Welsh seaside, in spring 1922: "The two huge windows of my room look upon the ocean—the waves are rumbling below, the sunshine is marvellous..." (*ibid.* 103). From Los Angeles, in 1928: "I am staying in a private wooden house on the shore of the sea. The Pacific Ocean makes a tremendous noise, booming, roaring, sometimes even shaking my bed at night..." (*ibid.* 115). At Pontresina in 1939, he climbed the peak of Languard which is over 10,000 feet high (*ibid.* 118); his first flight, in 1936, carried him to an almost similar altitude: "At a height of 2,400 metres (8,000 feet), in brilliant sunshine, over infinite stretches of fleecy, curly clouds... well, now I know what it is like!" (*ibid.* 128). Finally, just one picture of Mersin in Anatolia, in 1936: "This was a veritable subtropical region, where during my visit at the end of November the weather was as hot as at the close of August, where dates grow and sugarcane, where we wandered under pepper trees, under flowering and fruit-bearing banana trees, where the temperature never sinks below freezing." (Folk-song Collecting in Turkey).

Innumerable further examples such as these might be cited. They all go to prove that scenery and nature were the first to captivate Bartók's eyes. In his reminiscences, his son Béla wrote: "He loved nature in all its mani-

---

* *Bartók Béla levelei* (Letters of Béla Bartók, usually referred to as Letters I), edited by János Demény, published by *Magyar Művelődési Tanács*, Budapest, 1948, p. 57.

** *Bartók Béla levelei* (Béla Bartók's Letters, usually referred to as Letters II), edited by János Demény, *Művelt Nép* publishers, 1951, p. 85.

festations; he regularly went for walks and excursions. Whenever possible, at the end of each academic year, he left for the mountains, where he spent a month finding complete physical and mental recreation; the majority of his most significant compositions he wrote when thus refreshed, during the second half of the summer vacation. Among natural phenomena, he was equally interested in plants, animals, and minerals."

A direct connection between experience and work can naturally be but rarely demonstrated. That the "Evening with the Székelys" stems from the first Transylvanian collecting tour, is obvious from the dates (1907—1908); that "Night's Music" was inspired by a trip to the Plains, emerges from the reminiscences of Béla Bartók junior; it is also beyond doubt that the bird-note studies of his last American summer are closely related to the sylvan bird-song music of the Third Piano Concerto. Elsewhere the interconnections have remained hidden, but their actual presence behind almost every composition is becoming increasingly probable, in somewhat the same way as Beethoven's rambles around Heiligenstadt were perpetuated in the score of the Sixth Symphony.

Indeed, Bartók's nature-world is incredibly wide and colourful. Landscape description and illustration may here almost be regarded only as a first phase, a starting-point, even when its emotional content and dramatic significance are in the forefront from the very first; "Flowering" is already of this kind, so is the flower-garden and the pool of tears in "Bluebeard's Castle," and also the fabulous forest and swelling stream in the "Wooden Prince." These pictures display the traits that were to become increasingly characteristic of Bartók's later nature-music: he did not depict, illustrate, or decorate nature, but let it speak for itself, identifying himself with it; he has it speak from "inside" in the language of the river, the idiom of the forest, the dialects of valley and cave. It is, moreover, characteristic that the scenery is immediately peopled by living creatures—here attention may be drawn to the animal world appearing on the scene, from the innocent adventures of the "Little Fly" or the meek domestic animals of his "Spellbinder" and the birds, through the "Bear Dance" and the mythical stags of the "Cantata profana" to the procession of beasts of prey in the "Marcia delle bestie," where the living animal world would seem to conceal the threatening shadows of animal fiends, ready to intervene and destroy. Bartók felt close to these primeval beings; he evinced excited interest when speaking about the legendary world of Rumanian sagas, where the story tells not only of the rivalry of the sun and the moon, but of boys turned into stags and of fights against the mythical lion; "so many pagan memories," he cried, in rapture. In America it was once said of him that he understood and "spoke" equally well the language of cats, birds and lions, like Kipling's Mowgli.—But from the beginning this scenery includes man, with the immense, virtually unsurveyable range of his being, his fate and his significance.

What sort of man peoples Bartók's universe? The first thing that meets the eye is that this man, the ideal man, is an inseparable part of nature. Bartók was twenty-six when he described his own pantheistic creed in a letter: "If I were to make the sign of the cross I should say, 'In the name of Nature, Art and Science'..."* This point of departure, this classical trinity determined not only his work as a creative artist, but also his scientific activity, his entire human and moral attitude.

At the outset we quoted the observation of Aladár Tóth, the most eminent contemporary critic of Bartók's music, concerning the composer's relationship to the people and to nature. Let us add some further observations made by Tóth seven years later, in 1934**: "The peasant, who in everyday life remains in crude, direct contact with the elements, experiences from year to year the birth, bloom and passing away of life. He beholds them with the same childish wonder and ministers to them with the same simplicity as Béla Bartók." (Pesti Napló, Jan. 4, 1934). This, it is clear, will serve as one of the chief, fundamental explanations for what will be said in the further course of this essay. In his art and his studies just as in the people and his own heroes, Bartók always sought the laws of nature; thus he was led in this direction not only by his tours, collecting and reading, but his whole human and creative spirit also served such ideas.***

It has long been observed that Bartók's scientific system, his whole scholarly method, were far more those of a scientist than of a historian. "How did it happen, whence did it originate?" were not the questions to attract his interest; he was drawn by the problems of "what exists, how and why does it exist and in how many variaties?" Times out of number he betrayed that it was in full consciousness of this scientific bent that he lived and worked. It is common knowledge that the discovery of the ancient Hungarian folksong is linked to the names of Bartók and Kodály. Well, Bartók regarded folk music, the folksong, as a natural phenomenon. "We follow nature in our creative work, since peasant music is a natural phenomenon," he wrote in 1928 (Selected Writings, 1956, 213). Three

---

* ibid. p. 77.

** In "Pesti Napló", a daily Budapest newspaper.

*** The ceaseless scrutiny of the process of arising and of passing away belonged to Bartók's method of work, because his whole conception of the world was centred around his belief in natural philosophy. As interpreted by Goethe and Humboldt, life and the world, being organic phenomena, are a concatenation of organic correlations.

years later, in 1931, he said: "We profess ourselves to be scientists who have chosen as the subject of their study a certain product of nature, peasant music" (*ibid.* 315). And in another place: "This kind of music is really nothing other than the result produced by the transforming activity of unconsciously functioning natural forces in people uninfluenced by urban culture" (*ibid.* 186).

Later he went perhaps still further in linking nature and music, region and melody. A statement of his quoted by Agatha Fassett as having been uttered during one of their conversations in America, though apparently presented in a highly stylized form, is all the more believable in respect to its content: "I like to keep in mind all sorts of regions, and I like to clothe them in accordance with the changing seasons. Just as I like to invest songs with the colours of the countryside that has preserved them." In this world of ideas popular tunes come into being like bushes or waterfalls, the human community being little more than a medium for the manifestation of the creative power inherent in the Earth and the Cosmos. It would be easy to point to the survival of Rousseau's and Tolstoi's romanticism in these words and views, compared to which Kodály's folklore teachings may be said to express the concrete and realistic historical approach. However—and here it is necessary, to contradict numerous opinions on Bartók—this romantic ideal formed an organic part of Bartók's personality, imbued with an unequalled passion for knowledge and scientific endeavour. While searching for the laws of nature and striving to come close to nature, he suddenly—like Rousseau and Tolstoi (or among his contemporaries Giono, Ramuz, and others)—came up against conscious civilization, the town, artificial demands on life, the tussle of free competition, and the rootless world of the dominant strata, consisting, in Hungary, of the bourgeoisie and of feudal remnants simultaneously. He thus grew—as we would now say—into a "romantic anticapitalist." Already he united in his person all the contradictions of "romantic anticapitalism," for he was a delicate urban—soon a metropolitan—artist with a sensitive constitution, pampered by and at the mercy of civilization, metropolitan comfort, bustle and solicitude! Yet, at the same time, alert and tense, keen of hearing and sight, his visionary nerves enabled him to detect the approaching destruction of this bourgeois world, to sense the latent smell of death behind its civilization. It is true that research, experiment, publicity, the apparatus of science and art are urban privileges too, and Bartók was willing to accept them, but what he could not accept was the mercenary and warpingly commonplace life of the capitalist city. Since he was searching for natural man, for primitive man, who had remained close to the great laws of nature, he had to find the sought for and desired type in the peasant. All that was ancient, primitive, all that contrasted with the mechanized world of the metropolis was dear to him; in it he took refuge, held on to it with wild, demonstrative, often desperate defiance; he was determined to find the primeval world in the twentieth century! In an era of lies, delusions, deception and half-measures, he was going to find the *pure spring*, the golden age, the refuge of mankind. "Peasant and primitive," he wrote in 1931, "I employ both words to denote an ancient, ideal simplicity devoid of trash." Hence his personal conclusion that "the happiest days of my life have been those I spent in the country, among peasants..." (1928.) "As far as I am concerned," he wrote in one of his last articles (1943), "I can only say that the time I have devoted to such work (*i. e.* the collection of folksongs) has been the finest part of my life, one which I would not exchange for anything. The finest part in the noblest sense of the word, because I was permitted directly to observe the artistic manifestations of a still homogeneous, but already vanishing social structure. Beautiful to the ears, beautiful to the eyes! Here in the West (*i. e.* in America) people cannot even imagine that in Europe there are still areas where practically every article used, from clothing to tools, is made at home, where one cannot see stereotype, factory-made trash, where the shape and style of objects varies from region to region, often from village to village... These are unforgettable experiences; painfully unforgettable, for we know that this state of the village is doomed to annihilation... It will leave a great void behind it..." And later: "Now that these peoples murder one another on orders from above... it is perhaps opportune to point out that the peasants show no trace of savage hatred against other peoples, nor have they ever done so. They live peacefully beside each other; each speaks his own language, follows his own customs, and deems it natural for his foreign-tongued neighbours to do the same... Among peasants peace prevails—hatred against other races is stimulated only by the upper circles." This is Bartók's picture of the happy village, his fantasy of a golden age. But is it possible—the historian may well ask—that Bartók, one of the most sharp-sighted humanists of the age, should have failed to notice what his contemporary, the novelist Zsigmond Móricz, had perceived long before— that Hungarian villages, like the villages of Eastern Europe generally, were far from happy in the years from 1910 to 1920, that they represented a microcosmos struggling under the stress of mud, misery, and antagonisms in just the same way as the towns? Bartók deliberately idealized this world in order that he might escape to it, that he might say: "There is no one more fortunate than a peasant... the peasant supports gentry and clergy, soldiers and beggars... If there were no peasants, we should have no bread. If they did not plough, we should all starve... The peasant supplies all his own needs, preparing—and decorating—his tools, home and clothing. Music and songs he knows not from books. He has no need of city rubbish..." As we see, the words of this chorus (Of Past Times, 1937) and the text of the much later article correspond almost word by word. "Music and songs he knows not from books..."—no, they are suggested by nature, by instinct, by the primordial source.

And now let us quote from Bartók's famous creed of 1931: "My true ideal is... the brotherhood of all peoples, the establishment of a brotherhood despite all wars and contentions. This ideal I endeavour... to serve in my music; this is why I shall evade no influences, whether of Slovak, Rumanian, Arab or any other origin, provided only that the source be pure, fresh and wholesome." One cannot but remember that the words "source" and "pure source" had been written down by Bartók shortly before, in a major composition; and just as we recognized above the key to another choral work of his, the true sense of the "Cantata Profana," with its stags that drank only spring water, is bound, here as well, to flash across the mind. There is, moreover, a third great work on the same theme: a strong primitive man who has remained close to nature fights depraved metropolitan crime ("The Miraculous Mandarin"). It should be noted, though, that the metropolis of the Mandarin is in itself a demoniac, elementary natural phenomenon, a jungle fashioned as a metropolis. Reference to another early hero of Bartók's may be even more convincing—the Prince, who overwhelms the misshapen fiends of vanity and human meanness in the name of nature and with the aid of nature. We may note, at this point, that virtually all Bartók's grand works join forces in proclaiming the greatness and truth of man who has remained loyal to nature. Whether he bears the name of "peasant" (remember that Bartók always regards folk music as "peasant music" too!) or that of a Prince, whether he is dressed as a mandarin or appears as a mythical stag, is indeed a secondary issue, which scarcely affects the core of the composer's message.

What then is freedom, and who is free in Bartók's world? Man is free if he remains in close communion with nature and thereby with the great laws of life; in him there remains alive most effectively what it is worth while living for, it is he who has preserved human dignity. The Prince who overcomes nature through nature is free; so is the Miraculous Mandarin who is made invincible by vital strength, by the power of passion, and by independence from brigand society. The hunters of the Cantata Profana, who turn into stags, who will no longer brook the shackling intricacies of social conventions are also free, as is the peasantry, the peasant of Eastern Europe, happy and creative. It is, indeed, strange to hear this about the peasant of whom Bartók himself has sung "there is no man unhappier," who was rewarded by his masters with blows for every service and every gift, who "is ceaselessly harassed, allowed no respite as long as there is life in him!" The contradiction cannot be explained, but the contradiction itself leads us on to a fuller knowledge of Bartók's universe. Before taking this further step let us note that this peasant romanticism, the romantic and dreamy idealization of village life, also belonged to the tragic process of regression that gradually gained ascendency in the last years of the master's life. Again we have to refer to the records of Agatha Fassett (pp. 134—35, 170—71). In America, when Bartók recalled Hungarian peasant houses · or bread-baking in his mother's house, when he joyfully hailed paraffin-lamps instead of electric lights, he was longingly returning to a childhood that had been better, simpler, more primitive, and was nearer to the happy home, the golden age, the native country he had left for ever.

It is precisely in this manner that we can approach an essential feature in the life and creative work of Bartók. The search for the pure source, the primeval spring, primordial nature, the fundamental truths of life, led him to the requirement of pure form, pure structure and pure expression; it led him to the unequivocal musical formulation of *character*. This was the decisive turn which lifted Bartók's universe from among that of most of his contemporaries. As with Beethoven, his flight became opposition, and suddenly the solution appeared: the instincts must be liberated in a creative sense, the contradictions have to be welded into character. Here the word "character" suddenly assumes a double meaning: it denotes the essence of musical representation as well as the musical modelling of human character.

Haydn once told Griesinger, his biographer, that he had meant to draw moral "characters" in his symphonies. He may have expressed his idea hazily, but the sense of his words stands out clearly and definitely. In the period of enlightenment, aesthetes in general liked to avail themselves of the term, ever since La Bruyère—following the examples of antiquity—revived the portrayal of character, and the delineation of human characters began to fire the imagination of musicians too. Our view of Bartók partly corresponds with this interpretation, and partly it does not; in the notion of "character" we propose to include those types of themes and moods that belong together according to their contents and musical attitude. Bartók's "Night" themes, for instance, form such a character, furthermore the "Allegro Barbaro" type (particularly in the closing movements), the groups of dirges and dance phantasies, the peculiar monologue form, the development of which may be traced from the string quartets to "Music for Strings, Percussion and Celesta." These characters are marked not only by their representation of phenomena and processes but also by the fact that each summarizes the relation of man and the universe in a lasting picture. As with Beethoven, their development in the hands of Bartók took on two forms: elaboration of the basic themes and their "purification" by means of variations. We are familiar with the composer's important statement in 1937 about the significance of the technique of variation. "It is generally found," he said, "that I lay great stress on elaboration, that I do not like to use the same musical thought twice in the same form or repeat any detail unaltered; this explains my special predilection for variation and the transformation of themes. It was no mere game when I inverted the theme in my second piano concerto. The extreme variety, which is typical of Hungarian folk music, flows also from my own nature and aspirations." So much for the technique of variation which connects Bartók with Bach, Beethoven and Liszt on the one hand, and with folk music on the other; it should be borne in mind that variation is the basic creative method of folk music, and thus in Bartók's eyes the natural mode of composition. With Bartók, variation, however, stood also for something else: conception on an ever higher level, hence a gradual purification of the idea, a gradual catharsis, and thus, in the last analysis, a moral idea. We should remember here that from his early youth Bartók's favourite method of composition was to *vary the meaning of the same material*. Following in the wake of Berlioz and Liszt, this was his path to the fullest development of his personality already in his "Kossuth" and in the First Suite built on recurring basic themes. He achieved it in "The Ideal Portrait" and "Grotesque Portrait," which are contradictory elaborations of the same theme in two character variations, furthermore in the single-theme pattern of his works for the stage and his string quartets, and perhaps the most lucidly in "Music" and the Sixth String Quartet, where almost nothing happens but purification of the same material, the basic idea, and its elevation to increasingly lofty regions—as in Beethoven's last chamber music works. This organic unfolding of variation, this "natural" mode of creation, was a method of creative composition peculiar to Bartók and reminds us of his late statement interpreting his whole artistic development as the repetition and solution of problems on an ever higher plane. Obviously, it was here that Bartók attained the deepest and at the same time loftiest union with "nature."

However, only the sharply outlined type, the truly pronounced character, are suitable for varied expression. What matters is that both this variation and that, should be characteristic. Every new clarification, every transformation can only produce a profile which has in essence been lying dormant within. The expression "this variation and that" throws light on a fundamental, specific trait of Bartók's musical "characters": the constant dialectic tension of two poles, the permanent presence of lasting and ephemeral, rising and falling elements, the principles of dissonance and harmony. Beethoven throughout most of his life is supposed to have followed a twofold principle of form, the path dictated by a tendency to impulsiveness and appeasement, to dynamic activity and accommodating contemplation. With Bartók this twofold nature is perhaps still more organic, still more fundamental. In his frequently quoted and much discussed study on Bartók, Attila József made the apposite observation that the dissonant and the resolving principles constantly merge, while at the same time keeping each other alert; they call and challenge each other, lending a ceaselessly undulating motion to the whole thread of thought. This may well be where the chief quality lies hidden, which rendered Bartók different from his western contemporaries, the great and the less eminent experimenters.

However, as has been mentioned before, this dual character, thesis and antithesis, accompanied Bartók's development from start to finish. It is the dual form of matter, expressed in melody and rhythm, in augmentation and diminution, in diatony and chromaticism, or, if you like, in the Ideal and the Grotesque, the Prince and the corporeal Wooden Dummy. Let us recall that with Bartók, contrast and inversion were one of the most outstanding means for developing themes. The dual unity of theme and countertheme extends to this sphere too: they emerge from "here" and "there," from "above" and "below," from the "depths" and the "heights," incessantly arguing with each other, replying to each other, wrestling with each other or embracing each other, soaring upwards and bending downwards, appearing as a self-contradicting structure, assuming the form of a bridge, an arch, or a dome. Here we come upon *the character which, through its contradictions, rises to a higher union*, the Hegelian dialectic in Bartók's art. It is, moreover the "law of nature" itself, which Bartók evidently felt he could also bring to prevail in his works, thereby reaching the "pure spring" of which he had been dreaming all his life.

At this point all that had held Bartók captive at the beginning of his path found its resolution—the enthralling magic and thrill of nature, the concomitants of his affinity and strangeness to humanity: the struggle against space and distance so familiar to those who have travelled much, dizziness, anxiety, great childish fears, the "pavor nocturnus," the presentiment of permanent danger in general, the feeling of exposure to the "jungle" that inspired him in so many voices and works, and which left its mark on his whole conduct; here he himself became the mythical stag of the Cantata, which has learnt to defy for evermore the dangers not only of the huts but also of the brushwood, and has come to stand firmly on the mountain top.

*

The birth of every great work is affected by, and in turn guides, the fate of its genre at a decisive evolutionary moment. In taking shape, the career of every great artist sets in motion and determines the various historical phases of his art, possessing and representing, as he does, the forces that are about to grow into the decisive factors of the age. What is a social phenomenon thus becomes a personal initiative, and *vice versa*. In Bartók's universe, the picture of man and nature is a continuation and a modification of the picture produced by his predecessors. In the music of the eighteenth century, the representation of nature varied between the heroic and the idyllic, from Händel to Haydn; the art of Haydn and Beethoven expressed and brought to flowering the more personal, more humanly related nature of the bourgeois world. Then came the growing contradictions of bourgeois development, the growing distance between town life and village life, between rural simplicity and civilization, until the portraiture of nature, at the close of the nineteenth century and the opening of the twentieth, revealed how far man and nature had become divorced from each other. The artist was compelled to wage renewed battles for the conquest of the lost old unity or rather for the acquisition of a new, nascent unity. Some composers (Wagner) transformed nature into symbol and magic, others (Debussy) changed it into an ethereal fluid, which engulfed man's life in murmuring waves and the touch of which caused ecstasy and delight. One of the most astounding discoveries of the twentieth century was that of Stravinsky, in whose works around 1910 nature appeared as a barbarous, misanthropic compulsion at a time when other arts as well disclosed mechanicalness, technics, and demonized, fetishized mass motion as constituting the merciless and compulsory fetters of life. In the years between 1920 and 1940 the issue had already arisen as to whether man would succeed in reconquering and enlisting on his own side the seemingly overgrown, savage, bleakened forces of nature. With increasing poignancy the question was posed whether "human dignity" could be saved from the attack—first insidious then ever more open—of the ghastly forces of inhumanity. Our allusion to "seemingly overgrown" elemental forces is inspired by the fact that, while science and technique were advancing victoriously, the great majority of artists at that time stared with aversion, anxiety, estrangement and perplexity at the surrounding world that had become alien, a world in which questions were multiplying and answers becoming increasingly nebulous. Bartók saw the answer in an alliance with nature, with the elemental forces among which man—himself filled with elemental forces—must recover his brotherly place. What we call demoniac, elementary, superhuman, must be regulated so as to give it an inner and outer harmony and fitted into the concept of a moral world order. In the last analysis, this world order is but a new balance in which the laws of the inner and outer world are reconciled and become permanent allies.

In the music of the twentieth century, this solution has so far been achieved by the art of Bartók alone; that is why it could become the foundation of humaneness in its broadest sense.

PRECURSORS AND CONTEMPORARIES

AN EARLY BARTÓK-LISZT ENCOUNTER

Work on the relations between the music of Ferenc Liszt in his mature period and old age and twentieth-century music, with particular reference to Bartók's music, has been going on in Hungarian musical research for over fifty years. Bartók himself was the pioneer in this field. In an article entitled "The Music of Liszt and Contemporary Audiences,"[1] written in 1911, he spoke very highly of the later Liszt compositions, which were at that time little known and even less appreciated. In his inaugural lecture at the Hungarian Academy of Sciences in 1936—("Liszt Problems")—Bartók re-affirmed and enlarged on what he had written twenty-five years earlier.[2] The influence of Liszt's music on later developments constituted a separate section in this lecture. When Bartók declared that "in any number of more recent Hungarian compositions traces of Liszt's legacy can be discovered with absolute certainty,"[3] he was undoubtedly including himself among those who showed signs of Liszt's influence, as was clear from the subsequent sentence in the lecture.

The parallel between the art of Liszt and the art of Bartók had been drawn as early as 1940 by Aladár Tóth in his paper "Ferenc Liszt in the Development of Hungarian Music." Although in 1932 Zoltán Gárdonyi drew attention to the significance of Liszt's later style ("Liszt's Unpublished Hungarian Compositions"), it was only first analyzed with the care both its own profundities and its fecundating influence on European music merited by Bence Szabolcsi in his inaugural lecture in 1954 at the Hungarian Academy of Sciences, and then, following the lecture, in his book "The Twilight of Ferenc Liszt,"[4] which was soon afterwards published in several other languages as well as in Hungarian. This very important study was the first to throw a light on Liszt's influence on Bartók. Since then, further research has confirmed the

Liszt-Bartók resemblance so clearly illuminated in Szabolcsi's study. István Szelényi published his researches in a number of first editions of Liszt compositions, and the author of the present paper reported in an article which was published in German on his discovery of a Liszt-manuscript, in the musician's handwriting, the *Eighteenth Hungarian Rhapsody*, which presaged the style of Bartók.

It is no accident that the subject of these researches and in general the basis of the Liszt-Bartók comparison were very largely the compositions Liszt wrote in his old age. Bartók himself could hardly have known most of the work written by Liszt in his old age, and certainly not when he was a young man. It is worth noting, however, that in both his earlier articles and his lecture on Liszt, Bartók gave especial praise to the Liszt compositions connected with the Faust theme, the *Faust Symphony*, The *Sonata in B minor*, the *Danse Macabre* Piano Concerto, ranking them as works that would retain their influence for a long time. The aspirations and conflicts of Faust, the infernal powers of Mephisto to destroy ideals on the verge of fulfilment are the questions which found most valuable and most characteristic expression in the art of the aged Liszt, and this was precisely the theme, both in terms of content and style which is of absorbing interest to Bartók.

[1] See Béla Bartók: "Letters, Photographs and Music." Compiled and edited By János Demény, Budapest 1948, Hungarian Art Council.

[2] Cf. Liszt, *Hangnemnélküli Bagatell* ("Bagatelle without Tonality"). Compiled and edited from Ferenc Liszt's manuscripts by István Szelényi. With an introduction in Hungarian, German and French by the Editor. Budapest 1956, Editio Musica.

[3] Ibid.

[4] Szabolcsi, Bence: "The Twilight of Ferenc Liszt" (Translated by András Deák). Budapest, 1959, Publishing House of the Hungarian Academy of Sciences, pp. 134.

We are talking of a link: Bartók need not have had any direct knowledge of the compositions dating from Liszt's old age; it was obviously enough for him to have known the subject-matter expressed in these compositions—expressed in its final and almost ruthless simplicity—from Liszt's earlier and somewhat milder and more romantic phase. This was really enough, for both the aged Liszt and the young Bartók were temperamentally inclined to the broodings and speculations of lonely genius in the Faustian manner. It was inevitable they would both discover Faust in themselves, it was inevitable they would both give artistic expression to the struggle between good and evil embodied in the Faust legend.

Our own Liszt-Bartók parallel is connected with Faust. It can be followed through two "Bagatelles" composed for the piano, one of them being Liszt's *Bagatelle without Tonality*, and the other Bartók's *Fourteenth Bagatelle*.

*

The year 1908 was a turning point in Bartók's life and music. In 1908 works of an entirely different tone, introducing a new world of melody and harmony, replaced the compositions inspired by popular songs and later by peasant melodies. In the posthumously published *Violin Concerto*, the *Two Portraits*, the *Fourteen Piano Pieces*, the *Ten Easy Piano Pieces*, the *First String Quartet* and the *Two Elegies*, Bartók produced something unprecedently new, something that astounded and shocked the critics. At that time there were few who surmised that these works by the recently appointed 27-year-old professor at the Budapest Academy of Music would eventually come to be regarded as landmarks in the history of both Hungarian and European music.

But 1908 nowadays means more to students of musical history than the above list of Bartók's works. These attempts to find a new musical language were closely linked to a profound appraisal on his part of the deepest human and philosophical questions. In point of time, no doubt, the latter came first. Thinking about a new way of life must have preceded the desire to express it in art. The climax came after a spiritual crisis lasting several years, probably beginning in 1905, the year of the disappointing and disillusioning Paris competition for composers, and ended in 1908, when he was first attracted to Márta Ziegler, who later became his first wife.

The intervening three years were marked by the onset of a host of new experiences. It was a period of anguished loneliness, despite the attentions of many friends and well-wishers, and of philosophic meditation, nourished by this loneliness. Among those who gave him support was Dietl, professor of piano at the Vienna Conservatoire who had been on the jury of the Paris competition, and had revealed to Bartók in detail all the doings of the inept and impotent jury of that unfortunate affair. And far away—in Pozsony (now Bratislava, Czechoslovakia), Nagyszentmiklós and Budapest—there were warm-hearted correspondents like his mother, the Jurkovics girls, friends since their common childhood, and later Stefi Geyer, the concert violinist, an outstanding pupil of Hubay, all of them concerned for his welfare.

As we know from the letters to his mother dated August 15, 1905, and September 10 respectively, Bartók was taken around in Paris by Dietl. The flood of new impressions seemed to make him forget the recent failure, the blow to his pride as an artist. Some of them were bound to leave their mark on later compositions. Before attempting to analyze one of them, let us quote a longer section from the letter he wrote to his mother on August 15, 1905, from Paris. The description in this letter and the *Fourteenth Bagatelle* of Bartók seem to have common points of emotional and intellectual reference.

"...Dietl took us to a peculiar place of 'amusement.' The idea on which the place is based is so bizarre that it is worth describing at some length.

We entered a tavern called 'Le Néant.'

The first room was a dark little den; the light was provided by torches, and waiters dressed in the clothes of funeral attendants set our beers down on plain wooden coffins instead of tables, accompanying their action with rude remarks, the gist of which was that we were corpses, so would we please keep quiet. The walls were decorated with amiable inscriptions like: 'Corpses, hurry up and drink your beer because you're beginning to stink'. Above them were hung pictures depicting quite ordinary scenes: a battle scene, someone serenading his sweetheart, a rendezvous of lovers, etc. Every patron was given a thin candle.

A burning liquid suddenly ran into a glass tube hanging from the ceiling—and the room was flooded as if by daylight. Hardly had this happened when we had the frightening experience of noticing that our faces had turned ashy pale, our lips livid and our nails violet—in fact, we looked like corpses.

In the meantime the waiters in the room spoke to us in a funereal voice, and by the sharp light we could clearly see that every implement and piece of furniture in the room was made of human bones.

Now came the first attraction: the room was darkened again, the light being concentrated on the pictures of romantic subjects: the young lover and the soldiers gradually assumed the appearance of skeletons.

The second attraction was the following:

We went on into another, still smaller room, completely dark, on the wall of which opposite us was a small opening just large enough to see through it an open coffin under a bright light in the further room. Someone in the audience was invited to go across and stand in the coffin. Dietl—knowing what was to follow—volunteered without further ado. He stood in the coffin, wrapped in a white shroud up to the chin. All of a sudden, oh, horror, his face grew waxen and rigid, his eyes looked sunken, the flesh seemed to peel off his body and slowly he turned into a skeleton. A skeleton stood in the coffin!

He changed back in a similar fashion.

A pretty young girl also volunteered to submit to the metamorphosis...

...Don't imagine for a moment that the audience was impressed! Not at all! The whole 'tavern' seemed to be based on the idea of flirting with death, of mocking the fear of death.

One finds such strange things in Paris!..."

So, there was the theme of death in a Paris night club in 1905, whose mood probably mingled with other impressions it was to imbue a Bartók composition, the *Fourteenth Bagatelle*. But was it mere accident that twenty-three years earlier, in 1885, in the creative brain of Ferenc Liszt, then in the last two years of his life, a tavern scene also matured into a piece for the piano reflecting the same macabre death fire. István Szelényi found it in 1956 in the course of his researches at Weimar—and he was the first to edit it from the scattered manuscript pages—a piano piece by Liszt to which the composer had finally given the title of *Bagatelle without Tonality*. The original title had been more revealing: "Fourth Mephisto Waltz (without tonality)." This title (which does not refer to a piece identical with the later "Fourth Mephisto Waltz") points to the tavern scene in Lenau's Faust. This is a satanic waltz—a grim, forbidding and restless harmony, and a worthy companion to the other late Liszt compositions, preparing to cast off the outworn trappings of musical romanticism and don the dress of the twentieth century.

As far as we know today, Bartók at twenty-seven could not have known of the existence of this piece by Liszt. But we do know that at this period he was already making every effort to discover for himself the largest possible number of less popular Liszt compositions. We also know that the Faust theme of Liszt had begun to interest Bartók at an early stage in his career, for he had played the *B minor Sonata* (even if not fully comprehending its depth at the time) as a student at the Academy of Music, and then several times again; and in the article "The Music of Liszt and Contemporary Sources," written in 1911, he described the Faust Symphony as "a whole mass of wonderful thoughts, the planned elaboration of the satanic irony that first appears in the Fugato of the sonata (Mephisto)."

Of course, all this is not enough to explain the resemblance that can be detected between Liszt's *Bagatelle without Tonality*, written in 1885, and Bartók's *Fourteenth Bagatelle*, composed in 1908. Two people with similar human and artistic temperaments do not express themselves in works of similar form. The old man bitterly facing solitude and the young man sensing a lonely future both select the Bagatelle, that characteristic and apparently platitudinous piece of romanticism, as a means of at once conveying and disguising their emotions. It was at the end of the year in which he wrote *Bagatelle without Tonality*—the last but one year of his life—that Liszt made an allusion in so many words to the lack of understanding he found. This was when he "visited the place of Tasso's death with a pupil and pointed out to him the route by which the body of the great Italian poet had been taken to be decked with a laurel wreath at the Capitolium. 'They will not take me to the Capitolium' he added, 'but the time will come when my works will be recognised. True, it will be too late for me—I shall no longer be with you.' "

Twenty years later, beginning his career, Bartók was faced with the same lack of understanding, his failure in the Rubinstein competition. Even in the heart of Paris he wrote about being friendless: " . . . in spite of the fact that I have my meals in the company of twenty people—Cubans, North and South Americans, Dutchmen, Spaniards and Englishmen—and go on outings with Germans and Turks, I am a lonely man! I

may be looked after by Dietl or Mandl in Vienna, and I may have friends in Budapest, Thomán, Mrs. Gruber, yet there are times when I suddenly become aware of the fact that I am absolutely alone! And I prophesy, I have a foreknowledge that this spiritual loneliness is to be my destiny. I look about me in search of the ideal companion, and yet I am fully aware that it is a vain quest. Even if I should ever succeed in finding someone, I am sure that I would soon be disappointed." [5]

Apparently Bartók's prediction first came true three years later, in 1908. Stefi Geyer, the concert violinist, with whom he had shared his innermost thoughts, to whom he had revealed his deepest fears and meditations on the insoluble problems of life and death, God and immortality, the infinite and the purpose of life, to whom he had dedicated his 1907 *Violin Concerto*, and for whom he had composed a whole series of variations which were dedications concealed in his works,[6] this woman who had been spiritually so close, ceased to exist for him. By now she appeared perhaps only as a *Leitmotiv*, the *label* of a name in a code whose symbols had been agreed upon in advance, the person herself, whom the label represented having apparently passed out of Bartók's life. "*Elle est morte—*" wrote Bartók on the manuscript of the funeral music in the *Thirteenth Bagatelle*. And in the last line, symbolically the label also died: over the first soaring and then declining motiv Bartók wrote down: "dead—"

And then, suddenly, the same symbol, the intimate symbol in the funeral music of

5 See Bartók's letter written to his mother from Paris on September 10, 1905 in Béla Bartók Letters, Photographs and Music Scores.

6 For the argument that this motiv was not exclusively devoted to Stefi Geyer but became expanded as a reference to the "ideal companion" Bartók sought, and other questions connected with the Violin Concerto, cf. D. Dille: *Angaben zum Violinkonzert 1907, den Deux portraits, dem Quartett op. 7 und den zwei Rumänischen Tänzen. Documenta Bartókiana.* Vol. 2. Budapest 1965, Publishing House of the Hungarian Academy of Sciences, pp. 91–102.

the *Thirteenth Bagatelle*, spins round into a grotesque dance in the *Fourteenth Bagatelle Valse*. ("*Ma mie qui danse....*") reads the French title with its memories of Paris. The label motif—the Hungarian translation over the notes, saying "My Lover dances" makes clear the subject of the music—screams out in a savage Presto and then yields to the compulsive drive of the violently intensified waltz tempo. On the mistress he believed to be unfaithful Bartók invokes the doom of the girl who was made to dance to death—a theme familiar in many folk ballads. Now for the first time—but not for the last—(let us not forget its great successor *The Miraculous Mandarin!*)—he grapples with the cruel pace of the Dance of Death. The 27-year-old Bartók's dance macabre is haunted by the grim death music of the aged Ferenc Liszt. One does not know whether it is mere chance that both Liszt and Bartók gave the name "Bagatelle" to their piano pieces, that both of them give their macabre subject a waltz to dance, in which the outworn and rapid rhythms of the conventional waltz serve as an introduction and sometimes as an accompaniment. None the less, the fact remains that there is an amazing similarity in the story-content expressed in the same pattern.

This then is how presentiments and memories blended in Bartók's work: Ferenc Liszt's art, the acrid aftertaste of *Le Néant* and the *Moulin Rouge*, and the bitter personal experience of the young artist who found himself condemned to loneliness when the dear companion to whom the Violin Concerto had been dedicated grew as cold and death-like to him as the night club guest in the coffin, turning death-like in the sinister light. The influence of Mephisto took effect once again twenty years later, in the "Monstrous Portrait" orchestrated from the Bagatelle; and the same young composer was one of the first to act as an intermediary between Liszt's last works and the new age.

ISTVÁN KECSKEMÉTI

BARTÓK AND WAGNER*

"*Die Epoche der Weltliteratur
ist an der Zeit*"
(Goethe to Eckermann,
Jan. 31, 1827.)

Anyone who is familiar with Bartók's scholarly and literary work is aware that he wrote only rarely about himself, his works, his plans and "workshop practice." When he did, he usually concealed his own person behind expressions such as "modern music," "certain contemporary composers," etc. Knowing this we may confidently accept Bartók's following statement—without denying its general validity—as his own personal point of view, as an analysis of his own activities:

"The early part of the 20th century was a turning-point in the history of new music. The exaggerations of late romanticism were beginning to grow unbearable; certain composers were beginning to feel that it was impossible to go any further on this road; there was no other solution here but to turn completely against the 19th century." ("Influence of Peasant Music on the New Art Music," 1920–1931.)

This same thought, elaborated in greater detail, at the same time referring to the relationship between his own music and ancient folk music, appears in another study by Bartók:

"In my view we can find two common characteristics in all the modern music of our times which are closely related, one might even say, as cause and effect. One is a more or less radical departure from the music of yesterday, especially of the romantics. The other is a striving to approach the musical style of earlier periods. In other words, a loathing for works of the romantic period became common and consequently a search for modes of expression that were in the

greatest possible opposition to the romantic one. Composers turned—half deliberately, and half unconsciously—to the works of earlier periods that truly represented this antithesis." ("Hungarian Folk Music and New Hungarian Music," 1928.)

The question arises: could there have existed, after this, any kind of relationship at all between Wagner, the outstanding genius of the century of romanticism, and this "antiromantic" master of the music of our century? Naturally I refer to a spiritual relationship, any other was out of the question because of the chronology involved (Wagner died in 1883, Bartók was born in 1881). Although according to the usually reliable evidence of Bartók's mother, music was already playing a part in the little boy's life at the time of Wagner's death, his first meeting with Wagner's works had to wait for a good ten years. But from then on, the middle of the 1890s, for forty years a verifiable spiritual relationship existed between Wagner and Bartók, a many-sided, passionate relationship that manifested itself at times in wonder, at others in rejection and often in direct influence.

The scene of the above-mentioned "first meeting" was presumably Pozsony (Brati-

* This study appeared originally in a German version, in the "Parsifal" programme of the 1966 Bayreuth Festival (editor: Wieland Wagner). This enlarged English version is published by courtesy of the "Verlag der Festspielleitung, Bayreuth (Herbert Barth)."—I am quoting from the Hungarian edition of Bartók's articles (ed. András Szőllősy), his Autobiography (ed. Denijs Dille) and his letters (ed. János Demény and Klára Cs. Gárdonyi).

slava) then part of Hungary, where Bartók spent most of his time while at secondary school (1892–1893, 1894–1899). "Since I had begun to compose small piano pieces already at the age of nine and in 1891 (actually in 1892) I had already made a public appearance as a composer and pianist at Nagyszőllős (Vinogradov)," Bartók writes about these decisive years in his life in his *Autobiography*, "it was very important for us to move to a larger town. Among the Hungarian provincial towns at the time the liveliest from a musical point of view was undoubtedly Pozsony, and thus I had an opportunity, on the one hand, to take piano lessons from, and study harmony with László Erkel, the son of Ferenc Erkel,* until I was fifteen, and on the other hand, to hear a few—although not very good—orchestral concerts and operatic performances. Opportunities for practising chamber music were not lacking either, and by the time I was eighteen I had a pretty good knowledge of musical literature from Bach to Brahms. Where Wagner was concerned I had got only as far as Tannhäuser. In the meantime I had been composing industriously under the influence of works by Brahms and the young Dohnányi** who was four years older than I."

The last but one year of Bartók's secondary-school education coincided with the brief period when Bruno Walter, who later became world famous as a Wagner interpreter as well, worked at the Pozsony National Theatre. In 1898 Bartók—by this time he had been a regular performer at the town's various concerts for two years—played the piano transcription of the Tannhäuser Overture.

* Ferenc Erkel (1810–1893), composer, wrote the first significant Hungarian operas and composed among other works, the Hungarian National Anthem. His son, László Erkel (1844–1896), was active as a conductor and music teacher.
** Ernő Dohnányi (1877–1960), pianist and composer, teacher at the Budapest Academy of Music and later its director.

After finishing secondary school Bartók continued his studies at the Budapest Academy of Music (1899–1903). Here his teacher in composition was Hans Koessler, and his piano teacher was the one-time pupil of Liszt, István Thomán, a highly cultured man who first went to Bayreuth with his teacher as a youth. He acquainted young Bartók not only with the traditions of the Liszt school, but also stimulated his interest in Wagner, and placed a number of scores at his disposal.

Without a doubt Bartók's most important experience during the first year of his studies at the Academy of Music was his acquaintance with the Wagner works he was not yet familiar with. His letters to his mother who remained in Pozsony were filled with reference to Wagner. He ended his letter of January 12, 1900 with the *Rheingold* motive and a question relating to it. On January 21, he wrote that he had received the score of the *Valkyrie* from Professor Thomán. On February 18: "Last Monday, in one of the rooms of the Academy I studied the score of the *Rheingold* (legacy of Ferenc Liszt). I found many enlightening things in it (that I had never seen before...)." Then he dwelt at length on the instruments used in *Das Rheingold*. Somewhat later in a letter that has survived only in fragments: "Now I am studying the *Valkyries (sic)* this is much lovelier than the *Rheingold* (tell Aunt Mari, and that when I come home I shall play the "Ride of the Valkyries" for them)." The letter ends with four lines of music, sections of *The Valkyrie* obviously quoted from memory.

The 1899–1900 school-year ended with experiences at the opera, dominated by Wagner: "This week I went to hear *Mignon*, *Bärenhäuter* (Siegfried Wagner's opera), *Don Giovanni* and *Hamlet*. Today I'm going to *Tannhäuser*, tomorrow to the *Barber of Seville*, *Lohengrin* and *The Valkyrie* (certainly that). They are closing the opera season with *The Valkyrie*." (June 3, 1900).

Bartók's experience of Wagner was so

powerful during his first year at the Academy of Music that he recalled it in his *Autobiography* nearly two decades later: "Immediately after my arrival I flung myself with great effort into the study of those works of Richard Wagner that were still unfamiliar to me (the *Ring*, *Tristan*, *The Mastersingers*) and Liszt's orchestral works." His world grew more complete with his getting to know these works, but he was hardly able to draw any composing inspiration from them. He did not yet understand Liszt's significance, on the other hand he felt Wagner's art—this is revealed in a later study—precisely because of its perfection, to be a closed world, a round whole from which there was no road in any direction, and which could not be continued. "My creative activities... in this period were left entirely fallow," the composer recalled. "I have got away from Brahms's style. Not even through Wagner and Liszt was I able to find the new road I looked for. (I had not yet understood the significance of Liszt from the standpoint of the further development of music. I saw only superficialities in his art.) Consequently for about two years I worked on practically nothing and I was really known at the Academy of Music only as a good pianist."

The first Budapest performance of Richard Strauss's symphonic poem *Also sprach Zarathustra* pulled him out of this creative crisis. "...at last I glimpsed the direction that carried the new in its womb. I hurled myself into the study of Strauss's scores, and again I began to compose."

It was under the influence of Richard Strauss—and the Hungarian romantic art music heritage—that Bartók's symphonic poem *Kossuth* was written, whose Budapest first performance in 1904 suddenly turned him into a nationally famous artist in Hungary. Curiously it was Hans Richter, who had conducted the *Ring* when it was first performed at a Bayreuth Festival in 1876, who paved the way for Bartók's international reputation when he conducted *Kossuth* in

Manchester in 1904. The first meeting between Richter and Bartók—on June 27, 1903—was arranged by Karl Gianicelli, a faithful friend of the Wagner family who lived in Budapest, a teacher of the double bass at the Academy of Music. And it must have been Gianicelli again who made it possible for Bartók to go to Bayreuth in the summer of 1904 with the help of a Wagner scholarship.

We know little of the details of his stay in Bayreuth. In 1904, in addition to *Parsifal* and *Der Ring des Nibelungen*, *Tannhäuser* also featured in the programme of the Festival Theatre. In his only published account of it Bartók wrote merely about *Parsifal* (he must have seen it with either Michael Balling or Karl Muck conducting), but as a Bayreuth scholarship holder he undoubtedly received tickets to several performances. The fact that in Bayreuth he again met Hans Richter and played his new work for him, the Scherzo written for piano and orchestra, makes it quite probable that he was also present at the performances of *Der Ring des Nibelungen* conducted by Richter.

He wrote to his Hungarian poet friend, Kálmán Harsányi, on August 21, in Regensburg, already on his way home:

"I am writing these lines under the effect of *Parsifal*. It is a very interesting work, but it did not have as tremendous an impact on me as *Tristan*. Anyone who has the slightest bit of religious feeling in him is greatly moved by the story. I was disturbed by the constant praying on the stage. Despite my expectations I found much that was new in the music. It is remarkable that a 70-year-old man could have written such refreshing music as the temptation song of the nymphs in the second act—and without repeating himself. But then I shall write something about Bayreuth. I would only like to know, would you like to come here next year for a couple of performances? I played my Scherzo for Richter, according to him this is a scherzo *von und zu Übermenschen*."

His letter to Harsányi of September 18 indirectly informs us of the means Bartók used to yet get to Bayreuth:

"I found out in Bayreuth that those Wagner scholarships could be held not only by musicians, but also by writers, poets, etc. Perhaps you could apply for one as well. If you do not receive a full scholarship, then perhaps tickets for six performances (in view of the fact that the price of one ticket is 20 marks, this is not to be scorned either). The application has to be made by the end of Jan. 1905 to a Count Festetics, whose address I have already forgotten. It would be best if you turned to Professor Karl Gianicelli... at the proper time for information. A committee of four made up of the two previously mentioned gentlemen, Jenő Rákosi and Mihalovich, makes the decision."

The cold, objective tone in which Bartók writes about Bayreuth shows that Wagner was no longer in the focus of his interest. But it is curious that even in his "Strauss period" Wagner remained the yardstick of a composer's greatness for him. "Here I am studying all five branches of the art in complete solitude," he wrote on March 17, 1904 from Berlin to his Viennese friend, Dietl. "I have got to know some splendid Strauss songs. Yes, yes indeed, I can tell you: we have not had such a great master as Strauss since Wagner."

Bartók's Strauss period did not last long. His discovery of ancient Hungarian folk music, and his acquaintance with modern French music soon forced the influence of Richard Strauss into the background. And there was one more "encounter" of decisive importance in those years, in the first decade of our century: a meeting with Liszt's main works. "I began to study Liszt once more," Bartók wrote in his *Autobiography*, "that is his less popular works, such as, the *Années de Pélérinage*, the *Harmonies poétiques et religieuses*, the *Faust Symphony*, the *Totentanz*, etc.—and these studies, across a few, to me less sympathetic, external features, led me

to the core of things: the real significance of this artist was revealed to me, I felt the importance of his works to be greater from the point of view of the development of music, than that of Wagner or Strauss."

After that Wagner's name always occurred together with—or more precisely: in contrast to Liszt's—in Bartók's writings. The year 1911, the one hundredth anniversary of the birth of Liszt, provided an opportunity for the first time for Bartók to present his views on the two of them to the public. "It is curious," Bartók wrote in his article "Liszt's Music and the Contemporary Public," "what a large proportion of musicians, I could say the overwhelming proportion, is barely able to make friends with Liszt's music, despite all its novelty and splendour. I do not speak of those who *eo ipso* have an aversion to everything that is new and unfamiliar. But there were in Liszt's time, in fact, even today there are great, strong musicians who happen to abhor this master, or who have accepted him only very conditionally, or rather they just tolerated him. It is incomprehensible that while, for example, in our country they hardly dare to utter a word against Wagner, or against Brahms, although there are some things here and there that are objectionable, Liszt's music is wide open to attack."

In connection with Liszt's B minor Piano Sonata Bartók observed: "Liszt was the first to express irony through music. His Sonata was completed around 1850. Similar notes in Wagner (*Siegfried*, *The Mastersingers*) can be found only much later—perhaps precisely under Liszt's influence."

One of the most interesting sections of the article—and not devoid of exaggerations in its passion either—discusses Liszt's and Wagner's relationship, their relations as creative artists and friends. "It was not given to every composer," writes Bartók, "that like Beethoven, he should conquer all the difficulties by himself and achieve perfection in every single work. Only one person was worthy of the difficult office of being Liszt's critic, and that was Wagner. But Wagner repaid Liszt's affection with indifference, it was all the same to him whether things went well for Liszt or not, yet though from no one else, Liszt most likely would have accepted advice from Wagner." (We must not leave unmentioned the fact that in the depths of this conclusion there exist certain autobiographical references that the reader will understand at once when we compare it with a few lines of Bartók's article "Zoltán Kodály," written ten years later: "...I esteem Kodály as the best Hungarian musician not because he is my friend, but he became my one friend because he is the best Hungarian musician. The fact that I enjoyed the better part of the fruits of this friendship, and not Kodály, once again proves his splendid capabilities and sacrificing generosity... I can thank his amazingly accurate and quick judgement for the final, much better than original, formulation of any number of my works.")

One of the special characteristics of Bartók's compositions is that they contain large numbers of hidden autobiographical elements, lesser and greater quotations from his own and other composers' works, from Bach to Stravinsky. What is peculiar about these quotations—I discussed them in detail in my study "Quotations in Bartók's Music" —is that they were not addressed to the general public (as for example the *Tristan* quotation in Britten's opera *Albert Herring*), and can be revealed as a rule only as a result of penetrating analysis. But there can be no doubt about their being quotations. In his opera *Bluebeard's Castle*, for instance, Bartók quotes an ostinato motive from Bach's *St. Matthew Passion*. At the end of a scene, the *B-A-C-H* motive appears as a "scientific reference." Another example: in 1910 a French critic described Bartók, who was giving concerts in Paris, as a "young barbarian." Bartók's ironical reply was his famous piano work the *Allegro barbaro*, composed in 1911, which was based on one of the motives of a French composition—

Ravel's *Scarbo*, that had appeared in 1909. And a final example: he composed his Third Piano Concerto in the last months of his life, with declining physical strength but unbroken enthusiasm for work. The title of the second movement—a singular example in Bartók's oeuvre—is Adagio religioso. In the light of our knowledge of Bartók's ideology this "religious slowness" would be an insoluble puzzle if the music itself did not "reformulate" a movement of a Beethoven string quartet, the movement called *Heiliger Dankgesang eines Genesenen an die Gottheit...* (from the *A minor Quartet* op. 132).

What induced Bartók to quote in this way? For the most part certain historical, psychological and positional identities or similarities, with the evocation of which Bartók—one of the most solitary creative artists of the century—extended a hand to predecessors and contemporaries with whom he felt a spiritual kinship. (There are numerous examples of this gesture in his writings as well.)

In his music—and not all in the compositions of his youth, but in his mature works—we come across several references to Wagner, Wagner quotations; and what is more natural than that these are mostly just in his stage works. (Here and there, however, in his instrumental compositions also: in a statement made in 1941 Bartók himself calls attention to the "Wagner recollections" in his First String Quartet.)

Bartók's first work for the stage was his one-act opera *Bluebeard's Castle* composed in 1911. The work's libretto—by Béla Balázs—reconciles Maeterlinck's symbolism with the imagery of the Székely folk ballad, whose few words say a great deal and allow one to suspect a great deal more. The familiar tale deepens here into a tragedy of Man and Woman: Judit, the last love of the lonely Prince Bluebeard, seeks to know every secret of the man's soul. What she seeks she learns, but she loses her man forever. This dramatic situation refers in its roots to Wagner, to the conflict between Lohengrin and Elsa. And at one point, at one of the dramatic turning-points of the Bartók opera, this is what the music does as well. Here Bartók's music reminds us of Lohengrin's words: *Nie sollst du mich befragen...*

Lohengrin:

Wagner's theme circumscribes a minor triad, starting on its highest note and ending on the lowest, and repeating all this for greater emphasis. Bartók does the same, only his melody—to use the term applied by Ernő Lendvai—stems from the decomposition of what is called the "hyper-minor" chord:

Bluebeard:

The Wooden Prince—Bartók's ballet which was completed in 1916—begins with a picture of nature painted with broad brush strokes. This prelude expresses nature coming to life, "the beginning of all things"—with almost the same effect, and with the same means as Wagner used in the orchestral introduction to *Das Rheingold*. The principal difference here, too—as in the previous instance—lies in the tonal system. In Wagner's music the first five harmonics corresponding to a major triad are heard, and they swell into a tremendous wave. In Bartók's opening music—this again is "a single tremendous chord"—two more harmonic notes join the first five (in the instance of C basic note: f-sharp and b-flat), which modifies the major scale, or chord, into the "Bartók scale," the "Bartók chord."

This is the beginning of *Das Rheingold*:

And the 20th-century "reformulation" of Wagnerian music: the beginning of Bartók's ballet, *The Wooden Prince:*

etc.

Bartók's last work for the stage, *The Miraculous Mandarin*, is set in a den of robbers in the big city. Three ruffians force a prostitute to entice men up to the den, whom they rob. The first climax in the music: in response to the girl's enticing music a peculiar, mysterious figure steps into the robbers' den; a Chinese mandarin. He is the representative of a remote, alien world, his feelings are pure and natural, and his appearance in a decadent, modern big city has the same effect as that of the hero of Wagner's last stage work: *der reine Tor*, Parsifal. In Bartók's pantomime the temptation dance of the girl held captive by the forces of evil is reminiscent of *Parsifal*, of the scene of the flower girls, that part of the second act that had such a great impact on the young Bartók in Bayreuth. Despite the identical atmosphere, and the resemblance in the means employed, the listener does not feel Bartók's stage music to be Wagnerian, not for a single moment. Nature—which both adored equally—said different things to each of them. And who would be reminded by the nocturnal magic of Wagner's music of the mysterious dread of Bartók's nocturnal music? The heroes, the human relationships are revealed in entirely different aspects in the work of the two composers. One hardly finds an example in Bartók's compositions of an alien power's redeeming grace. His dramaturgy refers rather to Dante and the folk ballad: "whoever wishes to become a piper must descend to hell." In Bartók's words: "What is important is not the origin of the theme we elaborate, but rather how we elaborate it. It is in this 'how' that the artist's skill, his shaping and expressive power, his individuality are manifested."

After that Bartók dealt with Wagner's person and his works on only a single occasion: in 1936 in his inaugural lecture on Liszt at the Hungarian Academy of Sciences. These few splendid thoughts are a summary, as it were, a deeper revelation of his earlier views:

"I had once written somewhere: 'I feel that Liszt's significance in the further development of music is greater than Wagner's.' And I still hold this. I do not want to say that Liszt was a greater composer than Wagner. For in the works of Wagner we find greater formal perfection, a richer spectrum of expression, and a greater uniformity of style. Yet—Liszt's works had a more enriching influence on the succeeding generation than Wagner's. Let no one be misled by the great mass of Wagner imitators. Wagner solved his task in its entirety and in all its details with such perfection, that he could only be slavishly imitated, but one could hardly receive any inspiration from him towards further development. And all imitation is sterile—dead matter. On the other hand Liszt touched upon so many new possibilities in his works, without himself exhausting them to the full, that we were able to receive incomparably greater inspiration from him than from Wagner."

This was how a synthesis was born as the result of the clash between homage and rejection: the just and wise decision in Bartók's four-decade-long discussion with Wagner. From another of his statements we know that Bartók regarded the development of music as a single comprehensive process in which each epoch necessarily influences the succeeding one. Following Bartók's words written about Wagner, the references in his music to Wagner, the similarities that show through the differences in their times and personalities, perhaps finally it is no exaggeration to say: the two men are two links, not so far removed from each other, of one and the same tremendous historical chain.

FERENC BÓNIS

BARTÓK, SCHOENBERG, STRAVINSKY

The twenty years that have elapsed since Béla Bartók's death have furnished us with unquestionable evidence of our having lost in him one of the greatest creators of our age. Nevertheless, appreciation of his art has not always been unanimous; in fact, his rich and multifaceted work allows of very different, and often ambiguous, interpretations. Any sort of eulogy would be out of place and even harmful; still we must pose the question of whether a rightful place has been accorded to Bartók's activity and life-work in twentieth-century music history.

Widely consulted handbooks on contemporary music often show such a lack of understanding that, in point of fact, the picture they present of this genius of modern music is rather detrimental as well as distorted. In paging through the otherwise outstanding volumes of Hans Stuckenschmidt or Paul Collaer, for example, one finds that Bartók's work, in contrast to that of Schoenberg or Stravinsky, is dealt with only in the chapters devoted to the "national" or "folkloristic" schools. Such a classification, even if it is unintentional, constitutes a depreciation, for it argues implicitly against the universality of Bartók's art.

Pierre Boulez does Bartók an equal injustice—though we must recognize that, as a conductor, he is one of the best interpreters of Bartók's music—when he writes in l'Encyclopédie de la Musique (published by Fasquelle): "...It is undeniable that Bartók should be placed among the five great men of contemporary music, alongside Stravinsky, Webern, Schoenberg and Berg. His work, nevertheless, lacks the profound unity and novelty of Webern, the rigorousness and sharpness of Schoenberg, the complexity of Berg, and the vigorous yet controlled dynamism of Stravinsky." To me it would appear that, on the contrary, all these traits that Boulez mentions, are very much present in Bartók's work. If, taken singly, none of them seems to dominate as much as in the other composers, together they form a harmonious whole. It is precisely this combination of characteristics which gives his work its strength and richness and enables it to supply a universal answer to the questions of our age.

The group to which Bartók belongs in the history of music is that of the great synthesizers. In 1939, he confided to Serge Moreux, his French biographer: "...Again and again I ask myself: can one make a synthesis of these three classics (that is Bach, Beethoven and Debussy), and make it a living one for the moderns?" In fact, the synthesis that he envisaged only as a theoretical possibility was realized by him. Studies of his style and musical language have amply shown the elements he availed himself of in the rigorous discipline of Bach's counterpoint on the one hand and in the refined technique of Beethoven's last quartets on the other. And it has been equally well established that the orchestral sonority of his first mature works, with their *plain air* musical images resplendent in impressionistic colours, could hardly be imagined without the influence of Debussy. In his youth he had been subjected to the influence of such predecessors as Brahms, Wagner, Richard Strauss and Liszt. But none of these made as deep and long-lasting an impression on him as Bach and Beethoven, whose influence was to be with him throughout his life. Apart from stylistic details that are of interest mainly to the professional, he had something more in common with these great masters: their conception of art as a vocation and the deep responsibility they felt towards humanity.

It was this "first synthesis," bringing together the heritage of his great precursors, which enabled him to reach a "second synthesis": that of the major trends of his own age. He followed, with an indefatigable interest, all that was happening in Europe in the domain of music. After the first world war he had close connections with the avant-garde of Vienna and Berlin. He published several studies and articles in the periodicals *Musikblätter des Anbruchs* and *Melos*. His compositions were presented in private performances by the Viennese society, *Musikalische Privataufführungen* and, later, from the twenties on, at the festivals of the *Société Internationale de la Musique Contemporaine*. He often assisted as a pianist at these concerts, and he met the people who were foremost in music at the time—Berg, Webern, Stravinsky, Ravel, Szymanovsky. With Schoenberg he was connected only by way of correspondence. This did not prevent him from recognizing in Schoenberg the most important personage of his age.

At any rate, it is very characteristic of Bartók to have found his first models among the contemporary composers—to be exact, in Schoenberg and Stravinsky. This is why it is necessary to examine their relations to Bartók more closely. I think it will be understood here that their personal relations have at most a secondary interest, that what interests us above all are the artistic relationships that bind them and that are shown in their works.

It is well known that the point of departure for Bartók had been very close to that of Schoenberg: German traditions. Vienna and Budapest are too near each other not to have similar characteristics from the artistic and musical point of view. At the turn of the century, the two great romantic composers, Wagner and Brahms, exerted most influence on musical life in both these cities. Thus, it is not too surprising that the first efforts of Schoenberg and Bartók towards an expansion of tonality were made in the same direction. In the first ten years of this century these two were unacquainted with each other's works, yet it is possible to find parallels in compositions that date from the same year: Schoenberg's "Three Pieces" and "Six Little Pieces" for piano and his "Second Quartet"; Bartók's "Fourteen Pieces" for piano and the "First Quartet." At a later date when he wrote his treatise on harmony, Schoenberg cited a few bars from Bartók's piano pieces to demonstrate their parallel tendencies in renewing musical language.

It is even more significant that Bartók, after he became acquainted with various compositions by Schoenberg, did not wish to escape his influence. On the contrary, he even drew upon his theoretical elements and his means of expression consciously. The fact that Bartók reacted in such a sensitive way to Schoenberg's atonal essays indicates the importance and also the appropriateness of these tendencies. At the same time this sensitivity shows that his own attempts were directed along the same lines, independently of Schoenberg.

The relation of Bartók to Schoenbergian music is by no means limited to technical elements. It was under the influence of the expressionist movement that Bartók composed his first dramatic work, "Bluebeard's Castle." Since Schoenberg, too, absorbed a great deal of the vague symbolism of this movement and was, moreover, the first and most outstanding representative of expressionism in music, again we find a tendency in common. Parallel motifs can be clearly discerned in the two works dating from approximately the same period, Bartók's "Bluebeard" and Schoenberg's "La Main heureuse." Full of symbolic and psychological allusions, both of them confront the problem of the spiritual inequality of the sexes. The inconsistent character and parasitic existence of woman is contrasted with the completely consistent and creative character of man, and the conclusion is that there is absolutely no possibility of reconciling them. While there are no direct relationships between these two stage-works, it is evident that they had a common source: the current of ideas rising out of the atmosphere of crisis at that time.

The works of Bartók in which Schoenberg's influence is shown most clearly are the pantomime "The Miraculous Mandarin," the two "Sonatas" for violin and piano and the "Improvisations" for piano—in other words the compositions that originated between 1918 and 1923, a definitely mature creative period. Bence Szabolcsi, the eminent Hungarian musicologist, has written that "his encounter with the music of Schoenberg was not a transient phenomenon in the life of a young and enthusiastic composer; it became an enrichment of the artist who has attained mastery." In these works, the composer went to the farthest reaches of non-serial atonality, availing himself, in addition, of all the other means of expressionism in music: accumulation to excess of acoustic effects, melodic lines with large intervals, dissonant harmony bordering on acoustic noise.

Bartók, however, did not go further along the road that led Schoenberg to twelve-tone work. And yet the idea was always present in his compositions and he even developed it by constructing a tonality in an entirely new direction, which made full use of the possibilities inherent in the twelve-tone system.

As to the characteristic traits of this new tonality, this is not the place to go into detail. We shall note only what is most important to know: that it constantly and in complementary fashion uses all twelve tones of the chromatic system without recourse to the rigorous periodicity of the Schoenbergian technique. Within the framework of this free utilization of the chromatic scale there are certain nodal-points, which serve only to guide the perception of the listener, not being meant to suggest a definite tonality in the traditional sense. It is necessary to emphasize that these tonal nodal-points never occur on a single step of the scale, but are distributed equally over the chromatic octave. This, then, is the main component of Bartók's particular tonality, called a "system of pivots" in Ernő Lendvai's studies. It can be considered as a direct development of classic tonality, within the framework of the twelve-tone system.

Apart from the complementary use of the chromatic scale, the most typical feature of Bartók's technique of composition is his use of variation. For him, variation does not merely represent one of the given musical forms: it constitutes, in effect, the fundamental principle of his way of developing music. He expressed himself in this regard as follows: "You will probably have noticed that I attach a great deal of importance to the process of technical development: I do not like to repeat the musical idea unchanged, and never take up any part of it the way it was."

The technique of variation, which is, finally, one of the primary laws in Bartók's music, also comes close to Schoenberg's serial method as a creative principle. The series can be considered as another point of departure, the "basic set" in the musical process, and the composition is but its variational development. This is why forms of variation are so often encountered in the works of the Viennese school. Bartók's dedication to the variational method is of course a personal thing. Nevertheless, one may as well admit that this inclination was confirmed under Schoenberg's influence. The difference between the two composers is that while Schoenberg tends to follow the rules of logic, Bartók obeys those of music.

The second question to be posed here concerns Stravinsky's influence on the music of Bartók. It is well known that Stravinsky introduced himself to the European public with the three ballets composed for the Diaghileff's Ensemble. What shocked the bourgeois of the Western cities was the oriental dynamism of these works—particularly of "The Rite of Spring"—characteristic of primitive peoples. But, in reality, well before the "Rite," Bartók had formulated such a musical expression, full at once of explosive energy and overwhelming force, in his "Allegro barbaro" for piano.

He could not, however, divest himself of the influence of his Russian fellow-composer. While he had discovered this musical idea independently, later he was to draw upon the sources of Stravinsky's works in order to confirm his own ideas and enrich his means of expression. There are passages in his pantomime "The Miraculous Mandarin" which could not have appeared but for Stravinsky's influence.

This influence became even more marked in the twenties, by which time the style of the Russian composer had changed appreciably. The barbaric rhythm of Stravinsky's first period was transformed into a more controlled dynamism reminiscent of Baroque music. After the crisis, the overthrowing of old rules, the need of a new classicism, of a reconstruction of old values and of stricter forms, was felt. Bartók accepted and made use of this need in subjecting himself to the attractive influence of the music of Stravinsky and in experiencing the necessity of classicism. It was in 1926 that he composed those works which are closest to Stravinsky's: the "Sonata" and the "First Piano Concerto." The "Third Quartet" and the "Second Piano Concerto" also belong to this category, constituting as they do, Bartók's typically "neo-classical" series of works.

I must emphasize that Schoenberg and his followers were in lively opposition to this new classicism proclaimed by Stravinsky. It is all the more interesting that Bartók, after having gone in the Schoenbergian direction at the beginning of the twenties, began a few years later to orient himself towards the retrospective attitude of Stravinsky. Bartók himself supplies us with the explanation, not only with his works but also in a theoretical treatise. In a paper published in Berlin in 1920, referring to the *Pribaoutki* songs by Stravinsky, he demonstrated "the compatibility of music in which tonal elements are used, and atonal tendencies." Incidentally, he proved this in one of his compositions: In the "Improvisations" for piano it is possible to recognize Hungarian folk-songs hidden under atonal configurations of harmony and melody.

Even at this early period Bartók's remarkable tendency towards a synthesis of the most divergent and at the same time most important elements of his age is clearly observable. He worked to unite the new lines of modern music, as represented by Schoenberg's atonality, with a respect for both learned and popular traditions, and to unite as well the modern mood, as characterized by the feverish movement of cities, with the robust and instinctive rhythm of primitive peoples who are close to nature.

All this could no doubt be considered a sort of eclecticism by certain partisans of artistic intransigency, such as René Leibowitz or Pierre Boulez. However, with Bartók the emergence and eclipse of the various influences did not depend on fashion, on timeliness. Those he considered essential were never to be abandoned by him; they retained their life, incorporated in his own musical language, even when the immediate experiencing of them had lost its first meaning. The dodecaphonic elements, as well as the neo-baroque style, were never to disappear from his music, not even in the thirties, at the apogee of his career, though they did undergo transformations.

The influence of Schoenberg and Stravinsky that can be discovered in the works of Bartók cannot, for that matter, be considered exceptional. Like two opposite poles, these two great masters of the age exerted a magnetic attraction, so to speak; there was hardly a composer who would have escaped the influence of one or the other. Theodor Adorno, the eminent aesthetician and sociologist of contemporary music, believes that this polarization expresses the fundamental problem of the age. Schoenberg represents the progress and Stravinsky, the restoration: To this antagonism Adorno reduces the two typical tendencies. Even if we are not entirely of his opinion, we must admit that the polarization he refers to has a certain justification. Stravinsky's attitude, artistic and musical *par excellence*, is diametrically opposed to Schoenberg's ethico-philosophical position. Schoenberg symbolizes the consequences of a musical evolution carried to the extreme, Stravinsky the restoration of a sensual joy.

And Bartók's place in this magnetic field?—according to Adorno, it is to be found precisely in the middle, between the two poles. In the work entitled *The Philosophy of the New Music*, he writes that "Béla Bartók made an attempt to reconcile, in certain respects, Schoenberg and Stravinsky, and in density and fullness his best works are probably superior. This conception, while it would seem to be to Bartók's advantage, has implications that, in the last analysis, help to relegate Bartók's work to the periphery of contemporary music. This is why it is necessary to raise again, in a slightly different form, the original question: Is it possible to conceive of a third position between Schoenberg and Stravinsky, a position capable of uniting these two trends, exploiting their advantages without, however, being depreciated by the the compromise? The answers given by Leibowitz, Adorno and Boulez are, on the whole, negative. Even that of Schoenberg is. It is characteristic of this composer that, though he was not a professional aesthetician

like Adorno, he was fully conscious of this polarization of contemporary artistic conceptions. He even tried to express it in his unfinished dramatic work "Moses and Aaron." He himself wrote the philosophical text of this opera, using the biblical subject to conceal the problem of total separation between idea and interpretation. The protagonist, Moses, has the idea but not the ability to express it. For this reason God has appointed his brother Aaron to be his aide; Aaron is capable of interpreting his ideas to the people. When they work together miracles occur, but as soon as Moses withdraws to draft the laws Aaron is forced to act on his own and, in order to appease the disorientated people, he gives them the Golden Calf. Thus, interpretation alienated from idea even becomes harmful: Without Moses, Aaron leads the Jewish people to ruin. And Moses, what can he do without Aaron? Deprived of his interpreter, he is powerless even though he is still in possession of the idea. The only possible solution would be their reunion, but according to Schoenberg this is impossible: The separation is final.

Making use of the opportunity for an apt comparison, one might say that this opera of Schoenberg expresses the creative crisis of the composer and, simultaneously, of the whole period. The figure of Moses represents Schoenberg himself, the creator-philosopher completely conscious of the necessity and the righteousness of his idea but doubtful, at least theoretically, of the possibility of an adequate interpretation. This is why he left this work incomplete.

Carrying the comparison still further, one is tempted to identify the figure of Aaron with Stravinsky, who possesses an extraordinary facility for expressing sometimes not very profound ideas or arguments.

Like Schoenberg, who could not envisage the possibility of a unification or a synthesis of the two separate conceptions, his representative in aesthetics, Theodor Adorno, does not believe that the two creative methods, that of Schoenberg and that of Stravinsky, are compatible. As for myself, I believe nevertheless that unification of these two conceptions and creative processes can be and has been achieved—by Bartók. He was the creator who possessed the idea, like Moses, and at the same time the aptitude for interpreting it, like Aaron.

It seems to me, moreover, that in Bartók's art there is not a simple association between these two differing musical conceptions but an organic synthesis of them. Far from wishing to reconcile the two extremes, Bartók merely used them in forming his own creative system. He could never have done this but for the fact that his point of departure had been to maintain and at the same time to develop traditions. If he was able to achieve the synthesis of his age it was because he found a point upon which the heritage of the past and the revolution of the present—in Adorno's words, restoration and progress—were converging.

Apart from the European tradition, there was another factor that Bartók had been able to draw upon and that was the folk tradition. Folk music for him never served simply as a means of enriching his expression but was a means of establishing a philosoph-

ical basis for himself. It might possibly have derived from the naive nationalism of his youth and his subsequent romantic anti-urbanism and idealization of the uncorrupted village. But, starting from this basis, he went on to develop a deep conviction of the brotherhood of peoples and nations. His sources included not only Hungarian but also Rumanian, Slovak, Arab and even Far-Eastern folk traditions. He was probably the first composer in the history of music who, after having borrowed scales, melodies and even acoustic effects from the Orient, attempted to unite—on the basis of equality—the spirit of Oriental music with Western traditions.

Folk music of Europe, Asia and Africa alike furnished him with structural elements for his new language. But after being assimilated into his musical expression, it merged with the secular traditions of European composed music: counterpoint, variation, the crystal-like structure of the sonata or even the intrinsic laws of drama. Thus a "third synthesis" was created in the art of Bartók, parallel with his unifications of the European heritage and of contemporary ideas: the synthesis of folk music and the learned tradition.

JÁNOS KÁRPÁTI

LIBRETTI FOR TWO DRAMATIC WORKS

THE WOODEN PRINCE

*A ballet in one act**

by

BÉLA BALÁZS

THE STAGE

A grotesquely primitive setting. *Downstage
left, there is a hillock. A tiny castle is perched
on top of the hillock. It's a turreted toy
castle, with its outer wall removed so that the
interior is laid open to view—the kind one sees
in charming old Italian paintings. We see a
small room that contains a table, a chair and
a spinning wheel. (This is about all it can
contain.) We notice, in the right wall of the
room, a small window overlooking the country
below, and, in the wall at the back, a little
door. (One cannot help wondering how a tallish
person can possibly squeeze through it.) There are
two flights of stairs leading from the exquisitely
beautiful castle. The one curves down the hither
slope of the hillock. The other barely shows on
the far side. It obviously snuggles up to the
threshold of the little door at the back, pros-
trating itself reverently before it.*

*The little hill is girdled by a streamlet. You
shouldn't assume though that this is some tur-
bulent, choppy, shapeless body of water—no, silvery-blue wavelets, large, tender and round, are
ranged in it peacefully, showing up in candid
self-exposure, like the breasts of a hundred women
reclining. The hither path curves across them
over a bridge. The silvery-blue circle of the
streamlet is ringed by the black-and-green hoop of*

*a pine-wood. It is a vast forest, to be sure.
The trees stand in rows, four deep, motionless
and still. For here there is no rumpled, scrubby
brushwood. From the open arms of the trees heavy
green curtains are dropping, trim, one like the
other, as though they were rigid lines of well-
groomed ladies-in-waiting trying to hide and
shield something.*

*A road leads from the forest into the open
country (to upstage right). A big boulder lies by
the roadside (down centre). Up centre, there is
another hillock, crowned by another little castle.
The road runs right up to the gate, which is
shut—they don't let it run any farther.***

*Beyond that, nothing is seen, only a golden
sky. And everything is plain and orderly. This
is a world where Things have made a covenant and
are at peace among themselves. They have nothing
against each other any more. They have spoken
their last word and are now waiting for Man
to give his final answer.*

FIRST DANCE

Opening music sounds while, slowly,
the curtain rises. Everything is plain and
orderly, the music says, and things are
at peace. However, the music also speaks
of some great and silent, harrowing desire,

---

* The Hungarian original was first published
in the literary magazine, *Nyugat*, 1912, pp.
879—888.

** Roads have a tendency to surge into houses;
but people shut them out. Roads are dangerous
enemies of peaceful hearths.—The Author.

for in this peace Things have spoken their last word and are now waiting for Man's reply. It's a long, dismal waiting.

The curtain is up. As our eyes follow its rise, we behold, near the apex of the set, at the foot of the near castle, a tall woman sheathed in a g r e y v e i l. She is standing motionless, gazing afar, toward the yonder castle. Yet the grey veil falls over her face too. There is about her an air of suffering (could it be the suffering of that waiting?), of mystery and of terror. She obviously is not human, and yet one cannot help feeling a fondness for her.

Down below, at the foot of the hillock, in the middle of the forest, the little PRINCESS is at play. Her golden hair is topped by a gold coronet, a silver mantle hangs from her slight shoulders. Flowers in hand, she dances round the trees in wide-eyed wonderment. They do not stir. With nimble, coquettish and capricious movements she skips about among the trees. She is so lonesome and would like to make friends with the trees. But they do not stir.

SECOND DANCE

The music grows restless. Something is going to happen. The GREY FAIRY stirs: with her arms she draws marvellous, sweeping arches over the country. "Attention! All set—Now!"

At that, the gate of the yonder castle opens and there emerges from it the PRINCE. His curly golden hair is topped by a coronet, and a purple mantle drapes his broad-shouldered back. But, oh, he has a haversack slung over his mantle, and in his hand he grips a staff! It is a big walking-stick as tall as himself. Obviously, the PRINCE is off to see the world.

The PRINCE waves goodbye towards the slowly closing gate.

After that, he advances a few steps downstage. He opens his arms: "Oh, how beautiful, how wide the world!" He comes capering down the slope. "Oh, to go rambling—how wonderful!

The GREY FAIRY, leaning forward, watches the PRINCE as he approaches with gay, dancing steps. "So there you are. So you're coming at last. I have been waiting for you so long." She then comes down the hill. Her movements are fraught with mystery and majesty. She crosses over the bridge and enters the forest, where the PRINCESS isengaged in her child-like dance, not suspecting a thing.

The PRINCESS makes an endearing curtsey before the FAIRY OF The GREY VEIL and ingratiatingly dances around her also.

The FAIRY OF The GREY VEIL sternly points towards the castle: "Get back up there! Go home! Get along with you!"

The PRINCESS, sulking: "I won't! Why should I? I just won't go!" Suddenly she skips away like a cat and dances off. "Catch me if you can." The FAIRY opens her arms, from which veils are flowing like two grey wings. She seems to fly on them after the PRINCESS. She catches up with her, and drives her away with magic movements of her arms.

The PRINCESS, whimpering, runs for the bridge and, sulking and crest-fallen, goes slinking up towards the castle. But she turns about, scowling: "You'll pay for this. Just you wait."

The FAIRY OF The GREY VEIL keeps glancing back at the PRINCE, who is coming up the road, as she shoos away the PRINCESS. Her intention is quite obvious—she does not want those two to meet. While the PRINCESS, with bowed head, climbs up the hill, the FAIRY turns about, walks up to the edge of the forest and, with her arms wide open, greets the PRINCE as he arrives there. What is she up to? Surely she isn't trying to show herself off?

The PRINCE is about to reach the edge of the forest when he perceives the FAIRY

appearing in front of him. He stops in
his tracks, amazed. Who is this? What is
this?

The FAIRY OF The GREY VEIL
stands still, while a soft rocking starts from
her hips and goes rippling up over her
body to her finger-tips. Is it a summons?
It is a sweet summons if you understand
it. If you don't, it is a frightening enigma.
The PRINCE is puzzled and shrinks back
in dismay. But it seems as if he were with
much difficulty pulling his unresponsive
limbs out of some magnetic current. And
what happens now? As he comes to the
edge of downstage right he glances up
towards the hill and catches a glimpse
of the beautiful PRINCESS who is
about to enter her palace. And, bang, he
falls in love with her on the instant.
He runs forward, he runs right, he runs
left—he doesn't know which way to run.
He flings his arms open, goes down on
his knees, then jumps to his feet as if to
take wing. (One wonders, indeed, how such
a whirlwind love—listen to the music say
so—can fail to snatch him up and precipi-
tate him through the air.) His dance expresses a desire that makes him toss and
writhe. As if he were tugging at fetters
that bind his limbs. As if he felt shackled
by his own body, by the world at large!
The PRINCESS has not noticed him. She
has no idea that the PRINCE is already
there.* She knows nothing; and so she
enters her little castle (whose interior is
so agreeably exposed to view), seats herself at the spinning wheel near the window,
starts the wheel, and begins to work.
(Working at this time of day!)
The FAIRY OF The GREY VEIL has
seen what happened only too well. Impossible not to see it. The PRINCE wants
the PRINCESS, and wants her badly. The
tall figure of the FAIRY bows, she folds her

arms over her head and withdraws into
the forest, passing over the bridge and up
the hillock. Why should it hurt her so
much? What can she have been expecting?
The music conveys some sadness... And
up there, in the castle, the spinning wheel
is whirring away.

THIRD DANCE

(Grand ballet)

The PRINCE jumps up. "I'll go up
to her. It's the simplest thing to do." **
And he runs off, exultantly, towards the
forest. But lo! even as he is about to enter
it, what happens?

The FAIRY OF The GREY VEIL draws
magic circles with her arms. It's a command
from a haughty and mighty person. And
behold!

The FOREST stirs into life! The music
now speaks like an eerie wind, and the
trees sway to right and left, pointing their
branches at the PRINCE. A marvellous
sight! The trunks are swaying like supple
female bodies, and the branches are swing-
ing like the slender arms of women, and
the foliage flutters like so many green veils.
The trees seem to have turned into women.
The PRINCE recoils, taken aback, and
for a moment changes his mind. But he
looks up at the castle. "There's the Princess I've got to get up there by any means!"
After all, he is a prince and he will not
take fright at a living forest. He lays down
his big walking stick and makes a determined dash for the trees. But see what happens now!...
The FOREST moves! Four lines of trees,
like four dancing whirlpools, swirl around
the hillock. How will you get through here,
oh Prince? And so the dance struggle is on.
The PRINCE dashes against the magical
dancing forest and rebounds from it. He

---

* That is always the source of trouble. Princesses ever hang back till they can see a thing
with their own eyes. But by then the best part of it
has been lost. That's how it is.—The Author.

** This thought, as a rule, does not at once
suggest itself to princes in love—real-life princes,
that is.—The Author.

repeats his charge once, twice. Now he has got through the first ring of trees.

The FOREST's outermost ring of trees has stopped, as though petrified. The spell has been broken. Yet three more rings of trees are still swirling round the little hillock. The outermost danced most slowly of all.

The PRINCE finds this a kind of tag game. The dancing starts anew. He now finds it more difficult to get through between the trees: here, the roundelay goes faster, the whirl is swifter. Still, at one place, he manages to slip through.

The FOREST reveals that two of its rings of trees have already stopped. The trees are standing still, only their tops continue swaying. Is it because they cannot stop their motion on the instant? Or do they mean to say, "It's no use. No. No. No. No!" We shall see.

The PRINCE is very clever, to be sure. He has negotiated even the third ring of trees, which stand behind him wagging their tops. But the fourth ring! That's a different matter! Like dry herbs blown by the wind, like raging witches, the trees toss and swirl in front of him. But the PRINCE is not to be outdone. He is tossed and spurred on by love. Oops! He's got through, and has now come to the bridge. What now? He starts for the bridge. Now he is about to set foot on it.

The FAIRY—who has been watching the scene from on high and performing wonderful gyrations with her arms and body as though she was driving those trees round and round in whirling rings as a ringmaster drives his manege—now, for the second time, makes a sign in magic command. And lo!—

The RIVER rises in its bed, and its silvery-blue waves lift up the bridge and toss it backwards, against the slope of the hill. (Now, my Prince, there's a dance for you! A dance of the waves!) Silvery-blue veils float and flutter and stream. It is as though they were the undulating bodies of a hundred women. Perhaps they really are?

The PRINCE once again shrinks back. But he is not the sort to give in. He runs up and down the river bank, but this time to no avail.

The RIVER's dancing, undulating ring of babbling, rippling waves leaves no loophole. Indeed, the trees behind the PRINCE are still saying, "No! No! No!"

The PRINCE tired and beaten at last, slinks back through the trees, whose tops are still swaying, saying no. He walks back to where he laid down his staff and picks it up sadly. (My god, how very sad he is!) No use—the Princess cannot be reached. With his head hanging, he starts off to right.

The FOREST and The RIVER have stopped, and the bridge is now back on its pillars, spanning the river.

The PRINCESS—what has she been doing all this time? Why, she's been pushing the treadle and spinning the spindle. She's been doing nothing. *

She did not even know that the PRINCE was down below.

FOURTH DANCE

The PRINCE, however, turns to look once more. He cannot possibly go away without taking just one more look. He opens his arms: No, no, it is impossible to give her up, impossible to tear oneself away from her! He turns back. Again he starts for the forest. He stops dead—it's useless that way. "My god! My god! What shall I do?" He can see the little gold coronet through the window of the castle. "There she is! Oh, if she would but lean out and look down! If she but knew that I am here! How can I make her notice me?" He leaps high, stands on tiptoe—all in vain. Suddenly, an idea flashes through his mind. He takes off his coronet and turns it round, looking at it affectionately: "This is my glory, my emblem and ornament. You shall announce

* Indeed, there is nothing wrong about princesses not helping princes in trying to win their hearts.—The Author.

to her my presence." So he hangs his coronet on the head of his staff, climbs on the big boulder, and reaches the coronet up high. He waves his staff, "Halloa, Princess!" The PRINCESS looks up. She sees the coronet beyond the window and eyes it with curiosity, but without stopping her work to do so. After taking a good look at it, she pores over her wheel and goes on spinning the spindle with indifference. The music imitates a derisive, scornful humming. The PRINCE lowers the staff with the coronet. He grows excited, pricks up his ears. He feels sore: "What! Isn't this coronet enough for her? She takes no notice of it? Yet there's no other coronet to compare with this one in all the world. Never mind. She *will* take notice of me. She must. If she ignores my coronet, I shall show her something else." Thereupon he throws his fine scarlet mantle from his back and un-girds his sword. What is he going to do? In a trice, he ties his fine straight sword to the staff, crosswise, so that it looks like the skeleton of a scarecrow. Then he wraps his scarlet mantle around the sword and sticks the gold coronet on the staff. Why, now it almost looks like a real-life prince! If he were to plant it in the middle of a wheat-field, he might fool the birds. "Now, my Princess! Look who is here." He raises his coronet-topped, mantle-wrapped staff up high, proudly, triumphantly. This stand-ard is invested with all his insignia, his regalia, and under it he is standing on tip-toe —a plain, unadorned fair-haired boy.

The PRINCESS sees the regalia. Now that's something. The wheel stops; her little head turns with interest towards the strange standard—but that is all. After a while, the sound of the wheel turning and the spindle spinning is heard again. The music imitates a scornful, derisive humming. The PRINCE, exasperated, lowers his crowned scarecrow. What'll he do now? He is fuming with rage. And that odious humming noise! "That beautiful Princess up there cannot possibly remain quiet once

she knows that it is I who am here below! Evidently the dummy is still a poor one. Imperfect. It is not invested with my beauty. It just isn't ME!" In a fit of exasper-ation, he opens his haversack and produces a big pair of shears. Now what's he up to? Why—good heavens!—he is clipping off his fine, long golden hair! Then he takes the hair and arranges it as a wig on top of his stick and puts the coronet on top. But now the thing is the spitting image of the Prince! Seeing it from afar, his own mother would believe it to be her son. * Now then, he once again raises the wooden dummy. He does so neither haughtily nor with enthusiasm, just simply, as one will show one's best work to announce to the world: "Look! Here I am!"

The PRINCESS' humming wheel stops instantly. She jumps to her feet, amazed: "Oh! Isn't he good-looking!" She feels a rush of warmth to her heart. She is overcome with an emotion such as she never has felt before. She reaches her little hands through the window. "He is the most handsome Prince I have ever seen. I must have him!"

The PRINCE exultingly flaunts the dum-my and, hiding behind it, retreats with dancing steps, enticingly: "You'll come down! You'll come down!"

The PRINCESS leans out of the window, alarmed: "Is he going away? Oh, my God! I'll run after him." She runs out on to the road on this side of the hill, but catches sight of the FAIRY. She runs back into her little castle and flings open the door at the back. However, before leaving the castle, she snatches up a little mirror from the table. "Am I pretty enough? Will the handsome Prince like me?" She titivates herself like a kitten, gathering up her hair, which reaches to her knees, and lifting it on both arms as if to weigh

* Why, yes, that's what princes are like. They would strip off their skin to be able to make a true image of themselves—and no mistake.—The Author.

it. After that, she slips through the door. The FAIRY—now what has *she* been doing all this time? She's been standing motionless, watching that queer PRINCE invest a wooden dummy with all his ornaments and beauty. But having seen him cut off his hair and, waving the Wooden Prince enticingly, go dancing off, she furtively creeps down the slope of the hill and hides herself in the forest. Leaning forward she stares in front of her, on the watch like a beast of prey crouching before springing. What is she up to?

FIFTH DANCE

(Minor ballet)

The PRINCESS has also just come along the other path. She runs across into the forest and, smiling and coquettishly, dances towards the Wooden Prince, with whom the real PRINCE has reached the right-hand corner of the stage.

The PRINCE now draws himself up: "At last! You've come at last!" He sticks the Wooden Prince into the ground (its back to the audience) and steps forward from behind it, with his arms flung wide open, proud and happy ... But oh, what's this?

The PRINCESS, repelled and frightened, begins to flee from him. "Who is that ugly, ungainly, bald man? What does he want of a Princess like me?" (Oh, poor young Prince, you have no coronet and no hair.)

The PRINCE still smiling, his arms still open, pursues the fleeing PRINCESS. "Why, this is but a play of lovers." Oh, poor, poor PRINCE.)

The PRINCESS, her eyes fixed on the handsome Wooden Dummy, waves her hand at it and wants to get through to it, dodging, with dancing steps, the ungainly, bald man.

The PRINCE now understands. He bars her way! "What do you want? Where are you dancing? Why, that is but a wooden dummy! All the ornaments you see on it are mine! All that is me! Me! Me!" (Oh, you poor Prince.) And the chase is on.

The FAIRY—as though this were the chance she has been waiting for, when those two in their dodging and chasing come to the centre of stage, with the Wooden Prince standing, forsaken, backstage—comes out of the forest and runs across the stage to right, to the Wooden Prince, her grey veils fluttering ominously. Lo! Now she is treading softly round the dummy in a wondrous, magic dance. Is she casting a spell on the dummy? And now—look! look!—

The DUMMY begins to stir. The mantle is waving lightly as if filling up with body. The wig quivers as if it had settled upon a head. And look! The dummy raises an arm. The music is now full of crackling and pattering sounds as of gnarled twigs being broken. The Wooden Prince stirs and moves. (If anyone should think that some leggy actor has shot up out of the trap and got into its frame—all right, that's none of my business.)

The PRINCESS notices that the dummy has stirred and joyfully waves her hand at it, calling upon it alarmedly: "Come, help me! Let's get to each other! Look, this ugly, bald man wants to catch me." (Oh, poor Prince.)

The FAIRY makes another movement —giving the dummy a push—and then goes stealthily back into the forest.

The DUMMY, the wretched thing, is moving! It is dancing—if that is the word—towards the PRINCESS. It moves as though its every limb were breaking as it bends them. Well, a dummy's a dummy—anyone can see that. With one exception. The PRINCESS sees only the coronet and the mantle, and the curling golden hair—the very things princesses want. Let him dance!

The PRINCE dances with fascinating grace and bewitching sadness; his very soul is moving in his limbs. But it is all in vain. The PRINCESS dances to right and to left. It is like a game of tag, and it goes on for a while. Now! She has reached her partner, after all. That Wooden Dummy! Well, she asked for it.

The PRINCESS joins hands with the WOODEN PRINCE and tugs away at him, trying to make him join in the dance. And he does dance, bless him—every splinter and chip in his body is cracking and creaking. In this manner they go dancing out.

INTERMEZZO

The PRINCE stands there forlorn, without mantle and coronet, bald, looking on as the beautiful Princess dances off with the Wooden Dummy he has made. And he watches the creation of his own hands, invested with his own beauty so as to make it a herald of himself, dancing with his loved one, who, he is sure, has been waiting for him and been looking for him and no one else *. Oh, poor young Prince! For you, it seems, the game is up. Already, the dusk of evening is gathering about you; the surrounding country is turning gloomy, heavy and grey. It's all over. The poor PRINCE sits down on a stone lying by the wayside and buries his bald head in his palms. Nothing stirs. The music only is speaking; it says: "Wretched love. Contemptible princesses. A life like that isn't worth living." Yet nothing stirs. For all that soared and hovered has now sunken to the depths. Truly, his sorrow is like a boundless, monotonous wilderness—the music pours over it like a stray wind. Long the PRINCE remains sitting in that posture, while a heavy night is descending upon him. Maybe it will even bury him.

FIFTH DANCE

(*Grand ballet and apotheosis*)

But as the scene grows dark and darker, a sort of uneasy shudder passes over the

countryside. The FAIRY emerges from the forest. Her grey veils seem to light up. She starts moving, beckons to right, beckons to left—apparently issuing orders in quick succession. A mysterious bustling and whispering surges up in the music. Every Thing stands where it stood before, and yet it seems as if each Thing has changed its form. **

And now begins The FAIRY's magic dance. Now it becomes evident that she is Queen over all Things at this place. At first, she circles slowly round the huddled PRINCE in a wary, wheedling, endearing dance: "Now you are suffering. It is as it should be. Now you are turning away from Life. Now you are mine!" And she flits about like a will-o'-the-whisp, like a luminous magic bat. And whichever way she turns, the night turns ablaze with magic light. (The light of the moon must be like that, shining over the lunar regions.) And wherever she turns, a shudder passes over all Things, and they stir and respond in whispers. Once more she flits around in a faster circle, and the Things move and follow her. The green-veiled trees of the forest start off, and the silver-blue-veiled waves of the stream leave their bed. "Come on, come on, come here, all of you. Come and gather ye round my sad Prince." And the Things, forming a semi-circle, surge towards the baldheaded and unadorned, sorrowful PRINCE to pay him their obeisance. "Come here, more of you! I want all of you to come here! Now he is suffering. Now he belongs to us!" And it seems as if the slope of the little hill were sliding: all the Things that were on it—flowers and bushes and stones—come rolling down it; but they do so noiselessly and meekly. And little imps and elves are turning up from nowhere. For if so many Things can move, every Thing can.

* You have no idea how often this sort of thing happens to princes that make up wooden dummies.—The Author.

** This point needs to be explained. Such things take place every night. At night, objects take off their masks, and we see them do it, only we do not recognize them, as it is dark. All the same, we know that, at night, everything changes.—The Author.

And the Things, paying their obeisance, dance round the bald-headed PRINCE. And now the FAIRY walks up behind him and, softly, in a motherly way, addresses him; "Raise up your eyes, oh Prince, and look about you".

The PRINCE raises his eyes and lets his gaze travel around. "Ah! What's this?" It is like an awakening from a sort of sleep-reality into the world of dreams. "Where am I? How light my poor, anguished heart feels! Why, this is a different world! Where is my sorrow?" And he almost starts looking for his sorrow. Yet it is gone with the world that has gone.*

The FAIRY now steps in front of him: "You are in my land, oh Prince. This is my country here. Your sorrow is gone with the world that's gone."

The PRINCE, as in a dream, takes the FAIRY's hand. It is the way the dreamer and the sleep-walker move. "Oh, strange Fairy, I've had such great sorrow." And, with the passing, reposeful languor of sorrow, he places his other hand too in the FAIRY's, and lays his head on it. The PRINCE has surrendered.

The FAIRY strokes his head and makes a signal to the Things: "Pay ye homage to him! He is now our King." All Things pay their obeisance and prostrate themselves. And lo—

The FAIRY takes a wonderful head of golden hair from the calyx of a flower and gently presses it upon the PRINCE's head. Oh, this is more beautiful a hundred times than the one he has lost!

The FLOWER bows its calyx and dances off. ANOTHER FLOWER advances and holds its calyx under the FAIRY's hand. The FAIRY produces a splendid golden crown and sets it on the PRINCE's head.

Ah, this is more splendid a hundred times than the coronet he lost!

The GREAT MAGIC LILY advances and from its bell-shaped flower the FAIRY produces a mantle of petals and hangs it over the PRINCE's shoulders. She then makes a sign of command to her hosts. The PRINCE rises. Ah, he is more handsome a hundred times than his former self—now lost—ever was. Is it quite lost, one wonders?

All THINGS dance round the PRINCE, fêting him. The trees form into lines; the waves prostrate themselves before him as a solid path; and smaller flowers, imps and elves—a gay crowd of flitting out-riders—run ahead of him, up the hillside. The wave-path and the lines of trees lead to the foot of the hill.

The FAIRY now takes the PRINCE by the hand and, walking on the waves, between the lines of bowing trees, leads him over to the foot of the hill, where the trees and the flowers flock around him, forming a live arbour. "Here. This is your throne. You are now King here, King over the soul-comprehending."

The PRINCE lets his intoxicated gaze travel over the scene: This is triumph, pomp and splendour! No more suffering, no more night.**

SIXTH DANCE

(Minor ballet)

Thus, there is triumph and pomp and splendour, and the PRINCE, radiant, is standing at the centre of ALL THINGS, which are paying obeisance to him. And now, of a sudden, over on the other side (upstage right), there appears—
The PRINCESS, tugging at the Wooden

---

* Now there, my Prince, you can see the use of the world of dancing. If the world is bad it ceases to exist. Everything will dance to the throbbing of your heart. But this is true not only in the theatre.—The Author.

** This point too needs to be explained. Darkness is a veil that hides things; but once things have revealed themselves, there is no more veil, and darkness ceases to exist. For the PRINCE, for instance, the night has been dispelled.—The Author.

Dummy; she tries to make it dance; and dance it would, that miserable—
The DUMMY, were it not so hopelessly out of joint by now. Its coronet is cocked at an angle, like the hat of a drunk, its wig has slipped back over its nape, and its fine scarlet mantle barely hangs from one shoulder. The WOODEN PRINCE has broken down and is stamping through a rather extraordinary dance. The PRINCESS, exasperated, is egging her sorry partner on. She is angry with it, and boxes and tries to straighten it. Maybe she even hates it already. But there is nothing to be done about it, since she has chosen this one. Now, as she is struggling with the DUMMY she enters the alley of firs at the end of which the resplendent real PRINCE is standing. And as she catches sight of him, she stops and stands agape. She pushes the wretched wooden DUMMY away from her, and it crashes and slumps to the ground. She smiles at the PRINCE and stretches her small hands towards him. "This is the most handsome Prince, after all. I *must* have him!* And she starts towards him in a coaxing, coquettish, flaunting dance.
The PRINCE notices her and clutches at his heart. He cannot help it—she *is* the real Princess, after all. Yet he makes a reproachful gesture of refusal: "*Now* you'd like to have me, wouldn't you? It's crown and mantle and hair that you want. So go to your dummy! There it is! It's lying over there. Go away! I don't want you." And he turns away from her and walks upstage. The FAIRY goes with him, but not intimately, as before, not taking him by the hand. When the PRINCE clutched at his heart, she drew her hand away and stepped back, and now she seems to have wrapped herself up even more in her veils.
The PRINCESS grows alarmed: "Oh, my God! Is the handsome Prince going away? Is he angry? I'll run after him." And off she goes.

* Princesses think in such direct terms.—The Author.

SEVENTH DANCE
(*Grand ballet*)

The TREES bend towards each other, like so many "V"-s closing, barring the way of the Princess.
The PRINCESS dances round the inner circle thus formed, to get to the PRINCE. The TREES, however, put new branches in her way, and the mound and the PRINCE on top of it are separated from the PRINCESS by the asteroid pattern of intertwining V-letters. This is the same kind of tag game again. But the interlinked walls of the firs rise like a star-castle; and the dance of the waves meanders in between them.

EIGHTH DANCE

The PRINCESS, tiring of it at last, buries her face in her small hands und runs off, crying (to downstage right). But here she stumbles against the lifeless form of the wooden DUMMY and almost falls over it. She views it in disgust and exasperation. She kicks its coronet: "Is that the thing that deluded me?" She kicks its mantle: "Is this the thing that turned my head?" She kicks the wig: "Is this the thing I fell in love with?" Then, in her utter despair, she snatches her coronet off her head and dashes it against the DUMMY; she throws off her beautiful silver mantle. "I don't want these things! Better to have nothing!" But she does more than this: she whips out the big scissors from her belt—no decent princess goes about without her sewing things!—and cuts off at her shoulders her wonderful golden hair that reaches to her knees. "I don't want anything! If the Prince does not want me, so I may as well be poor and ugly, a despicable creature!" She then falls on her knees before the stone on which the Prince in his sorrow sat some time ago and throws herself on it, sobbing. (Poor little Princess! Anyone would now take her for a shivering, out-at-the-elbows little shepherdess rather than for a Princess.)

The PRINCE has found it impossible, after all, to preserve his equanimity behind his stockade of fir-trees. Still and all, it was with the utmost difficulty that he brought himself to turning his back on the PRINCESS. Something makes him tingle all over, and he emerges from the forest upstage. He himself does not know what he wants to do—just saunters along, to the tune of some sweet music. As he advances downstage, his eyes fall on the sobbing PRINCESS. Well, well, she isn't the haughty, coquettish Princess any more—she has shed all her ornaments. She has humbled herself.

The PRINCESS suddenly jumps to her feet. Her first impulse is to hide herself—it seems as if she wished to hide herself behind her little palms. She feels ashamed: "Oh, I am ugly and deprived of all my adornments. He will abhor me. No, no, I'd rather not let him see me anymore!" And, turning her face away, with mincing steps, she retreats to the farthest corner upstage, where she crouches shivering. The PRINCE follows her nonetheless. "When you came to me haughty and wearing your coronet and mantle and reached your little hands to me, I turned my back on you. But now you have humbled yourself and are like a poor shepherdess—now I will wrap my mantle around you and clasp you to myself." And he does just that. He bends over the crouching PRINCESS, wraps his mantle around her and lifts her up to himself.

The FAIRY has been following the PRINCE in dismay and warily, as though she had a foreboding as to the end all this is coming to. And upon seeing the way the PRINCE approached the PRINCESS, the way he bent over her, she cut sweeping circles in the air with both arms in a flourishing of wailing and lament: "Go back! Go back, my hosts! All is lost!"

ALL THINGS withdraw. The trees retreat to their place and the waters to their bed. "Go back! Go back! It's been all in vain! Man has deserted us and gone back to Man." And as the PRINCE has reached out his hand to grasp Life elsewhere, the Things again hide themselves in their state of benumbed lifelessness. And as the curtain slowly falls, the world resumes its simple, ordinary aspect. It again becomes ordinary and simple like the last word the Things have spoken and to which they are waiting for Man's ultimate reply. They still are waiting.

The FAIRY too has retreated to the hillock, her place of watch since long, long ago, and leaning forward, stands motionless, staring in front of her.

The PRINCE and PRINCESS, however, gaze at each other, and respond to each other, and are no longer concerned about the Things.

CURTAIN

Translated by István Farkas

THE MIRACULOUS MANDARIN

*Pantomime grotesque**

by

MENYHÉRT LENGYEL

Characters

MIMI
THE OLD GALLANT
THE YOUNG STUDENT
THE MANDARIN
FIRST THUG
SECOND THUG
THIRD THUG

SCENE—An upper-storey room: fantastic colours of squalor. Tattered wall-paper—bleak walls—comically crippled furniture—corners filled with odd things as in some shabby, disreputable old curio shop. In short: This is the den of three thugs, who use it as a store for stolen goods.

There is a door upstage with a window on either side. From outside, in a compound of vibrating street-lights and a mixture of confusing cries and noises, the life and hubbub of a huge city spill into the room.

I

MIMI and the three THUGS. The FIRST THUG is lying full length on the bed, the SECOND THUG is having a row with MIMI in the middle of the room. They have no money. He turns his pockets inside out—they're empty. The THIRD THUG eagerly rummages through the drawers of the dresser—nothing turns up. He too turns upon the girl. MIMI keeps shrugging her shoulders. Why can't they leave her alone? What do they want of her? It's not her fault. She can't help.

At this moment the FIRST THUG sits up on the bed: he is a big, grim-looking, reckless bully. He scrambles to his feet and walks up to MIMI. He grabs the girl's arm—and pulls her to him savagely. "No money? Well, you go an' get some!" MIMI, frightened, makes evasions: "What am I to do?" The THUG: "You go to that window and show yourself. Get someone to come up here—and we'll take care of him, the three of us".

The two other fellows are all for the scheme. MIMI is reluctant—fists are raised to her face. The FIRST THUG pushes her brusquely to the window. Then the three men take counsel quickly: they're going to hide—one under the table, another behind the dresser, and the third concealed beside the bed. They do so, then wait.

* The Hungarian original was first published in the literary magazine, *Nyugat* ("West"), 1917, pp. 87—93.

2

MIMI at the window. She looks out; she waves her hand; she winks; she smiles—no result. Suddenly, she starts. Looks back timidly. The three THUGS poke their heads into sight: "Got anyone?" She nods yes. The three men duck their heads again. They are waiting. Footfalls coming slowly up the wooden stairs. MIMI retreats to middle of room, her eyes riveted to the door, which now opens and frames—the OLD GALLANT.

He is a quaint dapper old man—tired, wrinkled face, but waxed moustache; shabby top-hat; coat shiny with wear and ironing; suspicious-looking spats over what were once a pair of patent-leather shoes; dirty collar; cheap, gaudy tie; withered flower in buttonhole.

He enters smiling with the assurance of a gallant. After a few steps, he stops, looks the girl up and down. He is delighted. Takes off his top-hat, places it on the table (hair, dyed and groomed with painstaking care, is smoothed over his skull), and, while eyeing the girl, begins to peel off his dirty gloves. MIMI stands still waiting.

Now the OLD GALLANT steps up to her and opens his arms, meaning to put them round her. MIMI takes a step back, looking at him inquiringly and, by rubbing thumb and index together, asks: "What about the dough?"

The OLD GALLANT ignores the question—makes another amorous move. MIMI, now holding her hand close under his nose, repeats her question: "What about the dough?"

The OLD GALLANT waves that aside; he smiles: "Money—that's not important. It's love that counts." He presses his hand against his heart—he is wooing her, showing off; he pinches her arm, her cheek, becomes increasingly fresh. MIMI, indignant, is hard put to it to keep him off when—the three THUGS spring foreward and attack the OLD GALLANT.

They form a chain from the table to the door, toss the old man from hand to hand and finally chuck him out the door. He tumbles down the stairs; and the thugs throw his top-hat after him—one hears the hard hat roll tap-tap down the stairs.

Resentment runs high among the occupants of the room. The old man is ridiculed, his wooing imitated. Once again the FIRST THUG confronts the girl menacingly: "Mind you do it smarter this time!" Again he pushes her along to the window, and again the three men hide themselves. MIMI at the window: action as before—she swaying her hips provocatively. The frivolous music conveying temptation and whose volume has been gradually increasing, suddenly becomes charming, gentle and childlike, because—

3

MIMI has caught sight of someone in the street. She leans from the window, waves her hand and smiles. Then she turns about, clasping her hands joyfully. A gay, light patter of feet surges up the wooden stairs... the door flies open and reveals... the YOUNG STUDENT.

Rosy cheeks, blond hair, broad tie, short pants, big shoes. He has come rushing up to the door, but now he stops and stands helplessly, not knowing what to do with himself; he is panting, blushes deeply and casts down his eyes.

MIMI is studying him, smiling—he's a nice boy.

The STUDENT, smiling too in embarrassment, looks up at the girl.

MIMI beckons to him to step nearer.

The STUDENT advances timidly.

MIMI: "Come here, little boy." She takes his hand—how smooth it feels! She strokes his cheek—how rosy! His head—how blond! She draws him closer to her and again pats his cheek: "You little darling. My, and how handsome and clean he is!"—She looks him up and down with delight. The STUDENT feels embarrassed and is awkward and sweet.

Now it strikes MIMI that this, after all, is but a victim, poor boy: she has got to try and find out what he's got on him. She puts her arms round him and light-fingeredly, quickly searches him. A glance at his hands—no rings; waistcoat-pocket felt—no watch; pockets of his jacket searched—there's only a handkerchief... She sniffs at it: it's scented!... She throws it away: Damn junk! Annoyed, she asks: "Why, have you got no money at all?" The STUDENT sadly shakes his head. Depressed, despairing and helpless, he turns to go when—she takes pity on him very much: Poor boy. "Come here, you little darling. No need to be sad like that. What a young boy... And how he's trembling... Come on!"

She throws her arms round his shoulders, caresses him, fondles him, mischievously pulls his ear, pats his cheek, then takes the boy's clumsy hands and puts them round her waist; they start waltzing slowly. Their movements gradually become more uninhibited... Cheeks begin to glow, their heads bow closer together—love burgeons in their hearts... The music grows more and more melting—they stop 'and look at each other, and laugh. They kiss.

At this moment, the three THUGS, who have been watching the scene with anger, jump out from their hiding-places, dash forward and pull the couple apart. The boy puts up some resistance—but, of course, he hasn't a chance against those three bullies, and they throw him out the door. He has disappeared from sight, but down the stairs and through the courtyard and beyond, above the noises of the street, his sobbing is faintly heard.

In the room the ruffians turn towards MIMI; they are very angry. She is sorry for the boy and cries. The thugs jeer at her: how is it that, of all the men she can have, she wants that little kid, that young nobody? Love, that's what she's after. And as if that's not enough, she feels sorry for him and goes and cries her eyes out for him.

The FIRST THUG draws his knife and threatens her: "Take care—I'll cut you up! If you don't do something this time—if you don't get cracking—you're finished. Get back to the window!"

MIMI, trembling, obeys. Once again the three THUGS hide themselves.

The faint lament of the sobbing boy can be heard still, and back at the window, as she resumes her soliciting, the motif of temptation, of lust-provocation is heard again and works into a crescendo, suddenly acquiring a pungent, spicy, exotic colour.

4

At the window MIMI starts. Alarmed, she takes a step backwards. The THUGS poke their heads forward: "What's the matter?" She hovers at centre, dismayed and hesitant. The THUGS urge her to get back to the window, and timidly she returns to it. The exotic music increases in volume; the stairs are creaking. Her gaze riveted on the door, MIMI, trembling, retreats to the table. The door opens, and the MANDARIN appears on the doorstep.

A Chinese. Broad, yellow face; shining slit eyes—an unblinking, fixed stare like that of a fish. He wears a silk skull-cap, from under which a long black pig-tail falls on his back. He is dressed in a richly embroidered, loose-fitting yellow silk coat, black velvet trousers and very fine boots.

He wears a twisted, many-stranded gold chain around his neck, the buttons of his coat shine, and he has many diamond rings on his delicate fingers.

He is standing on the doorstep, looking at the girl with an unblinking stare, a deeply serious look in his eyes.

She is frightened of him and edges

backwards. But whatever she backs into—the table, the dresser or the bed— the THUGS, from their hiding-places, push her back towards the MANDARIN. At last she plucks up courage and cautiously approaches the Chinese, who is standing on the doorstep. She timidly invites him to come nearer. The MANDARIN does not budge. She invites him once again. The MANDARIN moves. Slowly, at a steady pace, he comes to the middle of the room. She points at the chair, motioning him to sit down. The MANDARIN sits down. But fixedly, unrelentingly, a darkly earnest look in his eyes, his set face never registering the least emotion, he continues to stare at the girl.

Something's got to be done at last, and MIMI, awkwardly and shivering, begins her show. She dances and whisks past the MANDARIN in a provocative manner. She waltzes round the room and as she comes to the door, with a sudden movement —always dancing—she bolts it, then dances on. The MANDARIN continues to watch her with his unblinking, grave stare. She dances faster and faster—by now she has thrown off some of her shyness, her movements grow less inhibited, and, as a spin brings her face to face with the MANDARIN, seeing the oddly stiff, unmoving posture of the Chinese, she bursts into laughter, which increases in force and, dizzy with the dancing, dissolving in laughter, plops upon the motionless MANDARIN's lap.

With the laughing woman lying, wriggling and tossing under his nose, the MANDARIN slowly undergoes a peculiar transformation. A soft tremor passes over him from top to toe. A blush rises to his cheeks. A flicker of his eyelids breaks his beady, fixed stare, and he starts blinking ever more rapidly. His chest heaves, his breathing becomes difficult and broken. His hands twitch, and his fingers—in increasingly rapid flits—wander on to her neck and head... His excitement mounts. Minute reflex actions burst forth—a twitch, a shudder passes over him—and a sudden hot rush of blood passing through him starts him shaking all over. The girl looks at him—and gets scared... She stops laughing, jumps to her feet and backs away.

The MANDARIN rises, too. He stretches his arms and moves towards her. She flees... The MANDARIN follows her, his eyes riveted on her, his face distorted and imploring like that of a sick animal.

The chase is on... The girl flits between the table and the chairs, with the MANDARIN intent on her trail... He leaps, makes a snatch at her, falls... Down on the floor, he manages to catch her by the ankles... She tears herself free... He jumps to his feet—his awkwardness and clumsiness are falling away from him... are gone... He moves with more alacrity... becomes extremely nimble and alarmingly grotesque... Now it is he who moves provocatively, starting to dance with fantastic movements. A strange, grating noise rises from his throat. MIMI grows increasingly frightened of him... She is fleeing, he follows in hot pursuit. He jingles his money and makes greedy snatches at her. He almost reaches her. She slips out of his hands. He is crying— tears streaming down his cheeks... He is completely beside himself—spinning, whirling, with increasingly alarming speed... He is now like a huge spinning top, fanning a whirlwind around him... His yellow coat and pig-tail stream through the air. It is impossible to avoid him... He catches the girl and with a rattle of intense happiness in his throat sinks with her to the floor.

At this moment the three THUGS rush forward and fall upon the MANDARIN. They hold him down and release the girl. They search his pockets—the gold coins fall from them with a jingle and roll all over the floor; they uncoil the long gold chain from his neck, pull the rings from his fingers. All this is done with lightning spead. Having plucked him clean, they exchange glances—and already the decision is taken to kill him. They grab him as if he were a parcel, throw him into the bed and on him heap pillows, blankets, mattresses, rags, everything, so as to stifle him to death. Pause. Then they make a sign at one another: "Finished." The girl is standing by the table, shivering. A slight pause. Then the THUGS sigh in relief: "He's done for."

At this moment the MANDARIN's pale, yellow head emerges from under the blankets.

It is a head with glassy eyes that start out of their sockets and are fixed on the girl.

The three THUGS are taken aback. The MANDARIN isn't dead! They pull themselves together. All right, let's finish him off.

They throw the blankets from the bed and pull the MANDARIN out of it. As soon as his feet touch the floor, the MANDARIN bounces up like some fantastic ball and hurls himself at the girl.

Before he reaches her, the THUGS catch him and hold him down. They twist his arms back, holding him fast. The MANDARIN, apparently unconcerned about what's happening to him, continues to stare at the girl with goggling eyes—two torches fed by the flames of a terrific inner fire.

The THIRD THUG produces a long and blood-stained, rusty knife. He motions to his two friends that they should hold the Chinese fast. Then, pointing the long knife ahead, dashes against the MANDARIN.

He runs the knife into the latter's belly.

The skin rips, the body slacks—the point of the knife emerges at the MANDARIN's back.

They let go of the body and watch it fall—now he's sure to die.

For a moment the MANDARIN staggers, totters and stumbles—he is on the point of slumping (they are watching eagerly). Suddenly he regains his equilibrium, starts and jumps—and is at the girl again.

She flees, screaming.

Again the THUGS grab him and hold him fast. They too are alarmed and dismayed—all the more reason for doing away with him quickly.

One of the THUGS produces a big old-fashioned pistol. He aims it at the MANDARIN's head and fires. Big bang and smoke. The THUGS jump clear of the MANDARIN. The smoke lifts—a dark singed hole shows on the MANDARIN's forehead where the bullet passed through him. He staggers and totters—swings round and is once again at the girl.

He starts chasing her with grotesque bounds.

They seize him and hold him down.

This is something horrible. He has *not* died!

What is to be done?

Kill him! Kill him! You've got to!

But how?

One THUG points up at the chandelier.

That's where he's going to swing.

They lift him on a chair... they wind his pig-tail round his neck... And now one of the THUGS, standing on the table, strings the MANDARIN up on the chandelier by his pig-tail. The chair is kicked from under his feet—the MANDARIN is hanged.

The light goes out.

Darkness.

Silence.

Huddled together the three THUGS and the girl hold their breath in the darkness.

Suddenly a dim and eerie light looms up in mid-air.

The MANDARIN's rotund belly—like that of a Buddha, a fantastic sphere floating in the air—begins to shine.

The mystic light illuminates the whole figure of the man who has been hanged by his pig-tail—his big, yellow, round head, his eyes starting out of their sockets,—eyes that, in a stubborn animal glare and with terrible desire, are turned on the girl like a pair of electric searchlights.

The THUGS, shuddering and a-tremble, scuttle for shelter; they creep under the bed and hide themselves.

The girl stays in the middle of the room.

She looks at the MANDARIN—for the first time without fear—and smiles.

She beckons to one THUG: "Come here." As the fellow refuses to go to her, she walks up to him and drags him along: "You cut that mandarin down for me."

The THUG dares not touch the man.

She urges him more energetically, putting the knife in his hand : "I *insist* that you cut him down!"

At last the THUG, trembling, clambers onto the table, and with the knife severs the pig-tail.

The MANDARIN drops to the floor.

But again he rises and rushes at the girl.

She catches him in her arms. She hugs him and clasps him to herself in a long embrace.

The MANDARIN emits a rattle of happy fulfilment—he clings to the girl, and a tremor passes all over his body.

At this moment the wound on his belly and the hole on his forehead start slowly bleeding.

He is gradually fainting away; his hug slackens and his arms droop; his knees give way beneath him.

There is a happy look in his fixed stare, but slowly his eyes close.

A smile hovers on his contorted face.

His desire is spent.

Slowly the girl, triumphantly smiling, lowers the body on the floor—to the sounds of a quaint and strident, exotic music.

The MANDARIN is dead.

Translated by István Farkas

DOCUMENTS

LISZT AND BARTÓK

by

BENCE SZABOLCSI

In recent months the world of music commemorated the fifteenth anniversary of Béla Bartók's death. All through his life this great Hungarian composer of our century was closely and directly linked to the art of Ferenc Liszt. It was by interpreting Liszt's works that the young Bartók attracted attention at the Academy of Music in Budapest; his inaugural lecture at the Hungarian Academy of Sciences dealt with the problems of Liszt's compositions; and in one of his most interesting articles he investigated the effect the music of Liszt had on our contemporary public. But over and above this, Bartók's whole art is imbued with impulses received from Liszt. What he learned from Liszt, what he drew from the example of his great predecessor is clearly to be seen only today, when the late period of Liszt's art—for a long time scarcely known and practically never analysed—is being investigated and clarified by musical science. Only today can we see clearly how much the music of the twentieth century owes to Liszt's late and bold compositions.

The reforms of harmony with which the great composers of our time have extended the possibilities of musical idiom are to a large extent rooted in Liszt's innovations; the vocabulary of musical impressionism and expressionism was mostly coined in his workshop. However, it was precisely in Bartók's music that Liszt's initiatives, the boldest ones at that, found a succession and achieved realization. This applies not only to the elements of the idiom or form of music but to the whole artistic attitude and, not least, to the international position and task of the composer in summing up the music of the various peoples—a task of very wide scope and, it is no exaggeration to say, of revolutionary importance, destined to renew the whole range of expression in European music. Beyond the traditions of Hungarian musical romanticism, *this* was the great example in which Ferenc Liszt preceded Béla Bartók.

Only gradually did Bartók himself recognize this significance of Liszt's art; for a long time he struggled with and for this art—first as a performing artist, then as a composer and finally as a thinker and humanist. The first time he rendered a conscious account of this music was an interesting and significant date. It was in 1911 that the hundredth anniversary of the birth of Ferenc Liszt was celebrated in Hungary, and on that occasion Bartók wrote a "festive" article about Liszt for one of the Hungarian musical periodicals. At that time the public at large did not yet know that in the same year Bartók had completed his piano composition, the "Allegro barbaro," as well as his first work for the stage, his only opera, "Bluebeard's Castle." At this stage of his career as a composer it was not yet at all obvious that there were secret, inner links that joined his art with the world of his great romantic predecessor. On the contrary, even several years afterwards only the new things that were different from Liszt were observed in Bartók's music: the difference of idiom, the discovery of genuine folk music and the evoking of the tone of the Eastern-European folk ballads, a style seemingly so very remote from Liszt's. Today, beyond these differences, we can also see clearly what in Bartók's art is related to or parallel with that of Liszt and even that which proved to be related already when Bartók's first paper on Liszt was published.

And for this very reason, in addition to its historical significance, Béla Bartók's first personal appearance as a passionate partisan of the music of Ferenc Liszt is bound to rouse interest even today. The musical world, which is preparing to commemorate in 1961 the common anniversaries of these two men: the hundred-and-fiftieth anniversary of Liszt's and the eightieth of Bartók's birth, could scarcely choose a more beautiful and symbolic introduction to this double celebration than this, the fraternal homage of one great master to another.

LISZT'S MUSIC
AND OUR CONTEMPORARY PUBLIC

by

BÉLA BARTÓK

I t is strange what a great number, I might even say the overwhelming majority, of musicians have been unable, for all its novel and magnificent properties, to become fond of the music of Liszt. I do not speak of those who are *ipso facto* at loggerheads with everything that is new and unusual. There were, however, in Liszt's own time, as there still are even today, great and able musicians who absolutely abhorred his music or only accepted it with considerable reservations if, indeed, they went beyond just tolerating it. It is incomprehensible that in Hungary, while nobody for example dare utter a single word against Wagner or Brahms (though in fact there would be a thing or two to find fault with in their music, too), Liszt's music has been free prey to cavilling. From the man in charge of music at the Ministry to the student at the Academy of Music, everyone will find something in it to criticize.

We cannot say that the deterrent quality lies in the novelty and unusual features of Liszt's music, since, on the one hand, everybody has heard plenty of this music, and, on the other, the disapproving criticism stresses the point that it is "trivial and tedious." It may rather be Liszt's extreme versatility or multiplicity, his excessive susceptibility to all sensations from the most commonplace to the most extraordinary. Everything that he experienced in music, whether it was trivial or majestic, left a permanent mark on his compositions.

Even as a man he possessed heterogeneous features. His convictions led him to prepare to become a Catholic priest, yet he lived with a woman in a marriage unsanctioned by the Church; he was an enthusiastic admirer of ascetic Catholicism, yet loved the perfumed atmosphere of drawing-rooms; he was not loth to visit the dirty camps of the Gipsies in Hungary, yet felt at ease in the artificial life of the high aristocracy; everywhere he spoke of Hungary as his beloved motherland for which he was making

121

sacrifices, and treated the special music he had heard in Hungary with great devotion, yet he did not learn Hungarian although he was an excellent linguist. His musical life is similar. In his young years he imitated the bad habits of the commonplace artists of his time—by "improving, and arranging," polishing up masterpieces that should not have been touched even by an artist of Liszt's calibre. He was already under the influence of the more vulgar melodies of Berlioz, the sentimentality of Chopin and, even more, the stereotype effects of the Italians. Up to the very end the traces of these influences are noticeable in his work, lending it those traits that are called trivial. Later, when he had become acquainted with the pot-pourris of the Gipsies, he did not bother to distinguish between rarities and the commonplace; the Gipsy manner affected him, as such. Wherever he went he received musical impulses, through which his style became somewhat diffuse. Side by side with this triviality nearly all his works show a marvellous audacity of either form or invention. This audacity is an almost fanatical striving for what is new and rare. In his works, scattered among many stereotypes, he wrote much more that was new and ahead of his time than many other composers whose works are sometimes more highly esteemed by the general public. Let us illustrate this through some of his works. The earliest of his great compositions that offer so much is his Sonata for the Piano. Some dull introductory bars, the principal section of the exposition, the stops leading up to the recitativo-like music which precedes the development, the dark coda devoid of all exterior effects and—leaving the greatest to the end—the diabolically brilliant fugato... all this belongs to the realm of the most grandiose music. Side by side with this the sweetness of the andante in F-sharp major inserted in the development, or the sentimentality of the subsidiary theme formed from the principal theme, or again the empty pomp of the $^3/_2$ intermediate passage, naturally seem banal. In respect to form the work is absolutely perfect, which is rather rare with Liszt and is a revolutionary innovation.

Take another very well known composition, the Piano Concerto in E-flat major. As far as form is concerned, it too is a bold innovation, it too is perfect. Nevertheless in its contents it does not satisfy us at all, since its glitter is mostly empty indeed, some of its thoughts—however splendidly clad—descend to the level of a drawing-room piece. Diametrically opposed to this Piano Concerto is his gigantic Faust Symphony, with its host of wonderful thoughts and the planned development of the diabolic irony[*]

---

[*] Liszt was the first to express irony by means of music. His Sonata was written about 1850. Similar traits (Siegfried, Meistersinger) are to be found in Wagner's music only much later—possibly due to Liszt's influence. (Note of the Author)

(Mephisto), which first appeared in the fugato of the Sonata. These qualities render the Faust Symphony immortal, and yet something else disturbs us here: certain imperfections of form, particularly the hackneyed repetition of certain parts, the so-called "Liszt sequences." Scattered among similar sequences there are many new things to be found in the symphonic poems. In his utterly misunderstood Danse Macabre Liszt produces profoundly moving music, and we are greatly enriched by his B-A-C-H Prelude and Fugue and by the passacaglia-like Variations written on a Bach theme. The Années de pélerinage series, one of the smaller, less appreciated piano-pieces, contains some marvellous thoughts mixed with vulgar ones. The compositions that ought to be closest to us, his Hungarian Rhapsodies, are less successful works (perhaps it is for this very reason that they are so widespread and held in such high esteem). Despite a great many marks of genius, these Rhapsodies are mostly stereotypes; they represent Gipsy music—sometimes even blended with Italian music (the Sixth)—and as regards form, they are sometimes veritable conglomerates (the Twelfth).

The Liszt sequences mentioned above lead us to another point of criticism. It is these repetitions, after the same pattern and to be found in almost every work of his, that lend colour to the charge of tediousness. In this respect the trouble was that Liszt was far too much alone in his work. So much did he stand out from among his surroundings that nobody could criticize what he had composed but had to take everything as a divine present. Those who kept a greater distance and criticized him would say stupid things, so that Liszt was cut off from all acceptable and clever criticism that might have guided him. Not all composers are granted the gift, as Beethoven was, of breaking through all difficulties by themselves and creating perfection in each of their compositions. Only one person would have been worthy of the difficult post of criticizing Liszt—and that was Wagner. But Wagner returned Liszt's affection with neglect; he did not care whether another person's work would turn out more or less successful*, though it was surely from Wagner, if from anybody, that Liszt would have accepted advice. Thus it can to some extent be explained why Brahms, for instance, made such sharp statements about Liszt's music. That which was new in Liszt and in advance of his own age was unacceptable to Brahms, who had never composed anything reaching beyond his own period. That which in Liszt's work was perfect in form was generally a revolutionary innovation and therefore objectionable anarchism to the apostle of traditional forms. What

---

* In a letter of his to Frau Wesendonk he cannot find more to say about the Faust Symphony than: "I have heard Liszt's Faust Symphony; it is the Second Part, if any, that I like best." (Note of the Author)

would be left of Liszt? Trivialities both in form and in content—and that is why Brahms, in virtually raving fury, called Liszt's Dante, for instance, "Unmusik" suitable for the garbage heap.*

But, by its attitude of rejection, the public, which in the meantime has reached the age for which Liszt wrote his audacities, merely shows that it cannot distinguish between form and essence, that it does not possess a hearing keen enough to separate what is important from what is superfluous. When a composer is to be judged as a personality in musical literature, not all the stress should be laid upon forms, while great beauty—set ineffectively behind forms that may be imperfect—remains unnoticed.

In this connexion let me tell of a personal observation. I was student when I first came across the Liszt Sonata. I tried it, but at that time I did not take to it. I found the first part of the exposition dreary and felt it to be empty; nor did I notice the irony of the fugato. Of course, this was at a time when I did not understand Beethoven's last sonatas either. Soon after I heard the Sonata performed to perfection by Dohnányi. In spite of this I failed to understand it completely. Some years later I took the work up again —I was interested in its piano technique and in surmounting its difficulties. And while learning it, I gradually came to like it, though not without reservations. Later I once talked to Dohnányi about this Sonata, and it turned out to my greatest surprise that he had had the same experience with it.

This also shows that a certain kind of music needs getting used to; yet our public has not become used to Liszt's music to this day.

(Népművelés, 1911)**

---

* See Brahms' correspondence with Joachim. (Note of the Author)
** *Népművelés* was a periodical edited by István Bárczi and Ödön Weszely before World War I.

LETTERS TO BÉLA BARTÓK

The following is a small selection of letters written to Béla Bartók by various people over a period of 35 years, the earlist dated 1910, the latest 1945. The selection was made from the book *Documenta Bartókiana;* Vol 3. (German edition) edited, introduced and annotated by Professor Denijs Dille, and jointly published in 1968 by the Publishing House of the Hungarian Academy of Sciences and Schott's Söhne Musikverlag, Mainz, West Germany. (322 pp, including fascimiles and 7 pages of black-and-white photographs.)

Professor Dille who is one of the Directors of the Bartók Archives in Budapest writes in the introduction: "The principle of selection was a simple one. We did not look for "interesting" letters, what we tried to do was to use the letters to give some sort of idea of the variety of reasons why his correspondents approached Bartók, and in this way we meant to throw light on hiɔ life, his activities and his character, since letters from friends tell us as much about the character of the recipient as that of the senders."

Bartók was a meticulous correspondent, keeping practically every letter, note, bill and piece of paper sent to him. Professor Dille had a great wealth of material to chose from: "This volume contains only a small proportion of those letters which Bartók received and kept. Bearing in mind the many letters, notices and slips of no importance amongst his papers, one is tempted to presume that he simply kept everything and that it was merely a variety of circumstances that stopped some of the material from coming down to us. We are in no position to know how much was lost and how important it was. Thus whole years are missing from the correspondence with *Universal Edition.* When first looking through the major part of the material in 1959 (almost two thousand letters and cards) I was able to establish that some of the bundles were confined to one period, whereas others contained material from a number of years. It is thus impossible to establish how many letters were lost, and what their dates were. I had the impression—confirmed in some cases—that letters covering a definite period were sorted by Bartók himself, as regards the assorted bundles one cannot tell who tied them up, nor can one discern the principle according to which they were sorted. Two folders, one marked "pending" the other "answered and copies of answers" contained mainly 1939 correspondence. It is reasonable to presume that Bartók tried to answer each letter if at all possible. This does not mean though that he answered every letter personally. *Pace* the author of the Preface to *Béla Bartók. Ausgewablte Briefe,* ed. János Demény. Corvina Press, Budapest 1960, 10 per cent at least of his answers were written by his first wife, Mrs. Martha Ziegler; after 1935 (perhaps even earlier), a number of answers were typed. Official and unimportant letters were thus written by secreterial help, perhaps dictated by Bartók, perhaps he drafted them, perhaps he merely gave instructions."

Some letters, and parts of others had to be left out, however, because of their too personal character, and it is also a pity from the point of view of posterity, that the lifelong friendship and cooperation between Bartók and Zoltán Kodály did not, as Professor Dille says, quoting Kodály himself, commit itself to paper: "...he has told me himself that what they had to say to each other could be best expressed by word of mouth."

The sample from Professor Dille's volume printed below is meant to give just an insight into Bartók's private world, indicating the variety of information, concerns, requests, interests and feelings constantly reaching out towards him and claiming his care and attention.

p. 58, No. 26.

Villa Roma,
Kaposvár,
29th November, 1910

My dear friend,

I have received the folksongs—thank you very much. It was really very kind of you to send them to your admirer.

I hear that you are going to Veszprém on the 3rd; would it suit you to set out a day earlier, and to get off at Kaposvár instead of Dombóvár? To stay with us? (page 3) You do not even have to announce your arrival in advance—take a cab at the station and have yourself driven to us, to the Villa Roma on Mount Roma. We shall await you with open arms.

Our little guest Fenella has been invited for the same gala evening—to sing some of her exotic folksongs. We could go together to Veszprém the next day. You can also arrive in the evening, you are welcome at any time—The train leaves the central station at 3.00 p.m.

So, hoping to see you even sooner,

yours,
Jóska

Notes

Manuscript letter.

Address: Bartók Béla úrnak   (Mr Béla Bartók)
        zeneszerző tanár   (Professor of Composition)
        Zeneakadémián   (The Academy of Music)
        Budapesten   (Budapest)

Sender: Rippl-Rónai József (Kaposvár, Roma Villa)

József Rippl-Rónai (1861–1927), was a well-known Hungarian painter. Béla Bartók Jr., the son of the musician, owns a pencil sketch of his father by Rippl-Rónai. According to information from Mrs. Márta Ziegler, Bartók also owned two pen-and-ink sketches, studies of nudes, by Rippl-Rónai with dedications by the painter. These drawings were stolen during the period the family lived at No. 2, Gyopár utca. She also confirmed that Bartók never visited exhibitions of paintings, just as he also rarely went to concerts, but in 1910 he visited an exhibition by Rippl-Rónai. We do not know why Bartók went to Veszprém and to Dombóvár (where, as far as is known, he never collected songs), nor do we know whether he accepted the painter's invitation.

p. 115, No. 66

Aix-en-Provence
April, 1922.

Dear Friend,

I must tell you once again how much your Sonata moved me.[1] This is a noble work, pure and elemental. I regret I was unable to be in Paris for the whole of your stay. Please convey my admiration to Miss Aranyi. She is worthy of the work which she performs.

Yours sincerely

Milhaud

Notes

Manuscript letter.

Address: Monsieur Béla Bartók (Hotel Majestic) Avenue Kléber/Paris

Darius Milhaud (b. 1892), the famous French composer. On his relations with Bartók, see Milhaud: *Notes sans musique.* Juillard. Paris 1949, p. 232.

[1] Milhaud was present at the concert of 8th April, which was arranged by *La revue musicale* in the Théatre du Vieux Colombier. Bartók and Jelly d'Aranyi played his First Sonata for Violin and Piano.

p. 118, No. 67

My dear Bartók,

I am very sorry indeed that I cannot say good-bye to you today at Madame Dubost. May these few melodies take with them my friendship and admiration for you. You have given great pleasure to all young French musicians by coming to Paris to play your wonderful sonata[1] and all your piano works for us—thank you. I hope to see you soon again, either here or in Budapest. In any case do not forget to send me your "Improvisations" and your four songs as soon as they are published—I shall send you the "Impromptus". Another thousand good wishes from your friend,

Poulenc

14th April, 1922

Notes

Manuscript letter.

Francis Poulenc (1899–1963), French composer. Poulenc wrote this note in the form of a dedication on his composition *Le bestiaire.* Edition de la Sirene musicale, Paris.

[1] First Sonata for Violin and Piano.

128

p. 134, No. 84

Hotel Petersbourg,
Schlossplatz, Riga.
20th April, 1927

Dear Master,

I have written to Davos and to Montana[1], and have had the information asked for sent directly to Pest, to the Academy. I am certain that the thaw is over. I prefer Montana to Davos, it is sunnier and better for one's mood, because Montana is on the terrace of a mountain and not in a valley, like Davos. It is not much further from Zurich than Davos.

I have talked to the Baltic Concert Agency here about a piano recital; Müller is interested and would be pleased to sign you up if your conditions allow it.[2] Perhaps you will be kind enough to write to him when you have a concert in Berlin (or may be in Warsaw), so you could perhaps link them with playing here too. Müller would also like to receive a sample programme now.

In the Second Sonata I do not understand the fourth bar, after Fig. 1, (7/8). Isn't it like this? viz. first a group of 3/8, then one of 2/8 and then another of 2/8? "No! It is correct as it is in the music." (Comment added by Bartók later on the margin of the letter.) Couldn't the D before 12 in the second movement stand?

"Yes, it could!" (Bartók's comment)

Before 40 I would like to play it like this, because it sounds better: ...

...(What is this referring to? instead? this rather not! or to a quarter tone; that may go.) (Bartók's comment)

Respectfully yours,

József Szigeti

my address: 161 Boulevard Haussmann, Paris

Notes

Manuscript letter.

József Szigeti (b. 1892), Hungarian violinist.

[1] In June 1926 Bartók and his wife were in Davos together with J. Szigeti; in 1928 they were in Montana.
[2] It is not known, whether Bartók wrote to Riga, but there is no reason to believe that he gave a concert there.

p. 143, No. 93

Villa Paradon
Villerville sur Mer
Calvados.
18th July, 1929.

My dear Friend,

Please do not be angry with me for only thanking you now for your kind letter and manuscript, but the moving here and the planning of the next season have made so much work that I have only just begun to play my violin again. (And I did not, of course, want to write before having played the new version through!) (Incidentally, I have no accompanist for the next season, and this has put me in bad humour.)

I like the new ending[1] very much, and I shall only play this one (with orchestra or with piano); formally, and from the point of view of the inner rhythm, this is a very happy solution! (The piece now takes only abt. eight minutes).

I am delighted that we shall play together in London[2] on the 6th January, and I hope I shall be successful in arranging the Berlin concert! In Erfurt I shall play the Rhapsody on the 30th and 31st March, and am very hopeful you will be there. I suggested that the Berlin concert should take place on the 3rd April as a Sonderkonzert der Gesellschaft der Musikfreunde (special concert of the Society of the Friends of Music)[3], but they want it to be arranged at my expense, and I cannot agree to this. They will offer you a small fee. I believe that the following would make a good programme:

1. Piano: perhaps Frescobaldi, Galuppi etc.
2. Violin: Bach solo
3. Piano: Bartók compositions
4. Bartók's Second Sonata
5. a) Szigeti: Dances
   b) Rhapsody

I am afraid that I shall not have sufficient energy this summer to learn the Finale of the First Sonata (page 2). The "new" accompanist will require so much of my energy (teaching the repertoire, etc.) that I do not dare undertake any more work!...

When will the Rhapsody be published? I am going now to offer the first performance in Berlin to Kleiber,[4] but I am afraid that it will already be a bit late. Would it not be possible to send him the proofs of the score "for viewing"?

I hope that the first performance in London will be at the Royal Philharmonic Society on the 28th November, and the first performance in Budapest on the 22nd November, with orchestra, at my own orchestral evening.

Perhaps you will be kind enough to let me know what your plans are before and after the London concert, and also whether April 3rd in Berlin would suit you.

This is they way you mean the connection of the new ending to the old to be, isn't it?[5]

P.S.

Neither I nor Petri has received any money from the Ukranians so far[6]!... I hope that you enjoy the wonderful Montana very much, and that it will do your dear wife much good.

I was operated on by a fit-for-prison dentist in Gastein (resection), the needle broke during the sewing up, he looked for it, couldn't find it, sewed the gums up just the same, and since then the needle has moved up towards the nose, and now nobody dares to operate again to take needle out... A thousand warm greetings.

yours sincerely
József Szigeti

Notes

Manuscript letter.

József Szigeti, see letter of 20th April, 1927.

¹ This refers to a new Finale that Bartók added to the First Rhapsody for Violin and Piano, which he had dedicated to J. Szigeti. This new ending begins on page 21 of the printed score and carries the heading: Ending for "Seconda parte".

² Maria Basilides, József Szigeti and Bartók performed in the radio concert.

³ This concert took place on the date mentioned.

⁴ Erich Kleiber (1890–1956), well-known German conductor.

⁵ This refers to the new ending of the First Rhapsody; it does not, however, agree with the printed scores. After the first four movements a further four follow, then an asterisk that refers back to the second ending (which begins as the fifth and sixth movements; this may have caused the error).

⁶ In his book "With Strings Attached" (A. Knopf, New York 1947, p. 219) Szigeti states that he made ten concert tours in the USSR between 1924 and 1929, but "... with the tightening of the foreign currency export regulations, however (my fees had previously been paid in American dollars) these tours became more and more impracticable...)". Endre Petri (b. 1907), Hungarian pianist, Szigeti's accompanist was on this tour.

p. 226, No. 151

Albergo Dietetico,
Villa delle Ortensie,
Montecatini Terme
Viale Diaz.
My address from the 13th:
Grande Albergo de Breuil,
Breuil (Aosta).
11th August, 1938.

My dear Friend,

What appeared to have been a dream in the air in the Pagani Restaurant at that time has in the meantime solidified into something concrete through Benny Goodman (the world-famous "idol" of the jazz-clarinet mentioned at the time) paid a visit to me on the Riviera during his European "joy-ride". I took this opportunity and booked the afore-mentioned order with him on conditions to which he gladly agreed, and which amount to three times the sum then mentioned by you (one hundred dollars)! (I.e., my clever wife, whom I consulted in the matter considered 100 dollars too little and said: Let Benny pay three hundred, and as can be seen, she was right!)

So, please, send Benny Goodman at

320 Central Park West, New York City a registered letter in which you confirm that you will compose a clarinet-violin duet with piano accompaniment for him within a certain period, lasting some 6–7 minutes, the copyright of which will remain yours, but you give him the right to play it for three years, i.e. you will only have it printed after that period has elapsed. You also reserve playing rights on the gramophone for three years to him and me. You alone of course are entitled to the royalties for all performances, radio, and gramophone.

If possible, it would be fine if the composition were to consist of two independent parts (which could perhaps also be played separately), (like the First Rhapsody for Violin)¹, and we hope of course (page 3) that it will also include a brilliant clarinet and violin cadenza!

Mention in your letter as well that you are awaiting the records which he swore to send you, but it would still do no harm to remind him. (I told him to avoid customs complications when sending them.)

I can assure you that whatever a clarinet is physically able to do at all, Benny can get out of the instrument, and wonderfully (in much higher regions than the high note of the "Eulenspiegel"[2]!)

But to a certain extent the records will show you his sound and virtuosity. Do not be frightened by the "hot jazz" records, he has already recorded the Mozart Quintet with the Budapest Quartet, and the next season he will play Prokofieff's Chamber work for clarinet and strings in the New Friends of Music series.[3] The New York Philharmonic has also asked him to give a concert.

I should be very grateful if you would think at the same time of my "heart's desire". to orchestrate the string accompaniment of our Universal Edition publication![4] May I hope?

My summer is unfortunately far too eventful—for personal reasons: we are very worried on account of my daughter's ill-omened wedding-plans. I will not stop her by force, and we can no longer hope for a change of heart.

I have spent a fortnight here, and am now fleeing from the heat to the mountains, and then back to the Riviera.

Please remember me to your dear wife, and my old love to you.

Jóska

Notes

Manuscript letter.

Address: Méltóságos Bartók Béla (tanár úrnak)
Budapest, Csalán út 27.

[1] This explains why Contrasts was first called Rhapsody and consisted of only two movements: the first and the third; under this name and in this form the work was first performed in New York by Szigeti, Goodman, and Endre Petri. Although in the manuscript the date of completion is given at the end of the third movement as the 24th September 1938, a superficial examination will show that the second movement is written on a separate page which was later inserted into the manuscript. But this does not justify the assumption that the second movement was composed after the 24th September, since, in a letter dated 9th October, 1938, Bartók says clearly: "...two pieces... (in fact 3 pieces)..."

[2] "Till Eulenspiegels lustige Streiche" by Richard Strauss.

[3] Ouverture russe sur des thémes juifs, for clarinet, string quartet and piano (1920).

[4] Szigeti had asked Bartók to orchestrate the collection "Hungarian Folksongs" (Universal Edition, No. 8784) for violin solo and small orchestra. We have not found any indication anywhere that Bartók intended to make this transscription. As far as Contrasts is concerned, which Szigeti would have liked to have had orchestrated, the following fragment of a letter which Szigeti sent to Dr. J. Újfalussy, and which the latter was good enough to let us have runs: " 1st December, 1938. (. . .) To be sure, I am not very keen on the name Rhapsody (I have written about this in my letter); for I prefer the title "Two dances"! If at all possible, change this in the programme.

"As far as the orchestration is concerned, I have kept on thinking about at the matter, it could be done somehow. I even wrote a (3.) movement for the middle as early as September (Lento, 4'13" long) entitled "Pihenő" ("Repose"). I should be able to do it in January, so you should get the score approx. by the end of February. (. . .)" — This orchestration was never done; it should be noted that there is no mention of it in Bartók's plans, which R. Hawkes mentions in his letter of 25th April, 1939.

p. 137, No. 85

St. Moritz
22. VII 1927

Dear Mr. Bartók,

My fears have unfortunately come true; Wolff and Sachs[1] have advised me that it was impossible to put off the soloists who had already been booked for the winter, so that the concert in Berlin has come to nothing; and Hamburg as well, as the two would only have been possible together (same orchestra). About Leipzig[2], I have no final refusal as yet, but there is little hope.

I can only repeat how very much indeed I regret to have been deprived in this way of the pleasure of making music with you. I remember the evening in Frankfurt[3] with pleasure. With regards

yours sincerely,
Wilhelm Furtwängler

Notes

Manuscript letter.

Wilhelm Furtwängler (1886–1954), German conductor.

[1] Wolff und Sachs, the Berlin concert agency which arranged Furtwängler's concerts, and on which he appears to have been dependent for the arrangement of his concerts.
[2] The Leipzig concert did not take place.
[3] On the 1st July, 1927 Furtwängler conducted the first performance of the First Piano Concerto. It appears that it was not a success; it is even doubtful whether this cooperation was remembered pleasantly by Bartók. We do not have Bartók's letters to Furtwängler, but what the latter writes is not entirely dependable when compared to the information given by Bartók's manager; even if the manager interpreted matters to suit his own ends, one has the impression that Furtwängler did the same thing.

p. 203, No. 132

Budapest, 9th December, 1936.

Dear Master!

May I ask you to be lenient and forgive my omission. I am very much ashamed of not keeping my promise, and not reporting for the manuscript at the agreed time.[1]

I must not take up your time with chatter, but I have to apologize by giving some explanation. What happened was that on Monday night I wanted to write out my idea, considered interesting, on "Béla Bartók's Dissonance", so as to be able to show it to you when I called in the morning. Unfortunately, I overestimated my physical strength—I slept over the rendezvous, because I had worked into the early hours.

It would make me glad to learn that I did not cause you any annoyance, because in that case I could not only rejoice in not having done harm my own affectionate relations with you but also in what I had written.[2]

I shall ring tomorrow morning—please, leave a message when I should call for the manuscript.

Yours sincerely,
Attila József

Notes

MS letter.

Attila József (1905–1937), great Hungarian poet. This letter is published here for the first time in English.

[1] This probably refers to the manuscript of Bartók's study "Népzene és népdalok" ("Folk Music and Folksongs"), which was published in the periodical "Szép Szó", in December 1936 (Vol. III, No. 3, pp. 274–278); Attila József was one of the editors of the periodical.

[2] This text is possibly identical with the sketch entitled "Medvetánc" (Bear's Dance), which was published by Miklós Szabolcsi in "József Attila Összes Művei" (The Complete Works of Attila József), Vol. III, Akadémiai Kiadó (Publishing House of the Academy), Budapest, 1958, pp. 277–278.

p. 230, No. 230

Hotel Statler
Detroit,
10th September, 1938.

Dear Professor,

Yesterday, before I left Philadelphia, I received Jóska Szigeti's cable, which was an answer to my telegram offering to perform your latest work, the Violin-Clarinet Concerto[1] in Philadelphia. All I understood from Jóska's answer was that he does not dispose of the performing rights.

That is why I am turning directly to you with the offer to present the work twice (or three times) in Philadelphia and in New York. It must of course be a "first" performance in both cities. I would in fact very much like to give the first performance of all with my world-famous orchestra. Should this be impossible for some reason, I am asking for at least the first performance in America.

I have not yet had the opportunity to talk to the chairman of the "Victor" (His Masters's Voice) Company, but I am almost certain that it will be accepted for recording if Szigeti and Goodman play and I conduct it.

Because of the shortage of time, send a cable at my expense to Ormandy—Philadelphia Orchestra—Philadelphia, and let me know whether the first performance is available, and if so, how much the royalty will be for the first, second, and perhaps third performance in Philadelphia and New York. I must also ask you to let me know when the work will be ready for presentation.—

I recently accepted one of your latest Suites written for strings and percussion instruments[2] for performance.

Looking forward to your reply, and with warm greetings from my wife, I remain

yours sincerely,

Jenő Ormándy

P.S.

Please send your cable to Philadelphia, because I am only conducting a guest performance here, and will return in two days.

Address: Professor Béla Bartók (Zeneművészeti Főiskola)
  Liszt Ferenc tér (Budapest—Hungary—Europe)

Sender: Eugene Ormandy—Philadelphia Or-(chestra) Philadelphia, Pa.

Eugene (Jenő) Ormandy, the well-known American conductor of Hungarian origin, was a conductor of the Philadelphia Orchestra with Stokowski from 1936 and has been the permanent conductor of this orchestra since 1938.

1 See Letter of 11th August, 1938.
2 Music for String Instruments, Percussion Instruments, and Celesta.

p. 249, No. 164

October/November, 1939

Dear Bartóks,

I have again been "writing" a letter in my mind for a long time now, and many times—but it was never put on paper. And recent times have been so oppressive that it wouldn't have been helpful to write about the many fears and anxieties of which you too have had your share. Now that the first great shock is over, I would nevertheless like to talk to you now, to ask you what you are doing, how you are living, whether you are able to work, whether you are able to rejoice that for the time being our two countries are not in danger.

There was a small sort of panic here at the beginning, all the reserve officers were called up, and many others, the other auxiliary services (Walter[1] as well) are in the reserve and may be called up any day. So it is difficult to carry on a normal way of life; a good many sorts of food are rationed, eg. sugar, salt, fat, oil, flour, all fodder and corn, groats, noodles, rice; unfortunately I was not prudent enough and did not buy enough in advance, although it had been ordered by the state. We are not suffering any privation, but have to think what to cook. Teaching[2] goes on quite normally, but concerts are very uncertain. Walter especially does not know whether he should dare to risk it, for the time being nobody knows anything; the Tonhalle[3] intends to continue with all the concerts, but it will be hardly possible for foreign soloists, for instance, to come. —

The Lucerne Festival was wonderful; I admire and respect Toscanini more and more as a wonderful, ideal musician and man. The same thing happened with him as with Béla: I avoided him, was afraid of him, did not know what to say to him, i.e. I was unable to talk to him in an everyday way. Then I was put next to him on the last evening (just like Ditta to do it), and I sat next to him at table. We separated as great friends, to the envy of the others! — The Verdi Requiem, Coriolanus, Debussy's "La Mer", Smetana's "Moldava" remain unforgettable; perfect music perfectly performed, that is how I shall remember it. The many rehearsals 34—and 9 concerts were tiring enough, but we were still very sad when there were no more. We have just finished it, the last concert was on Tuesday, and on Friday the catastrophe fell... Fate was good to me in allowing me to live through this last summer and fill myself to the brim with beauty, harmony, with happy hours and serious music. — After Lucerne I turned over in my mind the idea of visiting Béla, we heard from Sacher that he was still there, but I was afraid to disturb him in his work, but things fell out differently: Jancsi, the son of my nephew Zipernovszky got stuck in France, came here and waited for the opportunity to go further: finally he returned to Budapest through Italy and Yugoslavia. I took advantage of this opportunity to send a penknife to Béla—will I ever be able to borrow it?—some chocolates to Ditta and the latest photographs to Péter. I hope that you have received them. Write soon, do not follow my example! — Puci4 is well, but she is sad and worried about the war. — She sends many regards to Péter.

Much love to you all.

Stefi

Notes

Manuscript letter.

Stefi Geyer (1888–1956), the violonist to whom Bartók dedicated the Violin Concerto of 1907/08.

1 Walter Schultess (b. 1894), Swiss composer, conductor and impressario; was married to Stefi Geyer.
2 Stefi Geyer was Professor of Violin at the Zurich Conservatoire.
3 The Concert hall in Zurich.
4 Daughter of Stefi Geyer.

21 Holland Park
London W. 11.
March 28, 1922.

Dear M. Béla Bartók,

I am just leaving London for Vienna, and thought I would like you to know how greatly I admire your work which I heard at the Aeolian Hall Concert last week, especially the Violin Sonata, which is a most sincere and remarkable expression of technique. I hope we shall have the opportunity of hearing it often, when it is published as I feel certain it will gain many adherents. I am so sorry I have not been able to talk to you personally, I hope that your stay in London has pleased you, and that before long we shall be able to welcome you again.

With my true admiration
Arthur Bliss

Telephone
Park 5296.

Rosehill Lodge, Porchester
Gate.
London, W. 2. 28/12/25.

Dear Bartók,

Very many thanks for the score of the Dance Suite which I have just received. I heard a performance of it quite recently and liked it very much indeed—although the performance itself was not a good one. I am glad to be able to become better acquainted with it.

It is good to hear from you after such a long time, and hope to see you over here again soon.

The Pro Arte quartet played your 2nd string quartet here a short time ago, at one of Mr Gerald Cooper's concerts; unfortunately I did not hear it, as I was in bed with influenza.

Please give my best wishes to both the Kodály's. I just received a visit two days ago from a pupil of Kodály—half Hungarian and half American—I forget his name; you will know him.

With best wishes to both you and your wife for the New Year

Yours very sincerely
Cecil Gray

Aug 16, 1945

Dear friend,

I arrived home about ten days ago to find your letter of June 6. I hope that now both you and Mrs. Bartók are enjoying a pastoral restorative summer free from all ailments.

It is indeed unfortunate for me that, despite our mutual sympathy, I have as yet had no opportunity to capture the stimulating influence and inspiration which would attend a more prolonged and intimate association with you.

When you mentioned the many musical plans you had made I could only pray for their early realization. As a matter of fact I may be coming to New York around Oct. 1.—for just such a feast!

Tony[1] and I played the concerto last Saturday at the Hollywood Bowl for some 18,000 Bartók-fans!!! It is a great country, you know, and sooner or later you will probably receive a commission from Billy Rose![2] Anyhow, it was most enthusiastically applauded and respectfully reviewed. We have some great plans or performing the work in London in November and recording it at the same time. Our most ambitious hope is to do it, with you in the audience, in Budapest! That may already be possible by November, in any case not Spring. As yet, we have merely planted and fecundated the seeds in our own hearts— but I trust they will soon sprout and rear their heads above the ground for everyone to see!

You have many admiring friends in London and a general public more than ready and eager to welcome you and your music. Boosey and Hawkes will certainly be right with you in promoting your works, especially in connection with their government—subventioned project at Covent Garden.

Do you expect to return to Hungary shortly?

Please convey my warmest greetings to Mrs Bartók.

Your devoted,

Yehudi Menuhin

Notes

Manuscript letter.

Yehudi Menuhin (b. 1916) the famous American violinist had commissioned a Sonata for solo violin from Bartók.

1 Antal Doráti (b. 1906) ("Tony"), the well-known conductor and composer of Hungarian origin, was one of Kodály's pupils.

2 Yehudi Menuhin has provided the following explanation of this joke: "Regarding the commission from Billy Rose, this was meant as a joke. Billy Rose (I do not know if he is still alive) was the very prominent theatrical producer in New York who put on shows of great lavishness. He aspired to culture, and commissioned a work by Stravinsky. The story goes that after the first performance he sent a telegram to Stravinsky saying 'YOUR WORK GREAT SUCCESS WOULD HOWEVER BE OVERWHELMING SUCCESS IF YOU PERMITTED US TO MAKE A SHORT CUT IN THIS WORK'—whereupon Stravinsky is supposed to have answered 'AM CONTENT WITH GREAT SUCCESS'. This is the background of my comment that sooner or later he would probably receive a commission from Billy Rose..."

UNPUBLISHED BARTÓK DOCUMENTS

The January 1961 issue of THE NEW HUNGARIAN QUARTERLY *(Vol. II. No. 1) contained a study by János Demény on Bartók research in Hungary. Our article has induced János Liebner, the well-known Hungarian 'cellist and musical critic, to disclose further facts about the life and work of Bartók, revealing the existence of a fifth movement to the Piano Suite opus 14, hitherto known as consisting of four movements, and to quote the complete text of the last radio interviews in Béla Bartók's life.*

A FORGOTTEN WORK OF BARTÓK'S

At the close of the year 1912, after his return from a tour to collect folk songs in Transylvania and the Northern Highlands of Hungary, Bartók again fell ill. His weak constitution was worn out by the two fatiguing journeys, but his ever active, searching spirit could not relax even while he was confined to his bed. He studied Eastern languages and Arab writing, in preparation for his subsequent visit to Africa where he wished to continue his investigations into the sources of the idiom of Hungarian folk music and to trace its assumed relationship to Arab peasant music.

That he might have the miserably poor peasants and nomadic shepherds on the fringes of the desert sing for him under the most natural conditions, Bartók spent several months living with them, sleeping in their small, circular, thatched mud huts, eating highly seasoned mutton stew and rice *pilaf*, drinking fermented palm juice and the slightly sour *cuscus*. He roamed about the Biscra region southeast of Algiers, became acquainted with strange and ancient string instruments played with a bow or plucked, and took down with his phonograph the peculiar music of the Arabs which almost defies recording, a major

second being divided into three tones instead of two semi-tones.

His journey was successful. In addition to its scientific value, the collected material enriched his creative art. The intonation of Arab popular airs merged into Bartók's music with no less unobtrusive naturalness, and welled forth in his compositions with no less fluency and freedom from any "foreign accent," than did the special, so different and yet fundamentally so similar, styles of Hungarian, Slav, Rumanian or, later, American Indian folklore.

*

The Piano Suite opus 14 composed in February, 1916, partly reflects this new influence. The musical idiom, mood and atmosphere of the third novement—its wild, impetuous, bewitching bedouin rhythm—incorporated the world of Arab folk music. This was, of course, no simple transcription of folk music, but its re-creation on a higher artistic plain, inspired by personal experience.

For several decades the Piano Suite, op. 14, was known as a composition in four movements; only quite recently has it come to light that originally the work was conceived as comprising five movements. After the first Allegretto, the following Scherzo movement was to be introduced by a slow Andante; then the Allegro molto of "bedouin" rhythm, which we mentioned above was to lead to the last Sostenuto movement of the suite. Ending with a slow movement, like the second string quartet composed in the same period, intermittently, from 1915 to 1917, the suite in its original conception already differed from the classical suite form terminated by a traditional fast movement. When Bartók published the work leaving out the Andante movement, this deviation became all the more conspicuous. Instead of the classical alternation of fast and slow pieces, the final version of the Piano Suite consists of three successive fast movements of varying character, to emphasize more poignantly the dreamy, *dolce* mood of the last Sostenuto movement.

*

The omitted Andante movement has been found by János Demény (the eager and devoted Bartók scholar) in the possession of Irén Egri, a pupil of Bartók's, who copied the five-movement version some time between 1916 and 1918 from the original manuscript at the music publishing house of Rózsavölgyi. She had studied the suite in this form, and that is how Bartók played it to her in the lessons. Later the work was printed without the original second movement, and Irén Egri cannot remember whether Bartók ever played or even mentioned the omitted movement. Presumably he may have withdrawn it when he changed his publishers, leaving Rózsavölgyi's for the Vienna Universal.

The Andante op. 14 is dreamy, transparent music, rising and sinking over a sustained F-sharp organpoint, moving, as if improvised, with delicately floating harmonies. The rhythmic pattern and melodic material point to the Scherzo that originally followed it, virtually preparing it; but, in atmosphere, the Andante displays more affinity to the last movement of the suite. Bartók may have been induced to omit it from the final version by the feeling that two movements radiating a similar atmosphere tended to jeopardize the varied, multicoloured wealth and unity of a work whose movements, though completely different in character, nevertheless formed a harmonious whole. This youthful work of Bartók's, fallen into oblivion, will hold its own also as a separate piece—just as the other movements of the suite.

The Andante op. 14 is a bagatelle of no more than a few minutes, yet it gives a faithful reflection of the master's modest and slender, yet gigantic figure.

BÉLA BARTÓK'S LAST AMERICAN RADIO INTERVIEWS

Béla Bartók's two American radio statements were made in 1942, the year of grave and exasperating financial straits ("...a terrible situation...") and inexorably progressing disease ("...no hope of recovery..."), at a time of darkest pessimism ("...I have lost all my confidence in people, in countries, in everything...") and creative barrenness ("...on no account shall I ever compose another work..."). From the tape his voice sounds tired and broken; several times he stopped speaking, hampered by frequent coughing and hard breathing. The first interview was short, embracing only one question and one answer. We do not know who the interviewer was, his question permits the inference that he was a journalist or radio announcer with a limited knowledge of music; at all events, he was a layman, not an expert.

*

INTERVIEWER: "Do you consider the Suite op. 14, which Mrs. Bartók is going to play next, representative of your abstract compositions; and if so, what qualities make it so?"

BARTÓK: "If by abstract music you mean absolute music, without program, then yes. The Suite op. 14 has no folk tunes. It is based entirely on original themes of my own invention. When this work was composed I had in mind the refining of piano technique, the changing of piano technique into a more transparent style, more of bone and muscle, opposed to the heavy chordal style of the late romantic period, that is, unessential ornaments like broken chords and other figures are omitted, and it is a more simple style."

That was all. Then Mrs. Bartók played the Piano Suite op. 14.

In the second interview the questions were put by a musicologist of the Brooklyn Museum; the third party at the interview was Tibor Serly, Bartók's pupil and faithful help during the last years of his life.

INTERVIEWER: "The Microcosmos, which Mr. Serly has transcribed for 'cello and string orchestra is such a vast work; I wonder if you could tell us briefly what it comprises?"

BARTÓK: "The Microcosmos is a cycle of 153 pieces for piano written with didactical purpose, that is, to give piano pieces which can be used from the very beginning and then going on; it is graded according to difficulties. The Microcosmos may be interpreted as a series of pieces in different styles which represent a small world, or it may be interpreted as a world, a musical world for little ones, for children."

INTERVIEWER: "Do you know whether Mr. Serly found it necessary to alter the material in transcription?—Perhaps Mr. Serly would be the best to answer that."

TIBOR SERLY: "No treatise or textbook has ever been written that so tellingly reveals the story of the development of musical styles as these brief, minute Microcosmos sketches. These miniature gems illustrate scale structures, chords, modes, forms, rhythms, harmonies, imitations and canons with dazzling ingenuity. Regarding the transcriptions we are to play, I have selected six to illustrate that they are more than piano pieces. As is often the case with the music of Bach, a more expanded treatment brings to the fore many actual and implied inner voices that are not apparent in the original piano form. Naturally voices have been shifted, contrapuntal parts have been separated into instrumental units and occasional sonorities have been filled out. Otherwise materially nothing has been altered, nor has anything been added."

The first question is somewhat vague because it does not define the transcriptions alluded to. We possess no information concerning Serly's transcriptions for 'cello and string orchestra of parts from the Microcosmos. We know two transcriptions, a series of five pieces for string quartet, including Overtones, op. 102; Wrestling, op. 108; Song, op. 116; Punch, op. 142; Tale of a Little Fly, op. 148; and a series of seven pieces for orchestra, including Overtones, op. 102; Bourrée, op. 117; Unisono, op. 137; Punch, op. 142; Tale of a Little Fly, op. 148; Two dances of Bulgarian Rhythm, op. 151 and op. 153. Serly, however, distinctly mentioned six pieces at the interview. Is it possible that there actually exists a still unknown third arrangement of the Microcosmos for 'cello and string orchestra?

I think that apart from being precious artistic and personal documents, Bartók's two statements before the American radio, notwithstanding their brevity, offer useful data to scholars of his life, his compositions, and life-work. The title of Microcosmos has been given various interpretations in the international history of music. According to some commentators the word stands for its meaning in medieval philosophy, implying that the individual mirrors the whole of the universe. Others maintain that the title expresses love for the minute organic world: "The collector is fascinated by the completeness manifested in the unique, attracted by the variety of species, captivated by the correlations between the regular and the extraordinary," Erich Doflein wrote in his study on Bartók and Musical Instruction. Others again find the sense of Bartók's title partly in the kinship between artistic compositions and creation, partly in the "balance of musical and pedagogical forces" (Jürgen Uhde, Bartók's Microcosmos). Conclusive elucidation of this much-debated question will be promoted by the double definition given by Bartók in the radio interview.

*

140

To the best of my knowledge, there are only three Hungarian recordings of Bartók's voice, beside the two American recordings in English. One contains the words of the *Cantata Profana* as told by Bartók himself; this record is in the possession of the Hungarian Radio. In the second, an account of his folk-song collecting tour in Turkey was taken down; this is the property of a Budapest sound engineer, who with his own gelatin recorder "illicitly" took down for himself Bartók's address on the subject, broadcast by Radio Budapest in the year 1930. The third, also a radio address, was put on record by the writer Sophie Török, the wife of Bartók's friend Mihály Babits, the poet.

JÁNOS LIEBNER

THE DISPUTE OVER BARTÓK'S WILL

Béla Bartók died on September 26th, 1945 in New York's West Side Hospital; only a few friends attended his funeral at the Ferncliff Cemetery, Westchester, Harsdale. Shortly before his death he finished his last composition, the *Piano Concerto No. 3*.

His last work, which was a farewell to life, was performed in Strasbourg in the twentieth anniversary year of his death, in a transcription for two pianos, by Ditta Pásztory, his widow, and Maria Comensoli.

Béla Bartók's widow, the pianist Ditta Pásztory, who never played in public after Bartók's death, returned to Hungary in 1946 at the end of the war. Her grief was expressed in this long silence. Last year, indeed, she took part in the recording of the *Piano Concerto No. 3* in Vienna, but still did not play in public.

This year, Paris radio asked her to give a wireless recital of some of Bartók's works. She accepted and following her radio concert in Paris, which was a great success, was invited to give a public concert in Strasbourg.

The long silence was thus broken. Ditta Pásztory accepted the invitation and played the *Concerto No. 3* with Maria Comensoli. It must have been a moving experience for those who saw and heard her play, heightened by the special character and spirit of the work—the farewell of a great genius. Béla Bartók had composed it for his wife, and twenty years later it was his widow who played it at her first public recital since his death.

The First Will

What happened to Bartók's will and his estate? I have been interested in this question ever since we commemorated the twentieth anniversary of his tragic death.

In 1965 I talked to a number of well-informed persons on the question. Among other things I wanted to know about the first will he made, and its date.

As everyone knows, Béla Bartók hated the fascist régimes of Germany and Italy and viewed with horror the expansion of their dictatorship throughout Europe. By 1940 he was already aware that this fate threatened Hungary as well, and consequently decided he would have to leave. He embarked on October 20th, 1940, and sailed with his wife for the United States.

In 1940, before leaving Budapest, Bartók made his will. In this he left his property, most of which was the copyright in his works, divided more or less in equal shares among his wife, Ditta Pásztory, and his two sons, Béla and Péter.

His sons—the younger Béla Bartók and Péter Bartók—remained in Hungary. Bartók went on his concert tour in the United States firmly resolved not to return to Hungary until the end of the war. His younger son, Péter Bartók, who at that time was still a student, followed his parents a little later, in the middle of the war, and after considerable difficulty joined them in the United States.

Béla, the elder boy, was the son of Bartók's first wife, Márta Ziegler. He was born in 1910, now lives in Budapest, is an engineer, a technical adviser, and at present also lectures at the Budapest Technical University. Péter Bartók is the child of Bartók's second marriage with Ditta Pásztory. He stayed in the United States after the end of the Second World War, became a sound engineer, and is ambitious to produce a complete set of his father's works on records with the participation of the finest artists of the time.

The Second Will

I later asked another expert about the circumstances under which Bartók's second will was made in the United States.

The Bartóks never settled down happily

in the United States. In the somewhat less than five years they stayed there, they changed their home five times. The difficult years in New York were further aggravated by Hitler's successes in the earlier years of the war. Bartók's determination to save his work from any control by the dictatorship added to his troubles.

Shortly after his arrival in New York, Dr Gyula Baron, a former Budapest professor of medicine, introduced Bartók to Dr Victor Bátor, the former lawyer of the Hungarian Commercial Bank of Pest, who had emigrated to the USA in 1938. Dr Bátor suggested that Béla Bartók should set up a trust under Anglo–American law, because this would be the most effective method of safeguarding his life-work, both in the interest of his heirs and of European civilization, in the face of all the uncertainties and risks of the war. According to the provisions of such a trust the testator leaves his estate to the two executors in trust for the legatees of the will. They were in fact responsible for the management of the porperty for the benefit of the legatees during the lifetime of the widow. Upon her death the trust would be dissolved and the estate would pass unconditionally to the two remaining heirs. Bartók agreed to the proposal. His obvious intention was that the trustees as American subjects would hold the copyrights, which would thus be protected from possible confiscation by the fascist dictatorship.

In the autumn of 1943 he duly signed the American will setting up the trust which was drawn by Dr Victor Bátor. In this he set aside the will he had made in Hungary and appointed Dr Gyula Baron and Dr Victor Bátor as trustees, with, however, far wider discretionary powers than was usual.

Two years later Bartók died.

The widow came back to Hungary. Péter Bartók remained in the States.

The New York Surrogate's Court duly granted probate of Béla Bartók's will and confirmed the trustees in their positions.

"Barely a Quarter"

Experts in international law all agree that the property was correctly managed by the trustees and in accordance with the terms of the trust, during the first two years. A little later Dr Gyula Baron resigned for health reasons, and Dr Victor Bátor was left in sole control of the estate.

For eleven years Bátor presented no accounts. When, finally, he produced them, it became apparent that the legatees, Ditta Pásztory, Béla and Péter Bartók, had received "barely a quarter" of the very considerable sums amounting from royalties. Three-quarters of the royalties were charged by Bátor to expenses. Neither the US law, however, nor the will itself authorized the trustees to charge the estate with the majority of expenses.

In the meantime legal proceedings had begun at the office of the Budapest State Notaries to obtain the administration of Béla Bartók's will; the case was finally heard in 1958, after it had been adjourned several times. In the final hearing in 1961 probate was granted to the plaintiffs. This judgment gave effect to the general dispositions of the New York will, but set aside the trust and the appointment of trustees as an institution unknown to Hungarian law. It therefore awarded unconditional possession of the estate to the three legatees.

The decision of the New York Surrogate's Court which recognized the existence of the trust and trustees is consequently in conflict with the decision of the Hungarian Court of Probate.

It is somewhat depressing that so many difficulties have had to be surmounted before the heirs of this great Hungarian could enter into their rightful inheritance.

Conflict of laws in such matters is unfortunately not uncommon. In some countries it is the nationality of the testator which determines the choice of law; the courts of his own country have jurisdiction. In others it is his last domicile which determines the choice of law, and these countries include the countries of the British Commonwealth as well as the United States of America.

It is accepted in Hungary that under Hungarian law probate of Bartók's will undoubtedly is subject to Hungarian law, since Béla Bartók died a Hungarian subject, his legal domicile was Budapest, and New York was only his temporary residence.

What happened after Hungarian judgment had been delivered? Dr Victor Bátor, under presistent pressure, finally presented his accounts on the management of the property for four further years to the New York Surrogate's Court. This account resembled the others, and the legatees again received barely a quarter part of the income. Naturally they challenged the accounts.

The Bartók Manuscripts

In the meantime Victor Bátor founded the "Bartók Archives" in New York, consisting of Bartók manuscripts, letters and other memorials of the musician, treated them as if they were his own, and in fact declared them to be his property. In these "Archives" were placed original Bartók manuscripts which in his first set of accounts were set down as part of the estate.

When the second set of accounts was presented, Bátor's duplicity over the manuscripts came to light. Bátor then declared he was willing to resign as trustee and return the manuscripts on the condition that his accounts were passed.

Negotiations for a settlement were however broken off when Bátor, in connection with the return of the manuscripts, raised new and unjustified claims to certain autograph manuscripts.

This is the point the negotiations have reached, towards the end of the twentieth anniversary of Bartók's death. Let us hope that the final disposition of the estate left by one of the greatest creative geniuses of our age will speedily be settled.

Settled, as Bartók intended in his last will.

Magyar Nemzet, December 25, 1965

Péter Ruffy

WILL

I, the undersigned Béla Bartók, at present domiciled in Budapest (29 Csalán út, II.), Professor at the Hungarian Royal Academy of Music, being sound in mind and after mature consideration, declare my last wishes in the following testament regarding all the goods I shall possess at the time of my death, and bequeath them as follows:

I.

It is my final wish as regards the copyright and the author's royalties on all musical and scientific works written in the past, as well as those to be written in the future, that all copyrights should be vested after my death, in equal shares, that is in parts of one-third each, in my wife Mrs Béla Bartók, maiden name Edit Pásztory, domiciled in Budapest (29 Csalán út, II.), and my sons Béla Bartók, domiciled in Budapest (2 Kenes u.), and the minor Péter Bartók, at present residing at Sárospatak.

The same is my wish regarding the distribution of the income arising from these copyrights; I desire that these also should become the property of the above named legatees, likewise in the proportion of one-third each.

My wish regarding the distribution of my income, should be altered as follows in the contingencies stated below:

A) It is my will that as long as my son Péter Bartók, a minor, has not completed his studies and has not found employment on the basis of his studies by which he can meet his needs and which will enable him to keep himself, my wife should receive a two-sixths share, my son Béla Bartók one-sixth and my son Péter Bartók, a minor, three-sixths of the income from my copyrights, in order that the latter may continue his studies uninterrupted and provision for him be assured. In the event of my wife's death during that period the income for distribution should, for the period determined above, go in the ratio of two-sixths to my son Béla Bartók and four-sixths to my son Péter Bartók. Should, however, this share of four-sixths be insufficient to enable my minor son Péter Bartók to finish his studies, I wish my son Béla Bartók to give, out of his share of two-sixths due to him, another one-sixth share to my minor son Péter Bartók until my son Péter finishes his studies.

I expect my son Péter Bartók to be conscientious in his studies and to do his utmost to find employment as soon as possible.

B) When making my will I took into consideration the fact that under existing law my wife née Edit Pásztory, domiciled in Budapest, is legally entitled to a widow's pension on the strength of my appointment as a State official. If, however, after my death, my wife should not, for whatever reason, receive a widow's pension, I direct that three sixths of the income arising from these copyrights should go to my wife for life, one-sixth to my son Béla Bartók and two-sixths to my son Péter Bartók while studying and unable to maintain himself, but apart from these provisions the principle of equal participation in the assets represented by the copyrights is to be maintained. When, however, my son Péter Bartók has finished his studies and is able to maintain himself unaided, the above division of the income from the copyrights should be so modified that a four-sixths share of the income should go to my widow while a one-sixth share respectively should go to my sons Béla Bartók and Péter Bartók.

C) Should my widow re-marry, I direct in any of the contingencies enumerated under B) that the income due to her from copyrights should not exceed one-third of the income. If as a result of this measure a part of the income becomes available for further distribution, then it is my wish that it should be used to equalize the shares in the income going to my two sons and/or to lessen the difference in the shares in the incomes to the advantage of that son who in the given situation is receiving the smaller share of the income.

II.

For the sale of the manuscripts of my musical works as well as the utilization and allocation of these assets I have concluded what is known as a trust agreement with the New York firm of Messrs. Boosey and Hawkes, Inc., and Dr George Hertzog, domiciled in New York, on May 15th, 1940, in New York, in accordance with the provisions of the law of the United States. I explicitly declare that I maintain all the dispositions made in the written agreement referred to concerning the sale of the manuscripts and the utilization of the income; those clauses of the agreement which refer to the utilization and distribution of the surplus, I interpret and change, respectively, in respect to my legatees in that I bequeath these incomes and/or the shares due to them, according to the stipulations laid down in Article I of the present testament.

III.

With regard to furniture, articles of personal use and the manuscripts of my scientific works, as well as souvenirs and works of art which are in my possession at present or which I may acquire until my death, I appoint my sons Béla Bartók and the minor Péter Bartók as my heirs in equal shares. Their rights of ownership are however restricted in that the right of use is exclusively vested in my wife, née Edit Pásztory, for her life, for it is my wish that these effects should be kept together and that she should enjoy the same rights of use as she had during my lifetime. After the death of my wife this right of use, which is a privilege vested in her person only, is automatically extinguished and the exclusive proprietorship and right of use are equally vested in my sons Béla Bartók and Péter Bartók.

Concerning the distribution of my possessions, of the two pianos which are in my possession I direct that my son Péter Bartók should have the right to choose one of them for himself and that this should be his, and the other one should belong to my son Béla Bartók.

IV.

With regard to the whole body of copyrights which are my property, it is my wish that in the event of the sale or transfer of copyrights all my legatees should act in agreement. I therefore direct that should one of my heirs wish to transfer his share of the property, he should only be able to effect this with the consent of the other two heirs. The purpose of this stipulation is to prevent the dissipation of the copyrights and to assure my heirs the protection of a permanent income.

V.

Should my wife predecease me, all the benefits due to her under the present will devolve on my sons Béla Bartók and Péter Bartók to be distributed between them in equal shares, regard being had to the qualifications under Article I/A. The same disposition is to apply should my wife survive me, and die at a later date.

VI.

Should I die when my son Péter Bartók is still under age, I designate chief physician Dr. Tibor Hajnal, domiciled in Budapest (13. Hadapród u., II.) on the strength of Par. 34, Act No. XX of 1877, to act as guardian for my minor son, Péter Bartók. If he does not wish to or is unable to fulfil this request for any reason whatever, I designate as guardian in the second place Vitéz Albert Koós, domiciled in Pusztaföldvár (László major, Szőlőspuszta), the son-in-law of my sister Mrs. Emil Tóth, maiden name Erzsébet Bartók.

VII.

Since I consider it as contrary to my last wishes if any of my legatees contests these testamentary dispositions, I therefore direct that that legatee refusing to acquiesce or accept the provisions of this will and contesting it to the detriment of the other legatees, should be restricted to the share of his inheritance regarding my entire property and its income which is compulsory by law.

VIII.

My funeral should be as simple as possible, without clergy. If after my death it should be desired to name a street after me or locate a memorial tablet which bears any relation to me in a public place, then it is my wish that

as long as the former *Oktogon Tér* and former *Körönd* in Budapest are named after those men whose name they bear at present, * and moreover, as long as there is any square or street in Hungary named after these two men, no square, street or public building should be named after me in this country, and no memorial tablet connected with me should be placed in any public place.

IX.

This testament was written and signed by my own hand and I herewith confirm that the contents convey my last will, as a proof of which I sign this testament with my own hand, repeating my statement in the joint presence of the two testamentary witnesses, Dr Ernő András, lawyer, domiciled in Budapest (7. Akadémia utca, V.), and Mrs Béla Csomós, domiciled in Budapest (21 Nagymező utca, VI.), who were asked to attest this document.

Given at Budapest, October 4, 1940.
Signed: Béla Bartók.
Mrs. Béla Csomós, testamentary witness,
Dr. Ernő András, testamentary witness.
Kjö. 35/1946 Vn. 1/1957.
This will was published this day:
Budapest, January 7, 1947.
Signed: Dr Keszthelyi, Notary Public.

* At that date the *Oktogon tér* was called *Mussolini tér*, and the *Körönd*, *Hitler tér*. Ed.

REMEMBERING MY FATHER, BÉLA BARTÓK *

My father, Béla Bartók, has been dead these twenty years. I did not see him die and was not present at his burial, hence he is still very much alive in my mind. Much has been written about him in the last twenty years, some of it untrue. It might be desirable, therefore, for members of his family to put down what they remember about him, all the more so because it is mostly in the bosom of their families that men reveal their true personality, when their children are young, and later when the children reach adolescence and independence. And that is why I record a few recollections of my father now.

My father lost his own father when very young; during his childhood, he lived with his younger sister, his mother—the bread-winner of the family—and his mother's

sister. They were a united and happy family, and an example of family life which inspired my father in the ordering of our own home life. My father, however, developed beyond the limits of that early domestic background; he was passionately concerned with all the new trends of the early twentieth century in art, political thinking, health, education, and other fields of human activity, and saw to it that all these influences for good were part of our home background.

Of all his qualities and virtues those which most impressed me were his love of nature, his sense of patriotism and ardour for national freedom, and his extraordinary diligence and capacity for work.

He loved nature greatly and everything to do with the natural sciences. He was most interested in astronomy—the "great Universe"—and knew all about the stars and the great constellations, which he liked to explain

* The Author of this article, Béla Bartók is the elder son of the composer, and an engineer with the Hungarian State Railways.

to us on clear nights. His wonder and admiration for the perfection of nature attracted him to many of its other manifestations as well: he collected insects, plants and minerals, and would arrange them with the help of textbooks. He did his best to make time for periodical visits to the Zoo, for regular walks, and occasionally for long excursions walking in the hills.

On his walks and outings he liked to take members of his family along with him. We were never tired of his explanations and comments; in fact, they stimulated us to such an extent that geography and natural history have remained among my chief interests, although I have chosen a different profession for myself.

He loved the sort of human beings who lived close to nature—peasants, whom he came to know mainly on his trips gathering folk music. He would take advantage of these trips to add to his collection of folk art; his home was furnished with carved and painted peasant furniture which he had brought back with him from Körösfő, in the Kolozs region.* He had fine collections of peasant embroideries, pottery and musical instruments. In folklore proper he was attracted above all by folk poetry.

He had a great devotion to children, he regarded them as the raw material from which a finer humanity could be shaped. His educational activities formed an important part of his whole work—witness his piano manuals, co-authored with Reschofsky; the cycle of works "For Children," which he revised several times; and the six volumes of "Microcosmos," composed with the most careful attention to detail.

As for the kind of education he gave his own children, he believed that they had independent personalities, and that education had mainly to rely on good example and on constantly stimulating their interest. He attached importance to regular physical exercise, plenty of sunlight and fresh air, abstinence from alcohol, and a frugal and

* Now part of Rumania. Ed.

modern diet based on vitamin-rich foods. I was still quite a little fellow when he started to give me art reproductions; he encouraged me to trace on the map the events described in the books I read. He would come back from his trips abroad laden with pictures, and would give us a detailed account of everything he had seen; it was from these accounts I began to know about the world at an early date.

He looked upon both his sons as friends, and expected a similar attitude from us. Believing it was for us to work for our own benefit, he would never hear us our lessons, nor would he ever call on teachers to inquire about our progress at school; yet he was pleased whenever we brought home good school reports, and he would ask us questions about what had happened at school.

He thought our decision not to choose music as a profession was quite natural; but he liked to ask us to help him with the arrangement of folk music or other minor matters of that kind.

He had a great love for Hungary and the Hungarian people—a love which constantly found expression in his work. In an early composition of his childhood—the "Course of the Danube," written at the age of nine—he greets Hungary with cheerful notes as the river enters the country at Dévény; then, as it leaves the country at the Iron Gate, a sad note is heard. Many years later, in his inaugural address on "Certain Problems of Liszt" at the Hungarian Academy of Sciences, he argued for the Hungarian character of Liszt's music.

His love for Hungary in no way implied contempt for other nations; the smaller a nation, the stronger his sympathy: he always took the side of the weak. He made every attempt to get to know other countries through their art, through their own languages, and in their own backgrounds when he went on collecting trips or concert tours. With incredible diligence he acquired proficiency in eight to ten languages, so that a fair proportion of the vast number of letters he wrote were written in the native language of his correspondents.

Giving recitals and piano lessons (he consistently refused to give lessons in composition), tired him chiefly because he always and everywhere insisted on giving his best. Five to six hours practising daily, or playing with his pupils, took up much of the time he could have devoted to pursuits dearer to his heart, particularly his work on folk music. He was only too delighted, therefore, when, in 1934, he was invited to join the Hungarian Academy of Sciences where, in collaboration with Zoltán Kodály, he could concentrate on systematizing and organizing the great work they had undertaken together.

He always looked for a flat in quiet districts, for any noise coming through the walls upset him beyond endurance. He always chose the most isolated room for his study, and tried to make it sound-proof by fitting on a double-door by some means or other. For his part, he took great care not to disturb other people's peace; when practising he would shut his windows, even on hot days, in order not to disturb other people.

The clothes he wore were plain and modest; he managed to keep them in good condition for many years at a time.

He ate sparely as a rule, and rarely drank alcohol. For many years a non-smoker, he only acquired the habit of smoking during the First World War. In later years, he made several unsuccessful attempts to break himself of the habit, and his failure to do so annoyed him considerably.

He had no recreations in the conventional sense of the word. He never visited the cinemas, cafés, or other places of amusement, and would seldom go to concerts. His principal pastime was—work. During the school-year he would leave the house very rarely—with the exception of visits to the family or to give his lessons at the Academy of Music. He read the newspapers avidly and would buy one every day, sometimes more than one. He was interested in everything in it, editorials, economic news, politics and the arts.

His manner with strangers was reserved and to some extent cautious, due to the tendency of some to intrude on his privacy. But those he conceived an affection for were fully appreciated; he was completely at ease with his relatives. He was very fond of explaining things, teaching people, showing them the results of recent research, recordings of folk music, etc.

He had a sure sense of vocation, but would never speak of it. He was modest and polite. On one occasion I went with him to Békéscsaba, where Mária Basilides, the famous contralto, and he were scheduled to give a recital. He noticed that his name was printed first on the poster, and Miss Basilides's second. He immediately complained to the concert manager, saying he deplored the practice of putting the names of the men before the names of women on concert programmes. Because of his diffident manner strangers thought my father a sombre, melancholy man; yet he had a good sense of humour, and enjoyed puzzles and riddles.

He loved his family above everyone else: some of his works express family affections. He would pay frequent visits to his younger sister, who lived in Békés County, where Julcsa Varga, Péter Garzó and their circle, people who figured in a number of folk songs from the vicinity of Vésztő, were personal friends of his. His "The Night's Music" took its origin from the same place; in it my father perpetuated the concert of the frogs heard in peaceful nights on the Great Plain.

He made a point of remembering all family festivals, particularly each of his mother's birthdays. When he or I happened to be away from home, he would always remember my birthday in a long letter, no matter how great the pressure of work. His last letter to me was written for my birthday in 1941. War, which he hated so intessely, and death, which he had wished so fervently to delay, combined to prevent him from writing any more.

From *Népművelés, January 1966.*

BÉLA BARTÓK

BARTÓK — PIANIST AND TEACHER

Few people realize that as a pianist also Bartók was among the greatest. The author of these notes studied under Bartók at the Ferenc Liszt Academy of Music in Budapest for three years (1924–1927), and maintained contact for a long time afterwards. During these three years Bartók either played excerpts from, or the whole of the compositions I was studying at almost every lesson, so that I had ample opportunity to appreciate those aspects of his character as an artist and a man which remained hidden from those who only saw and listened to him in the concert-hall. These impressions have accompanied me throughout my life.

Bartók was given his first piano lessons by his mother at the age of six. He was nine years old when he wrote his first compositions. Having lost his father at an early age, his childhood was difficult, but finally the family managed to leave the countryside for the town of Pozsony, now Bratislava, where Bartók could study music more seriously. His teacher at that time was László Erkel, the son of Ferenc Erkel, the composer, who taught him harmony and the piano. After his final secondary school examinations Bartók continued his studies with István Thomán at the Budapest Academy of Music.

Even though he betrayed a marked talent for composition, he first created a sensation as a pianist. He played Liszt's *Sonata in B minor* at a student recital at the Academy (given to commemorate the 90th anniversary of Liszt's birth, on October 22, 1901). One of his greatest feats was to learn Richard Strauss' *Heldenleben* from the score, and to play it before a group of dumbfounded teachers. Soon afterwards he achieved a great success with it at a concert of the *Tonkünstlerverein* in Vienna, January 26, 1903. The programme of his first solo recital, which he later played in several Hungarian and other towns, might also be of some interest:

1. *Schumann: Sonata in F sharp minor*
2. *Chopin: Nocturne in C sharp minor, Op. 27/1*
   Etude in C minor, Op. 10/12
   Ballade in G minor
3. *Bartók: Fantasy* (1903)
   Etude for Left Hand (1903)
4. *Schubert: Impromptu*
   Paganini—Liszt: Etude
   Saint-Saëns: Valse
5. *Liszt: Spanish Rhapsody*

Two celebrities, Godowsky and Busoni, were present at his first recital in Berlin (December 14, 1903). "Busoni came into the artist's room after the third piece and expressed his congratulations," wrote Bartók to his teacher. The music critic of the *Vossische Zeitung* described his as " . . . a strong personality. We could sense the background of emotional emphasis without which playing remains mere playing."

After such a start it seemed likely that an international career as a pianist lay before him. But though he possessed all the qualities needed for such a career, the development of his personality led him ever more irresistably towards composition. He had already composed *Kossuth: A Symphonic Poem* in 1903, which was first conducted by Hans Richter in Manchester. In the following year his *Rhapsody* for piano and orchestra was published as *Op. 1*. He entered the Paris Rubinstein Competition with this work, both as composer and soloist, and failed on both counts. The prize for composition was withheld, and the prize for piano was awarded to Backhaus, "a worthy rival, and then it's a question of likes and dislikes—whose playing the jury thought best," Bartók wrote to his mother from the competition on August 15, 1905.

This failure obviously depressed Bartók for a while. But he soon recovered. Paris opened all its beauties to him, and for four more weeks Bartók was busy absorbing new impressions. His letters give a vivid picture of the stimulus Paris gave him, and how his ideas ripened during those weeks. Soon after his arrival back in Hungary Bartók started out on his first trip with his close friend Zoltán Kodály to collect the folk songs of the Hungarian countryside and thus save them from oblivion. He entered a world full of miraculous treasures. It seems undeniable that the music and songs collected on these trips played a decisive part in this ultimate choice of composition as the cardinal task of his life. Already in the early works referred to and in his *First Suite* Bartók had expressed a firm belief in the necessity and possibility of a new, truly Hungarian music.

This was a highly significant period in Bartók's life, and it was at this juncture that something occurred which seemed to stand in direct opposition to his decision to become a composer. In 1907, when he was twenty-six, he was appointed a teacher at the Budapest Academy of Music. But he was not appointed to the faculty of composition, but to the faculty of piano. The contradiction, however, was more apparent than real. Psychologically it was quite understandable that he accepted the appointment precisely because at the bottom of his mind he already regarded himself to be a composer. Teaching the piano would save his best thoughts for his real goal: composition. About twenty years later I asked him how it came about that he did not teach composition. He answered with a characteristic wave of his hand: "No, no, it's just right as it is."

I shall come back to Bartók the teacher later. But first I should like to dwell on some concert impressions of mine relating to Bartók the pianist.

For Bartók did not abandon the piano. After a few years of silence he began to give recitals again, from 1919 onwards right up to the end of his life, when a fatal illness took hold of him. True, he performed his own works more and more frequently, but he also played the compositions of other men quite often, even in the thirties. It is characteristic of the spirit of those times that the recitals of one of the greatest musical geniuses of our time only attracted half houses. Official circles of the time despised the "half-witted" composer who, rather than seek the pompous gatherings of the upper tenthousand, preferred to walk the muddy roads of the Hungarian countryside, come wind, come weather, phonograph and music-paper in hand, who sat down at the tables of the poor, who took down their songs, without the least hope of financial satisfaction. Bartók's music jarred on the ears of official circles: they were ears habituated to sentimental "gypsy music" or the repetitive flatness of popular tunes. Concert audiences at that time were composed of the well-to-do bourgeoisie who—with rare exceptions—frequented the concert-hall out of mere snobbery. That is why the unforgettable recitals of Bartók were attended only by professional musicians and true music-lovers.

The first Bartók recital I heard took place on March 21, 1925. Here is the programme:

Liszt—Bach: "Weinen, klagen . . ."
     Variations
Beethoven: Sonata in E flat major,
     Op. 31/3
     Interval
Couperin: Les Fastes de la grande et
     ancienne Ménestrandise
     Les Lys naissants
     Le Trophée
     Le Moucheron
     Les Chérubins ou l'aimable Lazure
     Les Barricades mystérieuses
Bartók: Kolindák, Second Series
Kodály: Rubato, Op. 11/7
Bartók: Suite, Op. 14
Bartók: Sketches, No. 2, 4 and 6
Debussy: Ce qu'a vu le Vent de l'Ouest

More than forty years have passed since that day, but the grandeur of the evening still overcomes me when I recall it. I want to avoid superlatives, but the first words that come to my mind are "enthralling" and "stupefying." The very first D flat major chord of the opening piece sounded like at least four trombones, and the bass octaves rushing upwards pounded on my ears like a two-handed hammer. The atmosphere was created in a flash: elaborating on the basso ostinato theme of Bach, Liszt took his hearers through the whole span of human feeling, from the quiet tears of sorrow to the agony of clenched teeth and screaming pain. And yet the chorale at the end was so full of confidence that it almost burst with strength

and vigour. The intensity deepened even more in Beethoven's wonderful sonata. The first movement came to life under Bartók's fingers as fresh as awakening Spring itself. (Ever since I heard it played by Bartók I have been inclined to think that it has more right to be called the Spring Sonata than the *Sonata in F major* for violin and piano known by that name.) I hope the reader will not think that he is being faced with the raptures of a former pupil: at the beginning of the first movement, in bar 11

the *b* ornament, for all its shortness, was played espressivo, and with this added significance it lent an as yet unheard shade to the colour of the Rameau fifth-sixth chord. I had a similar experience when I heard Beethoven's *C minor Sonata* for violin and piano (Op. 30/2) which Bartók played with

József Szigeti at a sonata evening of theirs in Budapest. In the 17th bar of the Adagio the left-hand *a* note (marked with an asterisk) together with the *b flat* in the right-hand gave off such a wonderful dissonance that those who heard it played this way can never forget it.

The secret of this extraordinary effect lies not so much in the vertical small ninth of the *a* and the *b flat*: after all, Beethoven had composed it this way, and the vertical dissonance should have sounded the same whoever the pianist was. But it was the way Bartók led the *a flat- a-b flat* chromatic sequel that gave the *a* note immense significance: Bartók re-created the

classical alternation of the first and fifth notes. What he did was beyond all thoughts of interpretation: he took his audience into the very workshop of the creative process. He made the audience forget that the piano is divided into half-notes, he spanned the gap between the *a flat* and the *b flat* with a glissando that exists only in singing and in string instruments. All this, of course, was illusion; but it was an illusion of Bartók's own making.

The reader should not, however, think that Bartók's art as a pianist consisted of nothing but masterly individual sounds, that his playing consisted of a series of little bits. For all his minute workmanship (as with works by Couperin) he was one of the greatest pianists for the shape and form of the whole. This is only natural: as a composer he never blurred his lines, he held his material firmly together. As Béla Balázs aptly characterized him in one of his poems:

Indeed, your music is no lullaby
But a relentless construction of steel . . .

If I have rhapsodized over these sporadic impressions (and I could go on with more and more), it is to give those who never heard him *play* an idea of the many-sided creativity and wealth of Bartók's art as a pianist: this appeared in the tiniest details as well as the large overall form of the compositions he played.

I still possess the programme of another Bartók recital given on November 29, 1927. He began with 17th and 18th-century Italian masters: Frescobaldi, Marcello, Scarlatti, Rossi, Zipoli and Bella Ciaja, and continued with Beethoven's *Sonata in F major* (Op. 10/2). The second half of the recital was made up of his own compositions (among others his piano sonata composed in 1926). At an earlier recital, which I was unable to attend, he played all the 24 preludes of Debussy. I was present at two of his sonata recitals; he played with Marteau and, as I said, with Szigeti.

Bartók played as soloist with the orchestra fairly frequently in those years. The concert given to commemorate the 50th anniversary of Liszt's death was especially memorable (1936). All of Liszt's orchestral works with piano—the concertos in E flat major and A major, the Hungarian Fantasy, the rarely played, early Malediction and the

Danse Macabre—were performed by a number of Hungarian pianists. The highlight of the evening was the Danse Macabre played by Bartók. His playing corresponded completely to Liszt's intentions. (The author of these notes played the *Concerto in E flat major*.)

There is another orchestral concert I want to recall: the first performance, by the composer, of Bartók's First Piano Concerto in 1928, in Berlin. I was studying in Berlin at the time and was thrilled to be able to attend the rehearsals and the concert which—owing to the wonderful collaboration between the composer-pianist, the conductor, Erich Kleiber, and the orchestra—was an excellent one. And the reception? Cool, polite applause, boos and hissing here and there. After the concert, when I remarked what a shame it was that the reception was so poor, Bartók said: "Why are you so upset? When they book their seats they buy the right of expressing their discontent as well as their satisfaction. If they have the right to applaud, they also have the right to boo, haven't they?" He added qietly: "I myself wouldn't boo if I disliked a piece..."

The following incident is also characteristic of Bartók's greatness as a man. In 1930 he compiled a 60-minute programme of original piano pieces for four hands for Radio Budapest. The works he chose were Mozart's *Sonata in F major*, K. 497, and *Andante con variazioni in G major*, K. 501; Schubert's *Fantasy in F minor*, Op. 103; a piece from Ravel's *Ma Mère l'Oye*, and Stravinsky's *Five Small Pieces*. He chose me as his partner, and declared categorically that he would not think it fair to play all the more decorative first parts himself; he insisted that we should change places after each piece. He even added with a smile: "The listeners will have a hard job deciding which of us is playing first part." But I do not think it took them too long to guess.

To sum up Bartók as a pianist: Putting

it quite simply, the age-old saying held true of his playing: it was beautiful because it was true. It was true from two aspects. Bartók as a person always remained true to himself, he was one of the most immaculate, austere characters I have met—and the man is always inseparable from the artist. But his playing was true in a strictly musical sense too. Whatever he chose to play, every single work sounded genuine under his fingers, from the ideal tempos and phrasings to the most lucid larger outlines of each piece. The inner truth of his interpretation shone through the work as a whole as well as in the tiniest phrases, stresses and shades. His playing was devoid of all superficial, irrelevant flourish—Bartók was not a colourist when he played the piano. Probably this was the only deficiency in his playing, and it appeared only when—very rarely—he played works by composers like Chopin, whose colours and specific, instrumental sounds are inseparable from the fullness of the aesthetic effect. These pieces sounded somewhat strange, as if they had been carved in granite—but they were granite-masterpieces all the same. He prepared for his recitals with incredible devotion and deadly seriousness, even if those five to six hours of practice a day meant less time for composing. For Bartók it was *morally* inconceivable to mount the concert stage or face the microphone if ever so slightly unprepared. The musical experiences of the audience would probably have been just as magnificent if he had not prepared as thoroughly as he did, yet—as in other things—he never compromised. He had no other yardstick for himself—or for others—than the highest.

These aspects of his personality naturally revealed themselves in his activity as a teacher. He was never late for a lesson, he never stopped before it was time. When one pupil was unable to come, another pupil got a longer lesson. (On one occasion, I remember, he gave me a two-and-a-half-hour lesson.) He never tired of playing excerpts to his students. When necessary, he played a phrase 8 to 10 times. He often took ten minutes to clear up one single bar. His teaching was *par excellence* musical: although he never made light of the importance of technical details, fingering, variants, ways to practise, etc. he thought the purely musical aspects more important. He believed that at an advanced level the technical details must on the whole be worked out by the students themselves.

And here, to be fair—I have to say something else. I think it is clear by now how compelling and overwhelming Bartók's style as a pianist was. No one who heard him play could escape his magnetic influence. Well, this influence was, if possible, even greater when one heard him speak; when one saw the firm, blazing light in his eyes at arm's length. Bartók himself never wanted to impose his personality on his students, but close proximity to him made it impossible to avoid it. To adopt his essential greatness was impossible: that was *his* only. But many of us adopted what was external to his playing. By using the word "external" let no one think of Bartók as a *poseur*. There was no other person more remote from tricks of any kind. By the external qualities of his playing I mean his characteristic carriage when sitting at the piano, the fixed, almost stiffened state into which his creative efforts forced him. This was mostly due to his physique: he was a light, small, muscular but very bony person. He could exploit his small weight in a masterly fashion when he played, but all in all his playing was characteristically striking. His wrists and arms were all fixed. That is why he sounded, as I said, as if he had carved each piece in stone. It was combined with an unmatched clearness and plasticity of sound, a sound that was convincing from him alone. No one with a personality different from Bartók could make use of this sound convincingly—it was too specific, too unique to create a "school," like the schools of Leschetitzky, Philipp or the Hungarians Thomán and Szendy. These notable teachers, though far from Bartók's status as composers, could, precisely because their approach to the piano was not so extremely individual as his, create a school with their neutral (I use the word in its best sense) handling of the piano. Their "neutrality" could exert a fertile influence on the most diverse talents.

Bartók's activity as a teacher was not limited to his lessons at the Academy. Certain compositions of his are extraordinarily important in this connection as well. The first of these—written for teaching—was the series For Children (1908-1909). We know that great masters of all times have often created masterpieces when writing for the young. The small pieces of the For Children series belong to the most perfect piano-sketches of contemporary music. The folk tunes elaborated here are all enchanting, and over the whole emotional span of the human mind. Their treatment, especially their harmonization, is poetic and worthy of a genius, the melancholy or gay mood of the tunes comes across perfectly. These pieces preceded Bartók's other similar works "for adults" (e.g. 15 Hungarian Peasant Songs, 1914-17; Sonatina, 1915; Rumanian Dances, etc.) and they are of great importance: it was through these pieces that the public first learnt what harmonic and structural inspiration Bartók derived form folk music. But the didactic value of the series is even greater. The series not only covered in a melodious, very attractive form all the elemental skills of playing the piano (legato, staccato, leggiero, cantabile, double-holds, polyphony, etc.), but the musical quality of the melodies meant that young learners of the instrument could draw on a more nourishing food, more full of vitamins, as it were, at a time when worthless, repetitive "children's pieces" abounded.

The other series that Bartók wrote with a didactic purpose is the Microcosm. It is even more variegated and comprehensive. Twenty to twenty-five years had passed between the two series, and it is therefore no wonder that the style of the second is considerably different. During this quarter of a century Bartók had created a whole body of superb masterpieces, and after many years of struggle and labour his musical language had reached an extremely spare and concentrated state. Whereas the For Children series was primarily designed to give music to young pupils, and the teaching purpose was secondary, the didactic purpose of Microcosm was primary and this is especially evident in the first two books of the series. From the very beginning Bartók leads his young pianists all the way to the concert-pieces of the fifth and sixth books. The folk-song material is restricted in Microcosm, and Bartók deals with such elements of contemporary music as bitonality, mixture-chords or what are known as Bulgarian rhythms. These short compositions bear the stamp of Bartók's greatness as effectively as his most monumental works. Yet for all its merits I do not think it advisable that young pupils should study nothing but Microcosm for the first one and a half years of their study, as covertly suggested by Bartók in the Preface: this would inevitably lead to a one-sided approach. For a learner to be concerned with one master only for a long time is not admissible, even if that master should be Bach or Mozart.

And finally, a few words about Bartók as an editor. Along with Bach's The Well-Tempered Klavier he edited many of Haydn's, Mozart's and Beethoven's sonatas and other classical works. The most significant is undoubtedly the edition of The Well-Tempered Klavier. This edition conveys Bartók's greatness, seriousness and conscientiousness to the full. The divisions, the phrasings, the notes on dynamics and embellishments reflect to a great extent the characteristic way Bartók himself played Bach. Besides the accepted marking of musical stress he often made use of a $\wedge$ mark which in most cases means not so much a sharp marcato as a stress of an agogic, emphatic, espressivo character, of which I have already given examples in discussing Bartók's playing. Bartók's very individual approach to the piano revealed itself in the fingerings of the edition as well. Some of them can be said to be highly original and most appropriate. As a whole the fingerings bear the stamp of Bartók's own style of playing to so great an extent that the expert can reconstruct the editor's own approach to the instrument from them. Following a fingering the student arrives at the same style of playing as gave birth to that particular fingering in Bartók. And here I have to remind the reader of what I said about Bartók's enthralling but unique, inimitable style of playing: it is permissible, sometimes even advisable, for the student to alter some of the fingerings in this edition to suit his own talents and his own approach to the piano. (This, by the way, is true of all editions of musical works.)

I hope, in conclusion, that I have succeeded in throwing a little light on some of the less known aspects of my former master, Béla Bartók. My purpose has been to round out the accepted Bartók-image, so that, without idealizing it, it is wholly true. If Bartók were alive he would be the first to object to any idolatry of his person. Yet he was so great that almost any account of his virtues must ring true. He was not only one of the greatest musicians of our time; it is also true that there were few people who could compare with him in ethical and moral integrity. Everything he thought or did, every single note or word he put down, every sound he made at the piano demonstrated the highest moral principles and obligations, which his great predecessor, Ferenc Liszt, summed up in: *génie oblige*.

LAJOS HERNÁDI

BARTÓK AND ENGLAND

by

GERALD ABRAHAM

We in England have reason to be proud of the fact that the second performance of Béla Bartók's earliest surviving orchestral work, the 'Kossuth' Symphony, was given in this country only a month after its first performance in Hungary. This was at Manchester on February 18, 1904. With it began a long and friendly association; the English public has accepted Bartók's music more willingly than most contemporary music from the Continent and long acknowledged his undisputed place in the very front rank of twentieth-century masters; on his side, although (as I shall show) his attitude to England and the English was by no means uncritical, he seems to have regarded us generally with tolerance and even warmth.

Bartók was interested in the study of languages, not only for their utility, but for their own sake. As he told his American friend Mrs. Creel, he was particularly fascinated by 'the exotic languages'. But he was a real master of the more familiar ones, and he both spoke and wrote very good English. At what age he began to study English I do not know, but in 1902, when he was twenty-one, he told his mother that 'the English lessons are becoming interesting: we are now beginning to go through the history of English literature'[1]. And his attention was soon drawn to other English products besides books; on January 17, 1903, he writes:

Dohnányi has recommended a remedy for tiredness: Elliman's Embrocation. This remedy is also very good for all sorts of muscular pains (alleged!), such as: various forms of rheumatism, neck pains, etc. Obtainable of any chemist for 90 kreuzers. English and Hungarian instructions for use enclosed. These begin: Instructions for use of

---

[1] *Béla Bartók: Ausgewählte Briefe.* Collected and edited by János Demény (Corvina, Budapest, 1960). Letter no. 2. Unless otherwise stated, all letters and excerpts from letters in this article are translated by me from this collection.

Elliman's (Royal) Embrocation for muscular complaints of cattle, sheep, horses, donkeys and birds! That made me stop and think! to which group are musicians supposed to belong?

Very soon Bartók was to have an opportunity of putting his knowledge of English to practical use. In June 1903 he was introduced to Hans Richter, then conductor of the Hallé Orchestra at Manchester, who was on a visit to Hungary, and played him the 'Kossuth' Symphony on the piano; according to a contemporary account in the 'Pressbourger Zeitung' (January 23, 1904), Richter was 'so struck by the young pianist's warmth of expression and so surprised by the youthful composer that he immediately put Bartók's truly national symphonic poem in the program of his celebrated concerts at Manchester'. (It should be remembered that Richter himself was Hungarian by birth, his father having been cathedral Kapellmeister at Győr where he was born.) In August Richter wrote that the performance had been arranged for February 18, invited the composer to stay as his guest at his house near Manchester, and promised that the travel expenses should be met although he was unable to offer any fee. Bartók would appear not only as composer but as pianist, playing Liszt's Spanish Rhapsody (in Busoni's arrangement for piano and orchestra) and Volkmann's 'Variations on a Theme by Händel'—both chosen by Richter and not particularly approved of by Bartók himself. Bartók's first letter from England, to his mother (February 12, 1904), is so entertaining that it deserves translation in full:

Address: England
The Firs
  Bowdon
   Cheshire
    B. B.
    with the lines of
    Dr. Hans Richter[1]

Dear Mamma,

Now that I've safely arrived at Bowdon I should like to tell you something about my journey, etc. The Richters received me kindly. I have a room on the second floor. Anyhow I'm not in Manchester. Bowdon is 20 minutes away. In the afternoon the weather was very bad:

[1] In English in the original.

rain, storm, I couldn't see much of either Manchester or Bowdon. Richter's house seems a very pleasant place. Cheerful fires burn in the open fireplaces (English conservatism).

That reminds me of the awful state of the English railway-carriages. The smallest Hungarian local railway has better carriages than the trains here. Neither heating (instead of which you get a stone hot-water bottle) nor head- or arm-rests, narrow luggage-racks. There are no ashtrays, so the floor of the carriage looks like a pigsty. It surprises me that they bother about lighting and that even—bless my soul—separate brakes are fitted. Some trains have restaurant cars; but naturally one can only go to them and leave them at stations.

I am surprised to find that living here is not so dear. In London the fare for a cab is 2s/2d (= 1.40 Kr) as against 1.20 in Vienna. The porters are content with 30 kreuzers (3d) (d = penny). I've very quickly got used to English money and English reckoning; the big, well-worn copper coins (1 penny) are most peculiar.

Between London and Manchester there are only first and third class. (The comfort is equally 'excellent' in both.) For the latter I paid 16 shillings (10 gulden); the midday meal (or, rather, 'lunch') cost 2s/2d, Hungarian Apollinaris 8d, tip 3d.

I was very amused by the notices in the Dutch carriages: 'verboden te rooken', etc. It's been quite all right about the French cognac, which remains still untouched. The sea-crossing pleased me very much: a pity that, owing to the 'rŏf wind'[1], I couldn't stay on deck. So I let myself be rocked only below deck; then I sat down to tea (8d); after that I walked about again: I hadn't the least wish to go to sleep. However I had to (about 1.30 West European time); my travelling companions had long been asleep. About 2.30 I woke up: the ship was rolling quite a bit and the waves banged hard on the cabin wall. A pity that I was travelling alone. (But I don't think it would have done for you, because you like to go to sleep early.)

K(iss).
B.

According to the anonymous critic of the 'Manchester Guardian' (February 19), "Kossuth" was well played and "received with a fair amount of applause" but it is clear that it was by no means to his taste or that of the audience:

[1] Phonetically spelled English: 'rough wind'.

In the Symphonic Poem "Kossuth," which was the principal unfamiliar work played at yesterday's concert, Mr. Béla Bartók declares himself as an uncompromising disciple of the later Strauss, as a musician. His Hungarian patriotism appears in his choice of a subject, but not at all in his musical procedure. Of the national Hungarian melodies which have inspired so many eminent composers—in particular Schubert, Liszt, and Brahms—he shows no consciousness whatever in the course of his elaborate and ambitious orchestral poem. In fact the only previously existing theme to which reference is made is the Austrian national anthem... As to the manner in which that is used we shall have something to say in the sequel. The suggestions of Strauss, and in particular of Strauss's "Heldenleben," are too various and too strong to be accidental. Even the constitution of the orchestra, with eight horns, two harps, and one or more additional tubas, is Straussian. In the preliminary characterisation of the hero the procedure is exactly the same as in "Heldenleben" though there is no trace of resemblance in the thematic material. Passing to the dialogue between Kossuth and his wife, we are reminded of the "Hero's Companion," whose voice takes the form of a recurrent violin solo in the Strauss composition. Then comes the battle, quite as ugly as Strauss's, and open to one definite charge of a kind that cannot be brought against Strauss—the charge, namely, that the travesty of the Austrian Hymn is ferocious and hideous. There is nothing in precise correspondence with the section called by Strauss "The Hero's Works of Peace," Mr. Bartók's composition ending with the patriotic lamentations of a surviving remnant. It is, however, clear that the young Hungarian composer has been very strongly influenced by Strauss both in the fundamental conception of his Symphonic Poem and in his manner of putting it together. There is a slight hint even of Strauss's peculiar vein of musical invention in the dialogue between Kossuth and his wife, but for the rest the detail of the invention seems to be original enough... The mere fact that a young composer should attempt to follow in the footsteps of so tremendous a "Jack the Giant-Killer" as Strauss would seem to betray the consciousness of great powers, and the degree of facility in handling great orchestral masses exhibited by Mr. Bartók would be remarkable in anyone, and is doubly surprising in so young an artist. His themes, too, have life in them, and in certain cases awaken a hope that in course of time, when he shall have enough of the Straussian goose-chase, he may do excellent work...

As a pianist Mr. Bartók displayed powers of a less exceptional kind, but he was more satisfactory on the whole... The solo part (of the Liszt Rhapsody) Mr. Bartók played with technical power fully equal to all its demands, and his rendering did not lack geniality and charm. He afterwards gave two pieces without accompaniment—a very peculiar set of modern Variations, by Volkmann, on the theme of Händel's harpsichord piece "The Harmonious Blacksmith" that scarcely seemed to justify its existence, and secondly, in answer to an encore, a Scherzo of his own, showing some of the same tendency to harmonic extravagance as his orchestral piece, but piquant in rhythm and stamped with genuine if somewhat eccentric talent.

Two days later (February 20) Bartók played again in Manchester, in a concert given in the Midland Hall of the Midland Hotel. According to the "Guardian" critic (February 22),

The Chopin rendering had considerable distinction, though one rather considerable lapse of memory occurred in the course of it, and Schumann's "Aufschwung" from the early Fantasiestücke was artistically played... Mr. Bartók played (the Liszt Étude in E flat)

very effectively on the whole though here, again, there occurred a lapse of memory which compelled the pianist to fall back on improvising for a few bars. His own Fantaisie[1] was a piece in a meditative vein, original in harmony and colouring and decidedly attractive.

Bartók himself afterwards regretted that he had mislaid "the critiques from Manchester": "A pity! There were a few good and interesting remarks in them."[2] It is a pity also that he could not have foreseen that a later music-critic of the "Guardian," Mr. Colin Mason, was to become one of his most penetrating admirers and one of the leading non-Hungarian authorities on his music.[3]

Bartók disliked not only English railway-carriages but English etiquette and English millionaires (dislikes shared, of course, by many Englishmen). Perhaps he particularly disliked Austrians and others who aped English manners. Staying with the Vecseys at Keresztúr, at the very beginning of his folksong collecting in the summer of 1906, he had an Austrian countess as his fellow-guest:

The Countess is as cold as Franz-Joseph-Land at Christmas: when we see and hear her, the blood freezes in our veins. English etiquette rages at lunch. But I like dissonances, so I appear in the middle of all this frightful order—in summer shirt, without collar and cuffs, in shabby shoes... Woe to anyone at a meal who makes more noise with his food than a fly buzzing! For that sort of thing isn't done in England;[4]

Again in July 1908 at Argentières on the French-Swiss border he rejoices that, in contrast with Lucerne and Zürich, there are

neither a host of Grand Hotels nor hordes of lazy, idle, good-for-nothing English nor a network of cogwheel railways going everywhere; here (time is money![5]) the poor thirsting mortal gets unspoiled nature. Not of course in dusty Chamonix which Baedaekaer (sic) distinguishes with 38 stars, but in quiet, peaceful dear little Argentières where—"because it isn't the proper thing"—thank God the swarm of English millionaires doesn't come. Really, that's how it is![6]

After the Manchester visit of 1904, Bartók spent six days in London on his way home and the piano firm of Broadwood promised him—"on Dohnányi's intervention"—six appearances the following year, two of them

---

[1] This, like the Scherzo he had played two days before, is one of the "Four Piano-Pieces" (without opus-number) of 1903.

[2] Letter no. 19.

[3] I am indebted to Mr. Mason's colleague, Mr. Gerald Lerner, for drawing my attention to the article on Bartók's second appearance in Manchester which has been generally overlooked.

[4] Letter no. 37.

[5] This phrase is in English in the original.

[6] Letter no. 47.

in London, and also an evening recital.[1] Nothing seems to have come of this, however, and his next visit to London was apparently not made until 1922. He appeared first at the Hungarian Ambassador's, where a private recital was arranged for him by the Arányi sisters. (He had composed a violin sonata for Jelly the year before and was now writing a second for her.) He then went immediately to Wales to play for the Aberystwyth department of the University of Wales, whence he wrote to his mother and aunt:

Aberystwyth, March 16, 1922

Dear Mama and Aunt Irma!

Here I am on the west coast of England, on the seacoast of Wales. The two huge windows of my room overlook the ocean—the waves roar below and the sunshine is magnificent. This Aberystwyth is a little university town of 10,000 inhabitants; I have a concert here this evening. Yesterday[2] in London I had a "private concert" arranged by the Arányis at the Hungarian "Ambassador's" (Consul's?). Although it was not public, there was a notice next day in "The Times"—very favourable. But before that there had been announcements of my visit: in the "Daily Telegraph" and in the "Daily Mail", also in two musical papers. I have been awaited with great interest and received with much cordiality. My public concert in London is to be on March 24, when the financial risk will be the agent's. The day before yesterday's private concert brought in about 30 pounds, then I shall play twice more in family circles (10 pounds each time), and here at Aberystwyth I get 15 pounds (of which 10 will be pure profit). Considering that my journey here and back will not cost more than 15 pounds and that I am living here as the guest of a very friendly couple (up to now I have spent no money at all), and further considering that in Paris I shall get all in all 1,500 francs, it seems to me that I shall bring quite a lot of money back home. ∴. I go to Paris on Apr. 3. And now I must hurry off to a rehearsal (as I am also playing a Beethoven trio here).

If we assume that "here" means London, not Aberystwyth, the "friendly couple" were Mr. and Mrs. (now Sir Robert and Lady) Mayer, famous for the Children's Concerts they were just beginning to organize in England at that time. Under her maiden name, Dorothy Moulton, Lady Mayer was a well-known singer and an outstanding champion of contemporary music; she gave the first performances in London and (I believe) in Budapest of Schönberg's Second String Quartet with the Hungarian (Waldbauer)

[1] Letter no. 19.
[2] Actually the day before: March 14.

String Quartet, and it was through Waldbauer that she became personally acquainted with Bartók. He stayed with the Mayers at their house, 2, Cumberland Terrace.

Bartók already had a number of influential admirers among the London critics, e. g. Edwin Evans, Cecil Gray, and the French musicologist, M. D. Calvocoressi who had first met him in Paris in 1913 and had now settled in England. (The first Paris performance of the First Quartet was given by Waldbauer and his colleagues as an illustration to one of Calvocoressi's lectures at the École des Hautes Études Sociales.) Nevertheless, being a very modest man, he was surprised to find himself such a celebrity. "It is a great sensation," he told his mother (March 20),

> that the papers wrote so fully about my private concert (the one of March 14). The "Times" has written about it again; I enclose this; try and take it to A(lbrecht); perhaps someone can translate it for you. It's a great thing that the papers treat my visit as an extraordinary event. I really hadn't hoped for that. I have been introduced to a fearful lot of people and my head is absolutely swimming. Yesterday evening I was in unusually "eminent" company (to wit, purely musicians and critics) at the house of a wealthy singer. I also played. Today I lunched with some French. I had to speak alternately French and English (sometimes German); I blunder along as best I can, but this continual change of language makes me quite dizzy... Yesterday I was interviewed for the "Pall Mall Gazette" (an evening paper); tomorrow I am to be photographed for the newspapers.

The "wealthy singer" was, of course, Dorothy Moulton, who sang some of his folk-song arrangements to his accompaniment. He also played some Händel, his own Rumanian Dances, the Piano Suite, and the Improvisations, Op. 20.[1] On a similar, later occasion, Lady Mayer tells me, she

> gave a party for him at which he played some Beethoven and some of his own music, concluding with the "Allegro barbaro." Many pianists were present, and one of them—Benno Moiseiwitsch—commented that he was surprised that the piano was still on its legs. But those of us who listened more to the music than the playing sensed that here was somebody out of the ordinary, and in spite of his reserve and shyness we both felt very drawn to him... He was a very fine pianist, though *unerbittlich* in his demands on the instrument, himself, and the audience.

Other visits to England followed and, again through Calvocoressi, who was now advising the newly founded music department of the Oxford University Press, the project of publishing in England Bartók's collection of

[1] Note to Letter no. 97.

Rumanian folk-songs was mooted. In 1925 Hubert Foss, the head of the music department, visited him in Budapest[1] to discuss the matter. But, despite a long, interesting and sometimes angry correspondence extending over five or six years—which I hope to discuss elsewhere—nothing came of it. Only in 1931 the Oxford Press published Calvocoressi's translation of Bartók's book on Hungarian folk-song.

Two visits to London remain particularly in my memory: one in May 1934, when Bartók came over for the BBC performance of his "Cantata profana" and I had the terrifying honour of sharing his full score while Sir Adrian Boult rehearsed in the concert hall at Broadcasting House. (It was from Bartók that I learned that Holst had died the day before.)[2] The other was in June 1938 when he came with his wife to play the Sonata for Two Pianos. Again there was a party at the Mayers', where he played pieces from "Mikrokosmos," and this must have been the last time I talked to him, for it was his last visit to this country.

The *Anschluss* had already occurred and the Munich crisis was not far ahead. Bartók had no sympathy with Czechoslovakia, which he considered had treated his mother—who lived and worked in Bratislava (Pozsony)—very badly and which had for several years refused him the permission to appear publicly in Slovakia; but he was deeply shocked by Hitler's triumph and the behaviour of England and France. He recognized that it marked the end of a chapter.

[1] Letter No. 105.

[2] The only English composer who seems to have really interested Bartók, and whom he liked as a man (Letter no. 69), was Delius. In 1911 he published a sympathetic article on Delius which was reprinted by Szabolcsi in *Bartók Béla: Válogatott zenei írásai* (Budapest, 1948), p. 76.

BÉLA BARTÓK
AND THE PERMANENT
COMMITTEE ON LITERATURE AND ART
OF THE LEAGUE OF NATIONS

A subcommittee of the Commission for Intellectual Cooperation of the League of Nations *(Commission de Coopération Intellectuelle de la Société des Nations)*, the Permanent Committee for Literature and Art (Comité Permanent des Lettres et des Arts) in its reorganizing session on February 20, 1931, co-opted Béla Bartók. This is an event in the life of the great Hungarian composer which is well known from the Bartók literature. Recently the documents relating to the election, including a holographic letter of Béla Bartók, were found in the Hungarian National Archives.[1]

The election of Bartók was initiated by the Secretariat of the League of Nations. On October 2, 1930, a deputy secretary general[2] of the international organization, Albert Dufour-Feronce, wrote in a letter to Zoltán Baranyai, the provisional head of the Hungarian Delegation at the League of Nations, to make enquiries whether Bartók was ready to accept committee membership. As Dufour wrote: "The Commission for Intellectual Cooperation is seeking an outstanding musician for the *Comité des Lettres et*

des Arts which is soon to be formed, and here at the Secretariat we are considering whether your compatriot Mr. Béla Bartók would be a suitable person."[3] Immediately, on October 3, Baranyai asked Bartók in a telegram whether he would accept the appointment. The composer answered on October 5, "Accepting without obligation to work."[4]

It deserves attention that the other member besides Béla Bartók co-opted at the February session of the Committee was Thomas Mann. The Committee already counted among its members Karel Čapek and Paul Valéry; its president was the English professor, Gilbert Murray.

In Budapest this international tribute of respect to Bartók became known in mid-March 1931 and was also recorded by the Hungarian press.

Bartók subsequently obtained an invitation to the summer session of the Committee in Geneva and referred to this journey in a letter to Baranyai.

Budapest, III. 10. Kavics Street
May 8, 1931.

Dear Mr. Baranyai!

Couroy writes me that he heard I intend to submit a memorial to the Com-

[1] Hungarian National Archives (Hereafter: NA/Küm. (Ministry of Foreign Affairs). *A Nemzetek Szövetsége mellett működő genfi magyar képviselet iratai* (Documents of the Hungarian Delegation at the League of Nations in Geneva) 26/20.

[2] Also Director of the International Office of Intellectual Cooperation.

[3] NA. *Ibid.*
[4] NA. *Ibid.*

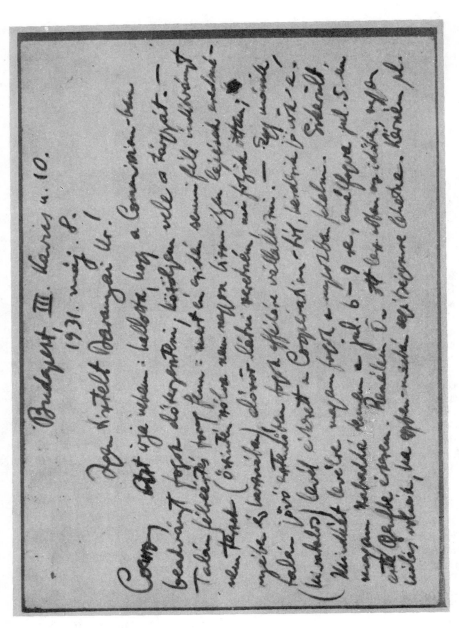

Béla Bartók's postcard to Zoltán Baranyai

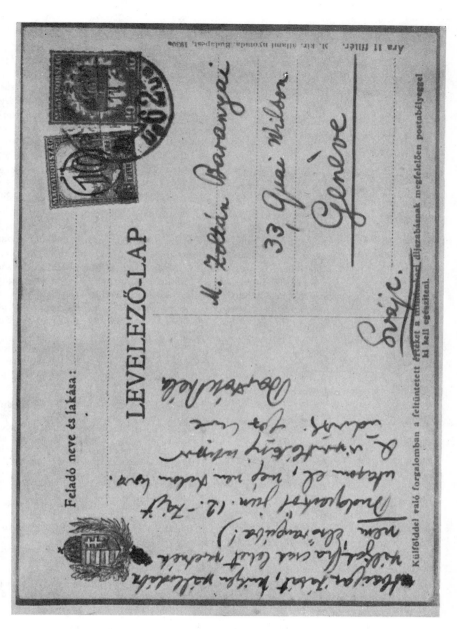

Reverse of Bartók's postcard

mission and asks me to let him know its subject.—There may be some misunderstanding because I am not proposing any resolution this year (to be quite frank, I do not have much faith in the results and usefulness of such steps). I should rather like to see first how things are going there; maybe I would undertake something of the sort next year.—Another (official) letter came from the Coopération asking whether I am coming. I shall answer both letters myself in a few days. I succeeded in freeing myself for July 6–9 and therefore shall arrive on the evening of July 5 in Geneva. I hope you will be there at that time; I would be greatly obliged if you could help me with one thing or the other. For instance I would ask your advice about which hotel to choose (if possible I prefer one that is *not* first-class).

I am to leave Budapest about June 12, I do not yet know where to. Anticipating the pleasure of seeing you again, with best greetings,

Yours sincerely,
Béla Bartók

János Demény, the well-known Bartók scholar, writes about Bartók's letters: "In general, all written statements of Bartók's are important and should be published, but the great Hungarian musician habitually expounded his ideological and political views in his letters only on few occasions and for few people. Therefore, those of his letters in which he does so—if only as an innuendo—have a special value..."[5] Bartók's reluctance to work for the Committee, which appears both in his telegram and in the above letter, can be explained not only by the pressure of work but, as the letter reveals, by his skeptical attitude towards "such steps" and the whole activities of the Committee. However a comparison of the

spirit emanating from the card with the lines he wrote to his mother about his doings in Geneva casts a light on the nature of this behaviour, its limitations and the individuality of Bartók. "So on Monday morning I first of all paid a visit to the Hungarian Legation. B. (Baranyai) is away on leave, so I spoke with his chief, the Minister (I believe *chargé d'affaires* is his real title), P. (János Pelényi). I asked for his opinion about the Toscanini motion.[6] I think he would have reacted very negatively if he had not been a diplomat, but as he is, he only courteously suggested not submitting it for the time being but first sounding out some members of the Committee..."[7] The same Bartók who on May 8 did not want to "propose any resolution" yet, was ready at the very first meeting of the Committee to speak up for Toscanini in support of the intellectual freedom endangered by the fascists.

The source of his misgivings concerning the Geneva spirit of "intellectual cooperation" in this epoch is illustrated by the

[5] Bartók Béla levelei (*The letters of Béla Bartók*). Ed. by János Demény; Zeneműkiadó Vállalat, Budapest, 1955 (p. 17).

[6] On May 15, 1931, in Bologna, Toscanini, one of the most prominent conductors of his age, was not willing to direct Giovinezza, the march of the Italian fascists. Therefore the fascists assaulted the grey-haired maestro on the open street. Presumably Bartók intended to take the floor in this affair. This is the more likely because the draft resolution of the New Hungarian Association of Music (Új Magyar Zeneegyesület), in which the Hungarian musicians protested against the criminal attempt of the fascists, was drawn up by Bartók himself. (János Demény: Bartók Béla pályája delelőjén (Béla Bartók at the Zenith of his Career).—Zenetudományi Tanulmányok (Musicological Studies). Vol. X. Akadémiai Kiadó, Budapest, 1962, p. 402.). In the Bartók literature this study gives the most detailed account of the connection between the composer and the Committee. The data in this article—if no other source is named—derive from it.

[7] Béla Bartók (Levelek, fényképek, kéziratok, kották) (Letters, photographs, manuscripts, scores). Collected and edited by János Demény.—Magyar Művészeti Tanács, 1948. Budapest, p. 122. This letter by Bartók himself has hitherto been our most detailed source on the days spent by the composer in Geneva.

following lines, written December 20, 1931, on the events in Geneva. "We were chatting about many nice things there..., but I should very much like to tell them that as long as it is utterly impossible to straighten things out in this world, economically and otherwise (so that, for example as a consequence of foreign exchange restrictions even spiritual products can hardly pass the various borders), it is absolutely useless to ramble on grandiosely about 'intellectual cooperation.' Of course I would have said it to no purpose..."[8]

Bartók was present also at the sessions of the Committee held in Frankfurt in 1932 and Geneva in 1933. The central subject of the latter was originally intended to have been *"Europa quo vadis?"* but this was changed at the last moment to *"L'avenir de la culture."* It appears that the initial scruples of Bartók concerning the work of the Committee were well founded. We know very little about the contribution of the composer to this work, but we may draw conclusions regarding the atmosphere which prevailed there in the middle of the thirties from the recollection of Thomas Mann: "At that time I was a member of the '*Comité permanent des Lettres et des Arts*' appointed by the League of Nations, and before the advent of the Third Reich took part in the sessions of this body in Geneva and in Frankfurt a/M. I contributed a written memorandum of political character for a discussion in Nice where I personally was not present. When read there, it caused something of a stir and later, under the title "Europe Beware!" was included in the collection of essays of the same title. I again attended the *Comité* meetings in Venice and Budapest, and in the Hungarian capital in the open session I made an impromptu

speech against the murderers of freedom and about the necessity for militant democracy—a declaration which was contrary, almost to the point of indiscretion, to the completely academic, and for the sake of the Fascist delegates, rather pussyfooting character of the discussions; it was, however, answered by the Hungarian public with an ovation that lasted for minutes..."[9]

Here, in the course of the Budapest session of the Committee, the figures of the two great artists, Thomas Mann and Béla Bartók appear together for the last time before our eyes.

The Minister of Education in the Hungarian government, Bálint Hóman, gave a gala dinner on June 8, 1936, in honour of the members of the Committee. Thomas Mann, however, who did not want to sit at the same table with the fascist Hungarian Minister, asked to be excused, giving "indisposition" as a reason. Lajos Hatvany, the literary historian and aesthetician of distinction whose guests Thomas Mann and his wife were during their stay in Hungary, then invited, to honour his guests, some Hungarian artists who sympathized with their point of view. One of the participants, István Péterfi[10] recalls the day as follows:

"Hatvany gave Bartók a call and explained the situation to him. He told him that Thomas Mann was indisposed. Bartók answered that he suffered from the same disease and had himself just asked to be excused. At the Geneva session of the *Comité* the friendship of

[8] His letter to János Busitia. Published hitherto only in German translation in "Béla Bartók — Ausgewählte Briefe." Corvina, 1960, pp. 149-150. Quoted by János Demény in his work referred to above: "Bartók Béla pályája delelőjén" (Béla Bartók at the Zenith of his Career), p. 403.

[9] Thomas Mann: Sechzehn Jahre. Zur amerikanischen Ausgabe von "Joseph und seine Brüder" in einem Bande. — Thomas Mann: Gesammelte Werke, vol. XI. S. Fischer Verlag. Oldenburg, 1960, pp. 674–675.
[10] István Péterfi, Hungarian musical critic. His wife, Mária Basilides, was one of the most prominent opera singers in Hungary between the two World Wars. These reminiscences of István Péterfi appeared in the periodical "Muzsika" in July 1959 under the title "A negyvenedik zsoltár" (The Fortieth Psalm), pp. 3–4.

Thomas Mann and his wife was the greatest joy for him and therefore he is happy to be able to pass another evening in their company...

"What was Thomas Mann like? Gentle, polite, quiet. As I observed the two men, him and Bartók, it could not escape my notice that in someway they very closely resembled each other. In both of them there was not only no affected ceremoniousness but also not even a shadow of condescending fraternization. From the way they talked to each other and shook hands when departing, one could feel how they respect, understand and esteem each other.

"And in this we all participated with them.

"We did not know then that in a few years Bartók too would leave us and death would come to him in the appalling loneliness of voluntary exile..."

MIKLÓS SZINAI

AN EVENING WITH THOMAS MANN
AND BÉLA BARTÓK IN BUDAPEST

by

YOLAN HATVANY

The League of Nations used to have an organization called *Coopération Intellectuelle*, one of whose bodies was the *Comité permanent des lettres et des arts*, of which Thomas Mann was a member. It was as a member of this committee that he visited Budapest in June, 1936. The official sessions were scheduled between the 8th and 13th of June, but we—my husband and I—had previously arranged to meet the Manns at the Vienna Westbahnhof on the 6th, proposing to cover the rest of the distance together by car. We had originally intended to drive them to Budapest by way of Lake Balaton, to show them a part of the country that they had not yet seen. However, the torrential rain thwarted our plans, and we drove straight home, without détours.

My memories of this journey always bring back the pleasantest feelings. It was in Vienna we learned that this was Thomas Mann's sixtieth birthday, but we were only able to celebrate the great event properly in the evening, after our arrival. The Manns, however, overcome by the emotional significance of the day, caressed each other's hands with touching tenderness during our journey. We passed the time cheerfully, in pleasant and thoroughly enjoyable conversation, so that we were home in almost no time.

The Manns felt thoroughly at home at our place, for they had quite recently been our guests on several occasions. They were familiar with the house and its habits, they liked being with us, so once again they preferred not to avail themselves of the hotel suite that had been reserved for them.

After dinner I handed Thomas Mann the mail that had accumulated for him. Every time he visited Budapest he received a large number of letters from admirers, asking for autographs and with all sorts of requests and questions. This time, however, the bundle was much more impressive, full of official envelopes embellished with the Hungarian arms, containing official invitations to luncheons, dinners and gala performances at the Opera.

Wherever he received his mail, whether in Budapest, Arosa, or his own home, Mann was in the habit of putting on his glasses and very carefully reading it all. As he looked through the letters and invitations we explained who the writers, who were unfamiliar to him, actually were, and whether he really had to accept or could afford to miss some of these tiring gatherings. He not only patiently listened to our advice and opinion, but in fact took it. All went well, until we came to a dinner invitation from Bálint Hóman, the then Minister of Education. My husband somewhat vehemently and none too diplomatically expounded who Hóman was, and tried to dissuade Mann, as the most important representative of those Germans who had been forced to emigrate in protest against Fascism, from attending the reception at the Gerbeaud Pavilion in the City Park. Mann, on the other hand, argued calmly and dispassionately, saying that this time he was in Budapest not as a private visitor but as the emissary of the League of Nations and a guest of the Hungarian Government. He could not offend his hosts.

The argument had almost reached a stalemate, when I suddenly remembered that Bálint Hóman had been in Berlin only a few days before and that the papers had reported the event. In fact—as far as I could recollect—they had even published photographs. I rushed out of the room, and among the papers that had been put aside I found the issue of the daily *Az Est* for May 27th, in which there was indeed a picture of the friendly handshake between Hóman and Hitler's Minister of Culture, Dr. Rust. This, I thought, would surely do the trick. I waved the paper triumphantly aloft, and when Mann actually *saw* the friendly smiles with which the two *Kultur*-Nazis greeted each other, he promptly and resolutely declared that he would not, even in his official capacity, meet a man who shook hands with Rust. My husband and I were delighted with this resolute and unequivocal stand, for we had been upset at the mere idea that Thomas Mann, the leading personality among the *émigrés*, might appear on a photograph with the same Hóman who had only a few days earlier been photographed with Rust.

The next day Mann wrote a letter to Hóman, politely explaining that he was indisposed and unable to attend the dinner. We sent the letter to the Minister by special messenger.

That was how Thomas Mann came to have a spare evening that night. Since he had already said on the way to Budapest that he would very much like to meet Béla Bartók, we asked him whether he would care to spend it with Bartók. He thought this would be an excellent idea, and my husband immediately rushed to the telephone to ring Bartók. Our phone had two ear-sets, so I quickly reached for the second, so as not to miss a word of the conversation.

"I am calling you, Professor," said my husband, "because Thomas Mann, who should have been at Bálint Hóman's reception tonight, has had to excuse himself, due to an indisposition. Since he now has a free evening, he would like to spend it in your company. Would you be free?"

After a short pause Bartók answered with delightful simplicity: "How strange. I should also have been at that reception, but I am also feeling indisposed."

"Would you care to come along to our place?"

"I shall be very glad to," answered Bartók. "Thank you. I'm coming."

*

It was the express wish of Thomas Mann that we should invite no one else, at all, for he did not want news of his feigned illness to get about. Consequently there were only Bartók, the Manns, ourselves and Béla Reinitz, the composer of the musical settings to Ady's poems and an ardent admirer of Bartók's, who were present, and my duties as a housewife did not preoccupy me too much. I was thus able to watch these two extraordinary men throughout the evening, and I was so intensely aware that this was a unique and wonderful experience that the very recollection still thrills me today, almost thirty years later.

BARTÓK'S ENTRY IN MRS. HATVANY'S ALBUM

After dinner, when the time came for Bartók to sit down to the piano, I felt rather embarrassed at having to make apologies, but since my husband did not allow music near him, they would have to come down to the nursery on the ground floor, where there was only an upright piano available. Bartók asked what make, and I told him it was a Förstner. He reassured me that that would be quite all right, for, he said, "a good upright is very much better than a bad grand." It really did seem to be all right, since, allowing for some short intervals for conversation, he played for almost three hours.

Wonderfully modest and thoughtful, he asked Mann after each piece what he would like to hear next. Mann, who expressed his admiration by murmuring "beautiful! very beautiful!" at intervals, named one Bartók work after another. Each time Bartók wanted to stop, saying that so much music had no doubt exhausted his listeners, Mann made his accustomed gesture of protest to say that he was not tired. "Please go on!" And so this little concert continued till the small hours of the night.

As I look back on that evening I see before me the thin, fragile figure of Bartók, his marvellous head that was translucently clear and brilliant, as though carved from a cube of ice. Thomas Mann's bony, angular face, like a German etching, was tranquil as he reclined at ease on my child's couch. And beside him sat Katia, that most suggestive and most significant of wives.

We held our breaths enraptured, watching and listening to them.

MANN'S ENTRY IN
MRS. HATVANY'S ALBUM

THOMAS MANN AND BARTÓK

from

THOMAS MANN AND HUNGARY

His Correspondence with Hungarian Friends

*

Incidentally, 1931 was a year of travelling in the life of Thomas Mann. He should also have visited Budapest to attend the PEN Congress, but due to his other preoccupations, he excused himself in a letter to Kosztolányi, the president of the Hungarian PEN. In July he attended the Geneva session of the Art and Science Commission of the League of Nations. Of interest from the Hungarian point of view was the attendance at this session of Béla Bartók, who in a lengthy letter, couched in rather sceptical terms, wrote to his mother about the unending meetings of the *"commissions"* and *"sous-commissions."* He also met Thomas Mann. His letter carries a reference to their encounter.

"Thomas Mann too, spoke a few times, always in German; he talked cleverly and in an interesting way..." Bartók wrote. And later on: "There was only one official lunch and one dinner—the lunch given by the secretary of the *Commission*, the dinner by the chairman. The lunch—in a hotel—was excellent, the dinner—in the chairman's lovely home—not so good. I found neither of them unpleasant, for I was able to talk to people who were to my liking. At the dinner I sat next to Mrs. Thomas Mann. I also talked a lot with Thomas Mann... I was made to play the obligatory 'Evening with the Székelys' and 'The Bear Dance.'"

Thomas Mann later again met Bartók in Budapest, at Hatvany's home. János Demény, the excellent historian of music and curator of Bartók's heirloom, sent a letter to Thomas Mann in 1953, asking him to write down his reminiscences concerning the great composer. Thomas Mann answered him on November 21, 1953, from Erlenbach near Zürich:

"Dear Doctor Demény,
Your letter of October 26 has reached me with considerable delay

after diverse roundabouts, via the Frankfurt publisher S. Fischer.

It is with great interest that I have noted your plan to write a book about Béla Bartók, whom I also sincerely respect and whose letters you have already published, and I only regret that I am hardly able to place any important facts at your disposal with respect to my encounters with the great musician.

The rumour that I met Bartók at Mondsee is mistaken. We first met in Budapest at the home of the banker Lukács—father of the critic György Lukács—in the middle 'twenties, as far as I can remember. I believe Bartók then lived at the Lukács's and we too were guests of the house. I especially remember an evening when Bartók's colleague Dohnányi was also present and where—thanks especially to the latter's humour in conversation and at the piano—the time passed very gaily. I was repeatedly together with Bartók at the sessions of the Permanent Science and Art Commission of the League of Nations; we were both members of this commission and the sessions were held in various cities, including Budapest. On this occasion my wife and I visited Bartók at his home, where he played us some of his recordings of African folklore music, which he had made on the spot.

Whenever I saw Béla Bartók, talked to him, or listened to him, I was always deeply impressed not only by his charm, but also by his superior and pure artistic personality, which was expressed even in the beautiful look of his eyes. I have never written about him, but then what musician have I ever written about, apart from the one I invented, the hero of 'Doctor Faustus'?

All I can say is that I am glad of your book, and that it will shortly be possible to read it in German too.

You write that you heard of my encounters with Bartók from Lajos Hatvany. Then the rumours which have been spread about our old friend Hatvany were false, and I am sincerely glad that your letter has enabled us to draw this conclusion. Please forward heartfelt greetings both from me and my wife to Lajos Hatvany.

With the best of wishes,
Your
Thomas Mann"

(The encounter at Mondsee did, in fact, take place—a letter of Bartók's bears witness to the fact. Thomas Mann must have forgotten about this session of the commission.)

*

PÁL RÉZ

A 1932 INTERVIEW WITH BARTÓK

by

MAGDA VÁMOS

Habent sua fata libelli. I do not know to what extent this saying is due to the convulsions that shook Roman history, in more than one case, however, it can, I think, be appropriately applied to the years that preceded the Second World War in Europe, and the period that directly followed it. Otherwise it would be hard to explain how one of the longest, perhaps the longest, interview that Béla Bartók ever gave could have sunk into oblivion.

More than forty years have passed. Now that *The New Hungarian Quarterly* is republishing this conversation with Bartók, which is apparently confined to musical questions, though it moves on many levels, an outline of its background, and the circumstances under which it took place may well be of some interest.

No decent man could remain indifferent to the moral pollution of the environment in the early Thirties. The Cantata Profana, composed in 1930, was a profession of faith in the innocence of art and the decency of man. It goes without saying that an important piece of music outlives by far the political tensions and constellations that prevailed at the time of its birth, contributing to it. They no longer count when listening to Beethoven's Third Symphony, and in the same way concert-goers will soon be unaware of them when attending a performance of the Cantata Profana. Beethoven and Bartók have much in common, to give just one example, possibly one of the most important, they were both committed men, as one says today, they both believed that an extraordinary talent commits to much that goes beyond mere self-expression. In Bartók's case, as in Beethoven's, this awareness was frequently formulated in non-musical terms. After finishing Cantata Profana Bartók wrote to Octavian Beu, a Rumanian fellow musicologist:

" . . . My real idea however, one of which I have been completely conscious since I have known myself to be a composer, is the brotherhood of nations, a brotherhood in spite of war and strife. I try to serve this idea in music, as much as my strength allows; that is why I do not shut myself off from any influence, be the source Slovak, Rumanian, Arab, or any other. But the source must be clean, fresh and healthy!... Others, not I, have to judge whether my style, regardless of the many sources, has a Hungarian character (and that is what counts). I, on my part, feel that it's there. Character and environment must after all be somehow in harmony."

This private letter, written in German, Bartók's German was as good and correct as his Hungarian, was followed that same year by a protest which the New Hungarian Music Society, on Bartók's initiative, submitted to the Societé Internationale pour la Musique Contemporaine as a draft resolution. Bartók himself formulated it. The decent stand taken by the Hungarian section of the society in the Toscanini affair must be particularly appreciated bearing in mind that Hungary at the time was formally allied to Italy, the country where fascist rowdies had the hide to demonstrate viciously against Arturo Toscanini, since he refused to conduct the Giovinezza at performances at La Scala. The one who gained from the whole affair was the Metropolitan Opera House, Italy and Milan were the losers. Bartók, at that time, did not yet consider emigrating as Toscanini had done. What he wanted to do was to preserve the intellectual heritage and the liberties of his country and Europe. The draft resolution formulated by Bartók demanded "a world-wide organization able to defend the freedom of art in an institutionalized way".

That is why, though a busy man, one what is more known to be taciturn and reserved, he took part in the deliberations of the Comité des Arts et des Lettres de la Cooperation Intellectuelle.

The Committee sat in Geneva, in the Palace of the League of Nations, between July 5th and 9th 1931. Bartók attended this meeting. He hoped to submit a resolution on the Toscanini case, but diplomatic over-caution aborted his intention. Bartók was the only musician attending the meeting, they therefore expected a special motion covering music from him. Considerable respect was shown him personally though, out of all those present, Thomas Mann only knew his compositions more or less well. A letter from Bartók to his mother shows that Bartók saw the importance of conferences of that sort not in the diluted and toned down resolutions but knew that "most of the profit lies in the fact that twenty-twenty-five people can meet, get to know each other, and talk to each other".

There is a photograph of the Committee sitting at a horse-shoe shaped table in the Conference Room. Bartók got his signed by the other participants. This photograph, bearing the signatures of Karel Čapek, Thomas Mann, Gilbert Murray, Paul Valéry, Hélène Vacaresco and others, has since appeared in a number of books on Bartók. He only established a closer relationship with Čapek and Thomas Mann and his wife. Bartók sat next to Katja Mann-Pringsheim at the official supper. "I talked a great deal to Thomas Mann as well", he wrote to his mother. Very likely neither Katja nor Thomas Mann were aware what a rare event they witnessed since Bartók only rarely showed an inclination "to talk a great deal".

Ten months after the Geneva meeting the Society for International Intellectual Cooperation held its symposium in Budapest and Esztergom. Even more people attended than at Geneva, perhaps the beautiful spring weather, or the Danube, or Hungarian hospitality attracted them. The *Nouvelle Revue de Hongrie*, a predecessor of *The New Hungarian Quarterly* published in French, issued a special number in May 1932 on this occasion. An hour-long interview with Bartók was considered one of the highlights of this issue, and indeed, it fulfilled the expectations attached to it; in the summer of 1932 *Le Mois—Synthèse de l'activité mondiale*, published in Paris, re-printed it in its entirety, a number of English and American weeklies published extracts, and the interview was translated into Hindustani as well.

It must be said that Béla Bartók is unlikely to have agreed to this interview if he had not considered it important that outstanding European artists and writers should build a bridge over an abyss in which hatred was eddying dangerously, if he had not considered that this organization assembled in the interests of intellectual cooperation had at least the strength of an intention or symbol.

He gave the interview to someone he had never seen before.

Perhaps I will be forgiven for saying a few words about myself, that is about myself forty years ago. I became a professional journalist at an early age. Unfortunately I was equally interested in literature, music and politics. That is how it happened that, right from the start, I wrote on home and foreign affairs, as well as writing book-reviews and music and dramatic criticism. My field in music criticism was strictly limited however, I wrote about operatic performances and *Lieder* recitals only, that is I did not even cover all of vocal music. Owing to the musical education of my youth I was much more at home in the German or Italian musical idiom than in the Hungarian one. It would be a mistake to deny that Bartók and Kodály's work had not yet borne fruit in Hungarian music teaching in the Twenties. As a rule not even the best teachers taught Bartók and Kodály's music. Margit Varró was my teacher at the time when I practised music and did not merely listen to it. She was an outstanding teacher of the piano whose books on new methods in piano teaching appeared in a number of languages. She emigrated to the United States before the War, continuing to teach there to a ripe old age. Bartók as well thought highly of Margit Varró's work, and that really was something. As time passes Bartók the composer is increasingly recognised as a classic, and Bartók the pianist tends to be forgotten. Whatever I may have said about the musical idiom my own aged generation was brought up in does not alter the fact that already in early youth, that is starting around the middle Twenties, I considered Bartók to be the most important pianist in Central Europe. The linear severity of his playing, the strength of the discipline controlling the demonic power inside him, showed the structure of a work more clearly than anyone else did at the time. It was as if a Shakespeare had shown himself to be the greatest actor even when speaking the words of other playwrights.

The piano opened Bartók's doors to me, both in a literal and a metaphoric sense. My teacher, Margit Varró, gave me a letter of introduction, and she also "introduced me" over the telephone when we arranged a time for me to call at Bartók's house in Kavics utca, in the Buda hills.

The path up to the Rose Hill house where Bartók occupied a flat on the First Floor was pretty steep. The ground above and behind was still free of buildings at the time. Silence reigned, and horizons were distant, the Danube islands and the outline of the town built on the Pest plain were within reach of the eye.

Silence and eyes that reached distant horizons: that was the first impression I had of Bartók as we shook hands. He had only recently returned from Egypt, his complexion was tanned by the sun, but his handsome figure still looked fragile, and in need of protection. His manner reminded me of outstanding mathematicians whom I knew, there was nothing "arty" about him. Simplicity, an effort to be precise, concealed wit—that is what I observed. The edge of his irony was playful rather than biting.

If I remember right we sat in two large leather arm-chairs, books, scores, magazines behind us, pianos in front of us. I had barely arrived and we had something to drink when Bartók's son Péter, who was eight at the time, burst in, showing no intention of leaving. His father told him not to disturb our conversation and he found a place under the piano opposite, between the pedals and right-hand leg. He crouched there right to the end without batting an eye-lid, observing us for a full hour. He came out from his hiding-place when we said good-bye. "Why didn't you ask me anything?" he said with a certain sound of reproach in his voice.

Then, like a little gentleman, he took me down to the gate, right down the steep slope of the garden.

I never saw Péter again. I met his father once again in the flat of Dt. Gyula Holló, whose patients we both were. Dr Holló was not only an outstanding scientist, but an outstanding man and amateur musician as well. His wife, also a doctor, was her husband's assistant. The Holló couple moved to New York feeling threatened by the Nazis, before Bartók and his wife did. Though there cannot be a moment's doubt that Bartók was prompted to emigrate by the unbearable state of the political atmosphere, the fact that Dr. Holló and his wife moved to America also played a role in his decision.

But that is another story.

As is one, which as far as I know remains unrecorded, concerning the desire of many politicians in Hungary in the months following the war, to invite Bartók to be the first Head of State of the new Hungarian Republic. Such plans were put an end to by Bartók's death in October 1945. The divided world of the time had stopped news of his mortal illness reaching Hungary.

The number of contemporary witnesses is dwindling, and these stories will perhaps remain unrecorded for ever.

Just as it is I alone who remains to vouch for the authenticity of our conversation. The interview was first recorded in Hungarian, then I translated it into French myself. Bartók carefully checked both the Hungarian and French versions and signed them. The MSS were destroyed, as were all the other files of the *Nouvelle Revue de Hongrie*.

A good many Bartók scholars have started work since then, others have continued with their labours. I had hoped that this major interview would also be dug out by them, but this did not happen. Much was buried too deep by the vicissitudes of time.

That is why, on the fortieth anniversary of the conversation, I myself asked the library of the Hungarian Academy of Sciences—Bartók had been on the staff of the Academy for the last six years of his stay in Budapest—to photocopy the original publication of the *Nouvelle Revue de Hongrie*.

T he sun-bathed crest of a hill dominating the town. Green meadows. Stairs cut in the hillside lead to a solitary villa: Béla Bartók's home. His room is fitted with peasant furniture of the land of the Székely. Letters and parcels from all parts of the world are stacked on the soberly carved timber table-top. At the age of twenty-five the young Hungarian composer, famous for his research into Hungarian folk music to which no one had responded with such intensity, had already captured the attention of the world of music; today, at fifty, he is one of the un-contested masters of modern music whose works are now becoming more generally admired.

Squeezed between two huge pianos in the maestro's studio, in whom a virtuoso, a scholar, a collector of folk-songs and a composer have merged to achieve an amazing equilibrium, we are talking of the relation of art-music and folk-music, of the role of Hungarians in music, and of the search for new ways, the great problem of all art today.

Béla Bartók is not fond of long speeches. A peculiar, not very modern, quality characterizes him: a respect for words. I almost said: a fear of what they may evoke. Even when speaking he is overwhelmed by the scruples of artistic creation. He stresses and chooses each word with the studied precision and anxious thoroughness of the scholar.

*

I began with a statement and a question. "While music is usually referred to as an abstract art, it is undeniable that it too reflects the artistic features of a given period. There exists, for instance, an intimate relationship between Debussy and the Barbizon school, or rather the impressionists. Similarly, Schumann has given musical form to the high fevers and the petty sentimentality of romanticism, and the dynamic conflicts and volcanic forces of the Revolution pulsated in Beethoven's music. Despite all individual and material differences an opera by Meyerbeer, a canvas by Delacroix and a poem by Victor Hugo create a stylistic impression—undefineable yet defined—which correlates them like parts of a single entity. Nowadays, or shall we say once again, a young and vigorous style appears to be more prominent in the arts—and here I am thinking of architecture and, maybe, literature in the first place. The names might differ. 'Populism' or 'neue Sachlichkeit' it does not make much difference what you call it, is here to stay. Neither sentimentalism nor romantic fervour seem to agree with the spirit of our time. At this point various questions will arise: what are the musical means helping to develop this style? What are its musical characteristics? Can it be felt in the new music as strongly as in the new architecture or new literature?"

"I do not think we can tell"—the Maestro said. "What we actually see is chaos: there are various trends, explorations, efforts, experimentations. Mere fumbling. There is but one trait which seems to be clearly outlined: a total rejection of the nineteenth century. But we really are too close to that to see things in the proper perspective.

"But you are a peak and from a peak it is easier to survey the whole, don't you agree?"

(Smiling). "A nice thought. As for myself: I know very well what I want to express. That much is true. But you cannot exclude the possibility that one who looks at things from a distance will see the peaks and the outlines more clearly.

Well, you seem to believe that harshness is the dominating tone in modern art. I would not say that. Disillusion? Simplicity? These are appearences only. In nearly every great modern musical work one may, in fact, perceive an effort towards a clarity of construction, a rigorous severity of composition coupled with a tendency to do without flourishes. At this point there may be a connection with the style you just mentioned. But modern simplicity is just a moment of condensation within a complex evolution."

"You have often emphasized how much peasant music has to teach, particularly from the point of view of this simplicity."

"That is right. The tunes of peasant music—in the strictest sense of the term—actually embody the highest artistic perfection. Still, whenever one discusses this subject it is indispensable to define one's terms. This is a point I keep stressing in my books and published papers. Even Ferenc Liszt, in the absence of scientific material and the necessary documents, operated with erroneous concepts when writing on Hungarian folk-music and on so-called "Gypsy" music. What is usually called Gypsy music— and maybe some day we shall be able to slowly convince the public of this— that is tunes played by Gypsy bands, are mostly compositions by dilettante members of the Hungarian middle class, town dwellers or landed gentry. Hungarian amateurs compose and sing these songs and the Gypsies merely play them. Anyone can observe that usually neither the Gypsy band-leader nor his musicians will sing. It is true that the Hungarian public will also play such melodies on instruments: piano, violin, cymbalum, but only at home or with friends. When it comes to performing this popular music in public, for money, that is the business of Gypsy bands, a Hungarian gentleman of old would never lend himself to so menial a task. True, times have changed but the dissemination of Hungarian folk-music and urban music has remained the monopoly of Gypsies. At most one could add that this music is played "à la tzigane" which seems to be the only original element contributed by the Gypsy nation to Hungarian art-music composed in the popular fashion.

Even here there remains a doubt and as for myself, I would be inclined towards the opposite view. Those who cannot imagine a Gypsy without a fiddle are gravely mistaken. Most of the Gypsies in Hungarian villages do not play any kind of instrument. It is true they have their own songs which they sing in the Gypsy language, but the melodies are usually borrowed from the neighbouring peasant population. Those few original songs sung on rare occasions by Gypsies in Hungarian villages have neither colour nor depth, and they have nothing in common with the tunes played by the Gypsies in towns. Incidentally, Gypsies have acted as performers in Hungary's musical life only since the 18th century. Still, even today the proportion of these musicians is rather low. Among Hungarian Gypsies no more than 6 per cent earn their living this way and their musical stock as well as style is by no means homogeneous. In remote villages they will play exactly the same pieces as the peasants and in exactly the same manner. The nearer one gets to civilization and the bigger towns, the more this style changes; finally, in big cities one meets those so-called "folk"-songs and those mannerism of execution known throughout the world by the name of "Gypsy music". It seems to me that this style and this manner were produced by the environment rather than by the character of the Gypsies', were it otherwise, the village Gypsies would play exactly in the same way as the urban ones. It is an open point whether the said manner of playing, customarily called the Gypsy manner, has been determined and shaped by the Hungarian classes just like their stock of tunes. I'm inclined to answer this question in the affirmative."

"You were just speaking of the excesses of the Gypsy manner. Maybe they are inseparable from the sentimental—sometimes shocking—exaggeration abounding in both the tunes and the words of pseudo-folk-music. Incidentally, nineteenth-century composers have freely borrowed from the elements of folk-music. Why, take Chopin who stands for the national romanticism characterizing his time, besides his own incredibly individual style. His Polonaises and other piano pieces of a Polish tenor have inspired similarly national works in other countries, national in rhythm and melody. What we are witnessing is a steadily spreading and systematic utilization of motives borrowed from folk-music, though in most cases the aim is just to achieve a decorative effect. Everyone knows that Hungarian motives are frequently encountered in Haydn's or Beethoven's music; and Liszt's Hungarian rhapsodies and Brahms' Hungarian dances art widely known. In the case of both of these composers the influence of Hungarian folk-music is often apparent. Towards the middle and the end of the 19th century the "national" element played an increasing role in European music, particularly with the Slavs and Scandinavians. It was precisely the utilization of the musical folklore by Grieg which had enchanted certain composers who came under his influence. Nevertheless we have reason to believe that in 19th-century music the famous "national" character was based on motives and tunes borrowed from the "popular" music of the upper classes rather than on genuine peasant music."

"This is so. The discovery of peasant music was left to the first years of the twentieth century. It is true that even last century, in western countries, folk elements lent colour and enriched great musical compositions, contributing something new and original; still, in the last analysis, these elements were treated in the routine manner and mostly mixed with romantic sentimentalism."

"Say sentimentalism and you've said prolixity. Peasants in general, and Hungarian peasants in particular, are sparing of speech. What, then, has led modern Hungarian music, art-music that is, to discover real Hungarian peasant music?"

"In the first place this: the great example of conciseness. An antique simplicity that will spurn all florid flourishes. Among Hungarians, and this is true also of their Rumanian or Slovak neighbours, and other East-European nations as well, peasant tunes show great conciseness, a clear-cut form, and neat outlines that cannot be surpassed. These melodies are the classical examples of the art of expressing any musical idea with the highest perfection, in the shortest form, and using the simplest and most direct means.
Much has been said about the intimate relationship between mathe-

matics and music. Whether this is mathematics or music, the most perfect form has been achieved when all that has to be said is said and not one iota more."

"It is true that in all human thought and art facility has its dangers. Often the spirit may spark to the disadvantage of depth; ultimately routine will kill the intensity of expression. On the other hand, real folk music, that is peasant music, gushes forth naturally from life's spring and from the great antique rhythms: thus it is, in the purest meaning of the word, the source to which one must constantly return."

"When twenty or twenty-five years ago, we were carrying out a thorough investigation of Hungarian peasant music in the field, many people were astonished, and they were sorry to see trained musicians, authors of original compositions, devote several years' intensive work just to collecting peasant music. These persons did not have an inkling of what it meant for us and —now it can be told—for the subsequent progress of Hungarian art music, to have had such a direct contact with peasant music. Still, the fact is that folk-art cannot have a fertile influence on a composer unless he knows the peasant music of his native country just as thoroughly as he does his mother tongue.

In this way folk music will flow through the veins of the composer and the idiom of peasant music will have become his own musical language which he will use spontaneously, involuntarily and naturally just like a poet uses his mother-tongue. In this country the most striking and magnificent example of this can be found in the case of Kodály. It is enough to think of the "Psalmus Hungaricus" in order to be aware of the victorious strength drawn by modern Hungarian art-music from delving into the Hungarian soil in the midst of roots that go deep and are alive."

"Don't you find that at the end of the last and at the beginning of this century, it was principally composers belonging to small nation or such as were at some distance from western civilization who marched at the head of musical movements? The motifs of western folk-music had been amply exploited by the great masters, so much so that the powerful impact of peasant music has, lately, benefited mainly the composers of Eastern Europe and of the small nations. Don't you agree that this explains much, and we should keep in mind that nowadays it is Hungarian, Russian, Czech and other national composers who represent progressive European music in the greatest number and in the most expressive manner; I would even venture to say that they are the most worthy of this European music."

"Let us beware of generalizations. The fact is that the impact made by the discovery of the peasant music of Eastern-Europe has been very strong and in many ways perhaps even decisive. What you have said sounds likely. Incidentally, it is interesting to observe that—as a rule—it is the small countries and chiefly the oppressed nations who devote themselves most passionately to the collection and study of their folk-music.

It is only natural that modern art-music, and not only Hungary owes much of its idiom to such research and to a knowledge of peasant music. This idiom and the particular characteristics which are the result of organic development will surprise reactionaries and may mislead many before they are able to understand their intricate relations. The melodic turns of East-European peasant music have led to new conceptions of harmony. We have elevated the seventh to the role of assonance for the simple reason that in Hungarian pentatonic folk-songs it is an interval with no less a role than that of the third or fifth. This equality, which our ears have often perceived in the sequence of sounds, we have also tried to make felt in simultaneity. In other words we have united the four sounds in a single assonant chord. Similarly, the frequency in which passages in fourths occur in our old melodies has inspired us to create fourth-chords, we have simply projected onto a vertical plane what used to follow on a horizontal one.

For instance, the fact that peasant tunes are not based on the stereotype pattern of the combination of triads has freed us from certain shackles, thus making possible, entirely new and free harmonies. We have been able to illuminate these melodies in various ways by greatly differing chords and tonalities. The fact that polytonality has appeared in Hungarian music, and in Stravinsky's works, can be explained, on the whole, by this possibility. It should be stressed that this has not been the result of a random change or accidental contingency but rather of an organic evolution having its roots in folk-music."

"Don't you find it interesting, Maestro, that the musical idiom is not the only thing to have been upset, but other arts have been as well. It appears that each period in art has its own favourite genre which flourishes at the time. Would you agree that the opera is stagnating, that it can be even said to be in a state of decadence?"

"This is so. No successful opera, or one which has proved viable, has been written since Puccini. Still, at this point the disadvantageous position of the small nations becomes more pregnant. In Hungary, for instance, the absence of good librettos has contributed a great deal to this stagnation. The composer's task is aggravated by the tyranny of the text, and in the case of a small nation the choice will necessarily be restricted. But in a general way yes, one may speak of the decadence of opera.

Incidentally, it seems to me that the fashion of suites consisting of short pieces, and generally the vogue contenting itself with short genres and forms must be connected with the faster tempo of the modern way of life. One may say, without exaggeration, that, nowadays, it no longer pays to write a long-winded work."

"It is striking that the element of parody should be so widespread in contemporary music and is still gaining ground. At this point I am not referring to the healthy ancestral humour of folk-art but rather to refined, even degenerate, parody, to musical coarseness, the cartoon, the petty grimaces, this mania of self-mockery. When all is said and done, shouldn't we see in this the expression, or negative proof, of an absence of real creative power?"

"That may be true to a certain degree. Right now these may be temporary phenomena only, striking our eyes. The taste for parody, incidentally, is not of such recent date as one might think. Berlioz, for one, was fond of it.

"Jazz indulges in such effects. Can it be that contemporary compositions are showing the influence of jazz?"

"(Smiling). What do I think of jazz? It is a clever thing, to which melody owes many of its happy elements and rhythms, owes much that is new, all valuable in their own way. True, the harmonies are mostly banal and poor."

"While we are at this point, what is your opinion on the future development of Hungarian peasant music? May we hope that it will not die out in this age of talkies, the wireless, the grammophone and jazz, threatened as it is by a multitude of alien influences?"

"Being a prophet is unrewarding. In any case it is worth mentioning that in addition to the old pentatonic style of Hungarian peasant music, tunes that are no longer sung except by old people, we have encountered a new and flourishing style, characterized by a lively, vigorous rhythm, and a symmetrical and orderly structure. These new-style melodies date from the last seventy or eighty years and several of them from the very 20th century. It is not likely that anything will arrest the development of peasant music. However, naturally, jazz may well leave its impact: certain features and certain elements of jazz may be absorbed by the powerful organism of peasant music only to be transformed and differentiated within it."

"A great many—and I don't mean laymen only—cannot or will not hear the melody in peasant music and its contemporary adaptations. But going on from peasant music to modern art-music, and I want to make it clear that what I am goig to say does not apply to yours or Zoltán Kodály's, music-lovers and even those who love the grand-style mostly have a confused feeling deep in their hearts that the works of the most progressive members of this school are wanting in melody. One might say that melody has been relegated into the background and invention—deliberately or otherwise—plays a lesser role. I should like to know your opinion, as that of one of the outstanding representatives of modern music. And at this point, could you tell me, which of these three elements, that is rhythm, harmony and melody, can be considered the most important today?"

"(Without hesitation). Melody. Today as ever. In my opinion those who find the works of modern composers to be poor in melodic invention are entirely wrong. Melody is still the "body" of the work just as it was with the old masters. If the public and those critics who are unable to get rid of clichés fail to notice this, why, it is the public and the critics who are at fault, not the composers.

After hearing an adaptation of a Székely folk-song, an English critic wrote recently that it was interesting but there was no use looking for a melody in it. Not to hear a melody in a folk-song! That is revealing. A folk-song without a melody: that is utter nonsense. But no matter how simple and clear the melodic line may be, once it clashes with the settled notions of the "initiates", they will fail to understand anything."

Bartók then discussed his working methods.

"Instinctive and conscious elements must be in equilibrium within the creative imagination. In my view the importance attached to the originality of the theme is one of the characteristic exaggerations of the past century. It is not so much the theme which matters but rather what the artist can make of it. All art has the right, even the duty, of looking for links and lessons in preceding ages. Let us recall how many formulae Johann Sebastian Bach, the greatest of them, borrowed from his contemporaries and pre-decessors. The big test of a real talent will be the form he lends to this loan.

The dominant current of modern music is based on the powerful impulse of folk-melodies expressive of the national soul. It is from that direction that rejuvenation has and will come. In the creative ages bent on inter-preting collective feelings, it is natural that the artists should draw from the great common source. But before folk-music can achieve its full artistic significance, it is necessary that, in the hands of a real creative talent, it should become capable of acting on the art-music. One thing is certain, those who speak of a poverty of invention and poverty of melody, are mistaken. Despite the arrival of the machine age the powerful stream of music throbbing with life's eternal rhythm will never dry up. And the source of this stream—particularly in the countries devoid of musical tradi-tions—will always be found in folk-music. Let me conclude with Zoltán Kodály's beautiful words: what folk-music means to us is no less than the organic life of a great national tradition."

BARTÓK TODAY

BARTÓK AND THE PUBLIC

Soon it will be fifteen years since Bartók died. The time is long enough to see the fate and influence of his art in a certain perspective. True, this perspective does not span centuries, nevertheless, the trend of development may be clearly discerned. His life-work is final, concluded, and cannot be further enriched; but the opinion, response, and demands of his audiences may—and do —change.

It would be commonplace to speak these days about the growing popularity of Bartók's music. I therefore prefer to give a few characteristic examples to illustrate the slow, almost imperceptible process of change in attitude, instead of presenting figures and data.

*

Let us first take a look at the older generation.

A year and a half ago, I had a conversation with an old lady, who was one of Bartók's childhood playmates. They lived in neighbouring houses, they were friends of the same age. Their friendship even came to be tinged with a kind of adolescent love—the boy composed his first songs for her and sent them to Nagyszöllős from Pozsony (now Bratislava) where he had gone to live. I made notes of what she could tell me about Bartók's childhood at Nagyszöllős. Then she asked:

"Is it true that all the world over he is mentioned along with Bach and Beethoven?"

Her question showed incredulity, although she apparently knew the answer. She knew, and yet she was amazed that the boy with whom she had played and the young man whose art she could never understand, had grown into one of the great men in the history of human genius. Doubt and amazement were nevertheless accompanied by an expression of admiring satisfaction at the thought that the strange boy

with the peculiar, stern look in his eyes had after all been right.

This reminds me of another picture of Bartók as a boy, described in his memoires by Sándor Albrecht, an eminent Pozsony musician who died recently. When he sat down at the piano at home, Bartók always played "Evening with the Székelys," because —as he explained—"this is the only piece of mine that Mama likes." Actually, his mother felt and knew that her son was a genius; but though she strove to understand his art she could never quite grasp it.

Let us skip one or two generations.

Judit is five years old. She has no particular liking for music, nor are her parents fond of it; she hears little about Bartók at home, and what is said is far from complimentary. Judit loves to draw and paint.

"When I grow up I shall paint pictures. As wonderful ones as Béla Bartók."

When we told her that Bartók was not a painter but a composer, she shook her head with imperturbable conviction. "No, Bartók painted, wrote poems, and made songs. He could do everything. He was like Sándor Petőfi."

I looked at her in astonishment. How did the child know so accurately where to place Bartók, I wondered. To my question of who had told her so, she replied indignantly, with evident contempt for my ignorance:

"Who? Why, everybody knows that."

I admit that this story does not reflect the general situation and that Judit's attitude is not based on thorough knowledge of Bartók's works. But, as a rule, Hungarian children learn to know the name of Sándor Petőfi long before hearing or reading his poems. And now another name has joined that of Petőfi. Children do not—cannot— know the source, yet they realize that the recognition of Bartók's greatness is "in the air."

Let us now take the most important age groups, the adult and middle-aged, in essence those who actually make up the majority of audiences today. Aversion, scepticism, and lack of comprehension are encountered, as well as appreciation, love, and enthusiasm. The most interesting phenomenon appears in the alteration that is taking place in the response of these age groups.

I have heard of numerous people who, actuated by superficial experiences or influenced by the opinions of those around them, assumed a negative attitude towards new Hungarian music. Upon closer acquaintance, however, they were amazed to find that they liked it.

For instance, quite recently I heard about a pretty, active, thoroughly modern young girl of 18—who, by the way, is first class at sports. A friend of hers, a young man, got her some tickets for a series of concerts of works by Bartók and Kodály. The girl likes music, but when she heard about the program she pursed her lips. At her parents' wish, she was to be chaperoned by her brother. On the evening of the first concert, they both got ready and went reluctantly, abusing the young man who had let them in for such questionable entertainment.

Then the miracle happened. They sat through the first concert, were impressed by the second, greatly enjoyed the third, and the fourth concert was attended by the whole family. Since then they have bought portraits of Bartók and Kodály, which are seen quite frequently on the walls of apartments of Hungarian professional people.

An old friend of mine has had a similar experience. He used to find Bartók's music inaccessible. (I remember very well when the "Cantata Profana" was broadcast by Radio Budapest round about 1942. A small party of 16- to 20-year-old boys and girls sat together, but the music was not to their taste and they shut off the radio.) Now he has watched the "Miraculous Mandarin" and later listened to a performance of the "Concerto". The "miracle" happened in this case, too. What used to sound strange, now thrilled his inmost being. He could not quite understand this music, it was still peculiar, unusual for him. Nevertheless, he found that it gave expression to some of his feelings and ideas. "It seems I have changed," he said, "I have had to go through a world of experiences to come to understand Bartók."

I do not wish to draw any far-reaching conclusions from these examples. However, it is a fact that a few decades ago Bartók concerts drew very limited audiences, whereas at present his compositions are among the most popular items on the concert programs.

*

I should like to add just one more example to those quoted above, about those who became devoted to Bartók's art in their youth, from 15 to 25 years ago; about those who, in pre-liberation Hungary, found in Bartók's music an expression of their discontent and their search for something new.

Much could and should be written about the meaning of Bartók and Kodály for that generation, which saw them not only as two great masters among the pioneers of an interesting trend in music, but also as symbols: symbols of all that was Hungarian and European. The preservation of traditions and the search for new paths, the rejection of the existing order and approval of a new one, the people and the ideas of revolution were blended in this symbolism. Avowed adherence to their art implied declaration not only of one's aesthetic attitude but also one's human, national, and political standpoint. I have known men and women to whom appreciation of Bartók was a precondition of marriage, because they could not envisage a lifelong partnership with anyone who disagreed in this. The same feature came to prevail in friendships: those devoted to new Hungarian music felt tied to one another by the bonds of a common movement.

One day it would be worth subjecting the political components of this movement to minute examination. Repressed passions came to the fore, and even if we find that they were not free from the shackles of nationalism and a romantic view of the people, it is evident that the art of Bartók guided considerable numbers to the left, towards the people, against fascism, and in the direction of socialism.

To speak with the members of that generation about Bartók today is an interesting experience. Many of them affirm that the way they now listen to and hear his music is different from what it used to be. When they were adolescents, surrounded by an obtuse public, they found that the most powerful attraction emanated from the novelty, the bold forms, the peculiar atmosphere of this music. Bartók was strikingly new, completely different from what had been recognized as music until then. It was this difference which pleased those who had become accustomed to a sense of aversion to everything which existed and was approved officially.

Take dissonance, for instance. Supercilious disparagement disposed of new Hungarian music by branding it as dissonant, adding sometimes that it sounded Rumanian. Its defenders knew the theory and could readily explain that dissonance and consonance were not perpetual categories ordained by God, but that harmony varied with various ages. They knew all this, to be sure. Now they confess that they were no less conscious of this dissonance than Bartók's adversaries but that was exactly what they liked, this spirit of revolt and the opposition they were craving for.

And today? I have heard many people say that those who at the time enjoyed Bartók's music on account of its unprecedented, extremely novel character and dissonance, are taken aback at the realization that the same compositions affect them quite differently and appear to be simple, self-evident, clear, and comprehensible.

In order to understand a composition one must hear it several times. The essence of music can be grasped or at least felt without any harmonic or formal analysis. Yet there is something that is indispensable and best expressed by saying that the listener must always sense what is coming.

Those who are not "accustomed" to the music of Bartók refuse to believe that there are people who know, or sense, what is coming—for example—in the "Miraculous Mandarin" even when they like the music, they think that it cannot be memorized, they have an impression of patches of music streaming forth according to a pattern of unfathomable logic and are astonished when they hear allusions to the world of melody created by Bartók.

The creative master lives in a world of his own thoughts, feelings, and aesthetic aspirations; so does his audience. And if the artist has a message to communicate, the audience is there to receive it. The relationship between the two, the development of this relationship, make art history. Message and reception are not always in agreement. The public often meets the artist only on one plane; various ages discover different aspects of the artist's message. At first hearing, Bartók, if one may say so, would seem to be more romantic and at the same time more expressionist than after repeated hearing. The novelty, the shattering strength of his art, which penetrates into the depths of the soul and the nerves, are recognized by the hearer sooner than its beauty, logic, and perfection.

It is as if Bartók had changed, whereas, in fact, we ourselves have changed. For the Hungarian public his art then represented the trend of extreme innovation; now, in the face of the latest western trends, Bartók will soon begin to count as a conservative musician. And although our knowledge of these endeavours is still deficient, in Bartók's art we have come to recognize with increasing clarity his moderation and classical infallibility. To many people in the Hungary of the Horthy era, the art and artistic program of Bartók represented a possible form of expression for suppressed revolutionary impulses. Since then we have gone through the horrors of war and seen the visions of Bartók assume the shape of terrifying reality. But we have also witnessed the downfall of fascism, a revolutionary social change, the sweeping away of feudalism, the foundation of a social order based on common ownership.

It is understandable that from the infinite and extreme intricacies of his art we at that time somehow responded to the element which revealed contradictions and opposed decay and destruction. I remember, the Music for String Instruments, Celesta and Percussion Instruments then acted on us as a drama of the nerves, concentrating every horror, fear, and dread of the age, and the struggle of our will to bring down everything with one powerful, culminating blow of our clenched fists. The relentless defiance of the last bars made us feel as if it were not the end but a beginning, a stubborn banging of the table, driving away terror and bringing promise of a new life. Today, this work has another message, or at least the proportions have altered. Frightening visions still loom, but the will that overcomes terror, compels it into order, and rises above it, is felt more keenly. We feel this victory not only at the end, but all the time while we listen; we sense the will to order whereby even struggle is resolved into beauty.

All these are subjective emotions despite the fact that they are shared by so many. It is nevertheless important to speak about them, because the emotional response of the audience is also significant. Those who learn to know the art of Bartók through such an approach, gain fuller initiation, because it includes this purification, this lofty freedom, and also the supreme victory. It is thereby rendered accessible to

men of future ages who will be spared contradictions and will enjoy victory, progress, and the experience and demands of creation. The art of the future will presumably present the problems of our age, the era that saw the revolutionary transformation of life, in a different way and in different dimensions, but Bartók's art with its monumental integration of extremes will suffer no eclipse.

This victory, advance, and purification can be truly understood today only by those who in the past understood the opposition, the revolt, and the protest against inhumanity.

*

In a recent statement, Igor Stravinsky refers to Bartók's work in connection with folk-songs as a pardonable but fundamentally unnecessary pastime for a great man. However, Bartók did not collect and search for folk-songs to while away his leisure-time or discover ideas to stimulate his creative imagination. This work meant much more for him: it was a means of expressing his aesthetic attitude and his view of the world.

I have found that for many people the incorporation of this view and attitude in the music of Bartók (and naturally of Kodály too) is of decisive importance. After the turn of the century, art searched for a way whereby to probe into the unknown depths of the soul, to penetrate into the unfathomed primeval layers of impulse, will, fear, and sorrow. The art of Bartók also says: what you are seeking is here, in the art of the people, in the will, the sorrows, passions, and joys of the people. They have always lived there, but have often escaped notice. Now, at the great turning-point of history we re-discover, accept, and identify ourselves with them, and, in the process, learn to find ourselves.

The message that reaches the listener naturally depends also on subjective elements. Many people hear this too in

Bartók's music. Others deny this relation to folk music and declare that its influence may be discerned only sporadically. The argument is not an easy one, for anyone who lacks knowledge of the people through experience can hardly understand those who have such knowledge.

The life-work of Bartók nevertheless provides evidence of close connection with the fate of the people. One might quote Bartók's words about the people, about serving the nation, about friendship among peoples. Or let us remember that he did not find it satisfactory to learn folk-songs from musical scores; he thought it best to go to the people, learn to know their lives, share with them the experience of their music. Bartók's fundamental experience was really derived from the people and not from folk music, pentatonic music, or any specific feature of folk music.

This was not an immaterial or adjunctive element in his art; it is that which made him become more than a mere innovator and has raised him to the height of personifying the great artistic aspirations of the first half of the century.

To quote the words of Kodály: "Bartók's works possess the mysterious, living, life-giving force which is absent from many compositions that are outwardly similar. For many musicians have in the past half century attempted to compose new music, that is to say, the new spirit arising universally has striven for artistic expression in many of them, but few have been able to evolve a lasting form for their message. Bartók is one of the few and has therefore become one of the composers whose works are played the most frequently all over the world."

Bartók embraces the extremes. He not only passes through the inferno but also shows the way out. His inferno is an awe-inspiring world, and it requires formidable strength to defy and vanquish it. The strength of one man is not sufficient, the whole people must enter the lists, the people who have gone through innumerable centuries of hell but have not been broken. It is by no means accidental that with Bartók the tone of strength and of serenity comes from the people, for instance, in the final movements of the "Divertimento," of "Music," of the "Concerto," promising resolution, and giving voice to direct folk motives.

This "mysterious force," this will, and the expression of action that overwhelms meditation, are understood also by those who fail to recognize their popular source and perceive them only as a power.

But knowing the source gives one a better understanding.

IVÁN VITÁNYI

BARTÓK'S HERITAGE

A composer's view

by

ISTVÁN LÁNG

Everyone who composes music in Hungary today, must confront Bartók. This means that Bartók's life and works—and here I am thinking not only of his compositions, research, teaching activity and performance on the piano, but also most emphatically of his personal attitudes—have become a yardstick which cannot be ignored. His monumental personality is undoubtedly not only a standard, but also projects a giant shadow that is difficult to throw off. It is certain however, that for us it was more important to acquire a basis of evaluation by which we could measure not only our own accomplishments but those of Hungarian music in general.

It is this Bartókian standard which definitively and unmistakeably—and in addition to the place he occupies in music history as such—relates Liszt for example, to the history of Hungarian music. These two great personalities supplement each other delineating their national characteristics even through they are remote in time from each other, and though the intellectual ties that link them, are difficult to trace.

It is undeniable however, that not a single significant contemporary composer could isolate himself from Bartók's influence. But one only feels that someone has not been able to step out from under this shadow, if one senses a direct Bartók influence, or to use stronger language, if a composer is clearly an epigone. Most of the time however, this is found only in less important composers.

More important however, is the fact that Bartók's works are a musical revelation with which one can form a direct communion. This relation can develop into a national style of composition, and can create a national music idiom which, as in Bartók's case, can be synthesised with the most modern composing techniques, and which is truly Hungarian in tone and yet readily understood everywhere. I believe that a Hungarian national school is being formed in Bartók's wake that shows similarities with the Polish situation, but its significance must be proved not only in Hungary, but primarily abroad.

*

In Bartók's composing an endeavour to lift prosaic matters into mythical spheres is always evident. This is unmistakeably clear in his stage works and in *Cantata Profana*. It is my opinion however, that the same is true of the Bartók tunes that make use of the folksongs of various nations.

For Bartók folksong never replaced the essential parts of a composition. He rarely used folksong in a composition as a substitute for the melodic material of various formal sections. He dug deeper than that. He synthesised the spirit of folksong with the most modern composing technique. This was how he built a bridge between the past and the present, for the benefit of the future, that is for us, in whose works folksong appears in the same abstract fashion as in German music after Bach, not in the voice but in tone.

Here I must mention the difference that is evident in folksong arrangements by Bartók and other Hungarian composers. Generally, folksong was embedded in bucolic musical material, even if depicting tragedy. Bartók emphasized the rustic elements. For him rusticity also meant leaving children's and lyrical songs in their original, naive charm, but expressing through harmony the harsh, crude and if you please, less civilized social medium and living conditions in which folksongs were born and in which the original performer lived.

*

Ernő Lendvai has shown that the rule of the golden section predominates in Bartók's compositions. At the same time, the laws governing classical form are also quite evident in Bartók's works. This duality somewhat resembles the phenomenon of interference in physics. Waves in a coinciding phase, reinforce each other while those in a displaced phase weaken each other. Perhaps the particular strength of Bartók's compositions is due to the fact that these dual laws of form construction pulsate together in a common phase multiplying each other's effect many times over.

Lendvai's research put the time concepts originally expressed in Bartók's compositions on an abstract level. In other words, whether he is counting in note values or searching for proportions according to bars, he ignores the natural agogics of the music, that is, equal note values are not really equal in practice. Since however, the formal plan in which the proportions of the golden section "interfere", is itself an abstraction, the result of the analysis is a synthesis of the two abstractions. It is my belief that detailed analysis would also reveal that the contrast between the time proportions of the music when it is actually played and the actual proportions of the formal plan equally multiplies the effect of both principles of construction. Perhaps at some time in the future it will be possible to measure at any given moment in a work how the two principles of form reinforce each other, lending particular force to the effulgence of the message.

*

Bartók's constant capacity for renewal is well known. Even so, what is the meaning of the frequent repetition of certain types of movements in his compositions?

The slow movements of the *Piano Concertos Nos. 2. and 3., Sonata for Two Pianos* and the *Concerto for Viola*, are generally constructed according the following pattern: after a first section in a slow, calm rhythm, follows musical material demanding a fast, virtuoso technique, sometimes dramatic and in a tense rhythm, returning in variations to the material of the first section. (This is also from a superficial point of view the form of the slow movement of Tchaikovsky's *Piano Concerto in B Flat Minor*.) Can this really be regarded as repetition, since the thematic features, except for form, do not bind the movements together? It is true that the central movements of the *Piano Concertos Nos. 2. and 3.* show further similarities in the responses between the piano and the orchestra. Indeed, the rubato in the reprise section of the *Piano Concerto No. 2.* even recalls a similar point in the *Piano Concerto No. 1.*, and the portrayals of nature's nocturnal rustlings and stirrings are similar in the middle sections of the slow movements of the *Piano Concerto No. 3.*, the *Viola Concerto* and the *Sonata For Two Pianos*, but, in my opinion, this is not a case of mere repetition. I rather think that Bartók "circumscribes" something over and over again, giving an ever more accurate reflection of what may perhaps have been one of his greatest experiences, the encounter with nature at night, or perhaps the abstraction of this encounter, the meeting of the man of intellect, the humanistic being with primeval, biological life, with nature. It is as if he were evaluating himself over and over again in the light of this encounter. These movements are like a series of self-portraits by a painter, and give a picture of the changes in the opinion of the artist about himself. This man-nature parallel can also be found in earlier Bartók compositions, in *Deux Images* (*Virágzás*—Blossoming—; *A falu tánca*—Village dance) this contrast is evident in two separate movements. An identical duality, even if concealed under the cover of drama, appears in *The Wooden Prince*. Within the slow movements mentioned above however, it is condensed within a single movement, and exists without the crutch of a programmatic title or of a verbal explanation of dramatic action.

The question inevitably arises: does the influence of folksong lie behind this demand for constant renewal, just as folksong itself appears in countless variations, existing side by side. These Bartók movements are also variations, and in a certain sense, supplement each other. Perhaps this is one of the highest forms of the art of variation of which Bartók himself was so fond. It is a principle of variation which is so complete, effecting all of his works, to a degree unparalleled in the history of music.

*

Nowadays, when the new form of conformism, a conformism of non-conformism is so fashionable, it would perhaps be valuable to call attention to certain features in Bartók's style which in their time also could have been regarded as conformist but without which the style would not have been complete.

Such for example are his respect for tonality even when atonality was the fashion, and his constant contact with folk music, even at a time when the other great contemporary master, Stravinsky, who also became world famous through compositions inspired by folk music, had turned away from it and gave rise to the belief that the relation between art and folk music was out of date. Another example is the synthesis of the most modern international composing technique with the most individual ideas at a time when in Hungary he was accused of de-nationalizing Hungarian music, turning it back to the time when it was replete with international elements, and through the use of alien folk melodies, stripping his music of its national character.

Always following his own path, Bartók assumed full responsibility for all his works. He retained his *Rhapsody* (piano and orchestral accompaniment) in his repertoire even when he had already performed his first two piano concertos. Perhaps the reason was that the easier compositions should pave the way for those which were more difficult to grasp.

*

Returning to the starting point, Bartók, the standard means first of all, that we should not bow before momentary fads. We should use every means to express ourselves as completely as possible.

LÁSZLÓ NAGY

BARTÓK AND THE BEASTS OF PREY

Not the splendid kings of the forests, nor those of the
air or water, no, these are not the beasts which lurk
and rage around our hearts; It is less dangerous to
entangle our hair in the lion's mane than to look with
kindness on the creature who has shed his humanity.
In the climate of the century this greatest of all beasts
of prey has multiplied prodigiously, spawning insidous
organisations and stripping great inventions of their
purpose. Over the girder-forests, the cable-jungles,
above the synthetic spindrift this brazen species parades,
and proclaiming itself morality, salvation open to all,
it recruits more beasts of prey, snatches more victims.
For the man of this century is ensnared by the
blandishments of the beasts of prey; it is Orpheus in
reverse; sweet music means taking their hand. Still
young, Bartók said—No! No false morality—no false
art! He tore away the seductive masks of the murderers
with the steel fingers of his music. For he is human
majesty—nature made him far removed from the jackal
quarrel. The Dragon-Slayer advancing in a new
rhythm one might say, but the significance of the
Dragon-Slayer is premeditated battle, predetermined war;
and Bartók is an independent star governed by its own
laws. He armed for no confrontation, nor did he seek out
the powers of obstruction and evil; and yet they
beset his way and his diamond head beat them back again
and again. Like a whistle of wind he swings in his
orbit, and through his art he triumphs. His life was
both satiated and bitter. He would have sought refuge
with the Greenland whales or the brute beasts
howling on the metallic soils of the Land of Fire.
Yet still he says no, mankind does not surrender. Not
to the powers of grief, not to the plague-lands. In
human love and human anger he went to his death.
And the beasts of prey have followed him even to the
grave. And where the stone was rolled away, pierced
by the music, even today they curse him and whimper and
try to free themselves in vain. For them Bartók is the
ineluctable hammer of fate; for me example and
redemption. Like the two shining outcasts—Attila József
and Ady. I see him on high—his hair glowing white-hot,
his eyes penetrating outer space. In his palm a watch;
he measures and controls the music of the universe.

Translated by Andrew Feldmár

BÉLA BARTÓK

On the 25th anniversary of his death

by

GYÖRGY LUKÁCS

These lines were not written by a musician, their author cannot even claim to be a connoisseur in music. So the experts are free to ignore them if they wish.

And yet I believe, or at least hope, that these non-professional lines have a close connection with Bartók's true significance, even if they are no more than suggestive hints and far from fully exhaust the subject. In any case, it is this true significance that inspires them.

The mere fact of being his contemporary provides no adequate excuse for this article, even in spite of the fact that—being a few years younger than Bartók—I also am one of those whose early years of development were overshadowed by the patriotic traditions which hardened into the rigid and obtuse academism prevailing after 1867. At that time only the first faint indications of the ideological revolution were visible. So if I claim to be a slightly younger contemporary of Bartók, it is first and foremost in terms of the community which stifled all genuine protest common to both of us in our youth.

And when the ferment of protest began it was Bartók, alone with Ady, who raised his far-reaching voice; he was one of those whose personality and creative work made the period from 1900 to the revolutions the truly great epoch of Hungarian culture.

After the collapse of 1848, Hungarian society and Hungarian policy followed "the Prussian way." Following Lenin's definition this meant that Hungarian capitalism and the development of bourgeois Hungary produced no more than slight changes in the economic, social and political hegemony of the vestiges of the past still surviving. The unequal alliance between the feudal latifundia and developing capitalism for the joint exploitation of Hungarian workers and peasants was then called liberalism, on the grounds that within this alliance, where the leadership of the feudal partner was always unquestioned, large-scale capital was no longer relegated to a social ghetto; on the contrary, it was sometimes tolerated even in the corners of the exclusive National Casino; and under this system the great Jewish-capitalist landowners duly fulfilled their allotted roles side by side with the big bank presidents of ancient lineage.

Capitalist Hungary, consequently, except for the brief episode of the 1919 revolution, remained the country of the nobility, a "gentleman's" country. Of course such a gentleman, as one of István Tisza's supporters said about his leader, was "a gentleman who worked." This meant that any one of the minor gentry, if he chose to go into business, could even rise to prominence in economic affairs, or if he chose to remain a simple country gentleman, a ministry or county official. Everyone knows that all the estates of feudal origin were only finally broken up and divided among the peasants in 1945.

Hungary was not the only country to follow this line. It was equally the destiny of the German nation after the sad end of 1848, and of the Russians until the Great October Revolution in 1917. But this social and political similarity produced different intellectual attitudes in each country. 1848 put an end to the radical trend in German thinking and German art which, from Lessing to Heine, had dominated those attitudes there. A new phase began in the development of German literature which has been aptly characterized by Thomas Mann as "power-protected intimacy." In Russia a definite revolutionary contradiction developed in the field of ideology and political thinking which characterized the great epoch of Russian literature from Pushkin to Chekhov. And if we consider the main line of Russian literary development we would be mistaken if we assumed the trend represented by Bielinsky, Chernishevsky and Dobrolyubov as the antithesis of the ultimate aims of Tolstoy and Dostoyevsky. The real essence of Tolstoy's and Dostoyevsky's work was the same sharp, uncompromising protest against the social bases of Czarist Russia as the direct attack waged in the criticism of the revolutionary democrats.

Hungarian literature (because we cannot speak of independent Hungarian philosophical thinking at that stage) embraces the major extremes of world development in a specific way. "Power-protected intimacy" was the ruling trend in Hungary as well. This is no exaggeration, but it is as well to make clear at the outset that this did not invariably and inevitably mean always a conservative and hidebound satisfaction with the long-enduring vestiges of feudalism in Hungary, nor with the capitalism superimposed on them. This kind of ideological backwardness was equally to be found in the German "alldeutsch" trend and Russian reaction, extending to the "Black

Hundreds." But I am now speaking of something fundamentally different: the basic frame of mind here is an attitude which could perhaps be best described as a state of mind reluctant to grumble or show discontent.

*

Honest and sincere political thinkers, at least the best of them, despite the difference in the degree and clearness of their vision, perceived the great deformation of human beings through the alliance between the remnants of feudalism and the beginning of capitalist production. Feeling and thought protested against it, but they believed *a priori*, that even theoretically, any possibility of radical opposition leading to or encouraging action was hopeless. The abdication which sprang from this attitude was one of the essential features of "power-protected intimacy" and ranged widely, both subjectively and objectively from open desperation to cynical resignation, at which point the man and the political thinker comes to a full-stop, renounces all intermediate attitudes and becomes a cynical and active supporter of the regime he despises. A glance at German developments after 1848 will show us the evolution of Richard Wagner in the ranks of the "power-protected," he who was a revolutionary in 1848 and became a follower of Feuerbach and later of Schopenhauer; it will show us the fundamental and deep melancholy of Brahms which had its origins there, and the self-ironical humour of Raabe and Fontane.

In Hungary 1848 was also the point of departure for "power-protected intimacy" as a dominant trend. It is hardly necessary to mention Zsigmond Kemény and Mór Jókai in this context, men who in all other respects were so different from each other, although there is no doubt that not only their direct impact, but also these effects considered as a model, have influenced the development of Hungarian thinking up to our days.

János Arany, who ought be mentioned here as the first great representative of this very typical attitude, was never a born revolutionary by nature as Petőfi was. It is however remarkable, and worthwhile pointing out, that during the revolutionary years which brought so many personal disillusionments to Petőfi, Arany was the only one with whom his relation remained without conflict to the end. And of course the true image of Arany is only complete if we bear in mind that his relation with Petőfi was never shaken or even questioned. Arany's belief that 1848 could never be repeated was no mere passing mood, and he never even considered the effect of an eventual revolutionary protest on his personal life. But an understanding of the truth of 1848 and the fact that it could never be repeated became the basis of Arany's outlook and thinking in his last years. And there are some perceptions in "The Love of Toldi" which on occasion go farther than the more revolutionary parts of it written before 1848. The only disillusionment of the ageing hero in "The Evening of Toldi" was King Louis's personal conduct. But "The Love of Toldi," which basically rejected the former attitude of protest, called him "the king of knights"—a very exact class characterization.

This is not the place to analyse these very profound inconsistencies. After all, I am only attempting to sketch the background which shaped the significance of Bartók's œuvre through its very contradictions. There is only one more thing to add to the image of Arany: in his manhood and old age, which were considered by Hungarian liberalism as the eternal and classical manifestation of what a poet's attitude should be, he deeply despised life in Hungary as it was around 1867. It is perhaps enough to quote here the well-known stanza of the poem entitled "Epilogue":

> When a gentleman horsetrader passed me
> Who spattered me with mud
> I never argued.
> I stood aside and wiped it off.

And it is no accident that Arany's "Album", his farewell to poetry, ends with these lines:

> Comus did not stay with me,
> Nor the gentle Muses
> Only unsmiling
> Naked misery.

Many have been aware of this "power-protected intimacy" in the works of Kálmán Mikszáth but they do not generally conclude with this definition. With Mikszáth these contradictions are perhaps even sharper than with Arany. It was Mikszáth who painted the most realistic, the most cruel test and the most cynically damning picture of Hungary in the epoch of the Tiszas. That is why we respect him as the most significant master of Hungarian critical realism. And we should therefore make it our business to understand, in analysing his poetic attitude, what is perhaps the biggest paradox in the development of Hungary: how could it happen that Mikszáth, the writer of such criticism, became the best-known writer of an openly admitted reactionary epoch, and why did he not become an outcast like Ady in the eyes of the Tisza epoch? His criticisms were no less sharp than those of Ady.

The most complex representative of the Hungarian "power-protected intimacy" was, undoubtedly, Mihály Babits. It would be an oversimplification to remind the reader that Babits rejected the first real poems of Ady which attacked the whole feudal establishment. But even these emotional motivations have to be investigated. Babits wrote to the friend of his youth, Dezső Kosztolányi, who felt the same about them: "I wonder if Ady comes from an ancient Hungarian family?... Even if that is so, he should handle this subject with love... I am a Hungarian, from a Hungarian noble family (yes, I am proud of it!) on the side of both my mother and my father: and my grandfathers on both sides have been county officials for many years (is there a more Hungarian occupation?): my father was the first of the family to take service with the State, but he was still the true type of the Hungarian gentleman and man of law."

It would, of course, be quite wrong to trace a direct connection between the more mature declarations of the later, mature Babits on what he considered the true substance of Hungarian culture and the right lines of its future development, to his somewhat callow outburst, but it is also true that Babits's attitude of mind on the essential characteristics of the Hungarian people never quite rid itself of this basic premise. It would be very interesting to follow up and analyse this development factually from phase to phase. It would show that his early article in *Nyugat* contrasting the petty bourgeois parochialism of Petőfi, which according to him was closely connected with his revolutionary attitude, with the distinguished sensibility of Arany, was by no means fortuitous. He describes this quality in a very characteristic way: "In those who always carry their past within them, the basis of their conscientiousness is their attachment to the past and a moral consistency."

Here, again, is not the place to illustrate the development of Babits, and the ripening of his opinions. I must add, however, that when he no longer rejected Ady he consistently tried to fit him into the historical development which, in his opinion, formed the unchanging and unchangeable essence of the Hungarian nation. His later writings, his attempts at autobiography, his essays written for the anthology "What is it to be a Hungarian?" consistently followed the same line. And this attitude remained, even when he voiced a powerful protest in his "Book of Jonah" against the fascism that was preparing in Hungary.

*

For the sake of clarity in this important matter I must criticize myself as well. When (in 1941) I enthusiastically welcomed this very fine poem I also discussed in some detail Babits's contemporary statements on his attitude and his views on Hungary. I recognized in my explanation the contradictions in them, I based this powerful anti-fascist demonstration in the main on individual moral motives. I had not then fully understood that he rejected fascism chiefly on the grounds of its objective nature, because fascism—unlike the nineteenth-century reactionary trends which respected and developed historical continuity and historical traditions—was a special type of reaction which, as the still unconscious ideology of the new phase of capitalist evolution, was not simply a further development of the old conservative trends, but indeed was often in sharp opposition to them. I should have seen this all the more because I actually quoted the following excerpt from Babits's autobiography, which had been recently published: "I am part of the old intellectual era in which the bond with the nation was a sacred and spiritual bond. This present epoch despises the spirit and spiritual bonds. Those who call it 'epoch of nationalism' do not really know this unhappy nineteenth century, which created modern national communities by simply giving the different elements equal rights and seeing that they shared in the common culture and tradition. Our century dissolves these spiritual bonds, it prefers the physical bond of race or the class community of interest." So the final philosophical viewpoint of Babits remained the same, he even enthusiastically idealized the transitory epoch which Arany despised, the Prussian road to capitalism.

All this by no means lessens the poetry and beauty of "The Book of Jonah" and its moral and social significance. But it demonstrates at the same time that the final philosophical foundation of Babits's anti-fascism was his attachment to the essentially conservative "power-protected intimacy." We know that the conservative Stefan George emigrated to Switzerland as a silent protest against Hitler. Babits did not keep silent, he spoke out and this, from every point of view, makes him considerably superior to his German contemporary. But this just and legitimate evaluation cannot and should not wish to conceal the final ideological foundation of his attitude which is very similar to the other's.

I have taken a devious route to reach Bartók himself. But this detour was necessary. If we wish to evaluate correctly how "power-protected intimacy" was overtaken by revolution we must not devalue these opposite philosophies and artistic trends by vulgar simplification.

It is only on the basis of these considerations that one can compare the "Russian" trend in Hungarian thinking, Csokonai, Petőfi, Ady, Attila József and chiefly Bartók, with the best and most progressive manifestations of the "Prussian way." Ady's famous article, "Petőfi does not compromise," was the first proclamation which was conscious of this contradiction.

Of course if we—quite rightly, I believe—draw a parallel between this trend in the Hungarian development and the great Russian revolutionary trend, we shall have to bear in mind another difference which is apparently only a difference of genre. The Russian form of development included all the important domains of poetry and thought: epoch-making creative work in the novel, drama and comedy appeared in the course of this development. The same trend in Hungary was almost exclusively confined to the best representatives of lyric poetry and the subjective type of literature, and then—in the works of Bartók—it reached its deepest expression and most exquisite manifestation in music.

*

The problems of genre, as everywhere in the development of world literature, are based mainly on philosophy of history. The medium in which any people in a given period wishes to give conscious expression to their self-knowledge, the criticism of their past and their present, and the way their future development lies, offers many types and very different possibilities of expression, and not only in purely artistic terms. The structures of and directions taken by the movements which create these differences are closely connected with the social foundations of these movements, and particularly with the extent to which a protest movement can penetrate the life of the masses. From this point of view the domination of lyric poetry in Hungary is *a priori* a reflection of the social weakness of its radical movements. It is not that the particular Hungarian development did not know the exquisite forms of expression provided by epics and drama: such forms of expression are very well known in Hungary. But the Hungarian writers who thought it their mission to describe the fate of their people purely objectively, could not, just because of their knowledge and experience, be resolute and combative opponents of the remnants of feudalism and emerging capitalism. The lonely lyric poet who, despite eventual fame, has to rely upon his own personality and the exclusive and direct manifestations of his ego, can draw the fundamental accent of his verse from this very situation. When Petőfi wrote his great ode about his desire to die for world revolution he opened with a meditation on his personal death, and the desire for revolutionary martyrdom grew out of this, and not inversely. And Ady, for example, reproachfully summoned the "lingering, languid red Sun," addressing it like a loved woman.

Only music is able to objectivize this deepest subjective attitude into a vision of the world without weakening the subjective verse of the lonely lyric poet. Music, indeed, can even augment and intensify it into a protest by the world against its own condition. So the unique place and significance of Bartók in Hungarian culture is built to a great extent on the fact that he was a musician. I wish to give an objective, generalized basis to this statement, and consequently would like to refer here to an important category of my aesthetics, viz. undetermined objectivization. This category has its source in the very substance of art. The extensive and intensive objectivity of the heterogeneous world can only be expressed by art through a process of homogenization which starts from man and returns to him. This process or homogenization, however, prohibits in advance the direct objectivization of certain decisive elements of reality. So literature cannot sensibly and directly represent people and facts, painting and sculpture cannot illustrate real movement and expressed thought, and music cannot exactly be perceived by thought, it is compelled to remain in the realm of pure feeling and experience, which cannot be articulated in a determined manner.

In the development of art, as everywhere, these insurmountable obstacles to the possibilities of expression do not constrict but, on the contrary, broaden and deepen the possibilities of artistic expression. The true basis of the creation of types on the scale of world history very often starts here. The dissolution of Renaissance culture can only be expressed in indirect phrases, but in the later works of Tintoretto, in the music of Monteverdi it finds a deep and unified expression in a unique artistic way: neither contemporary Italian literature nor philosophy were able to convey this picture. This undetermined objectivity makes this exquisite typicalness possible where many concrete and directly perceptible determined elements disappear or at least fade into the background; these are the elements which make the change of an epoch manifest even in daily life. These elements are then replaced by the deep and poignant human emotions through which the beginning of a new era can mean a memorable turning-point in the development of the human race, in the historical development of man as a human being.

This level of creation, which is rooted directly in the artistic limits of the forms of a genre, appears really as a problem of content. Merely to eliminate or obscure the direct forms of historical change only degrades art into dullness. Where undetermined objectivity ignores these symptomatic directly objective forms not for profound reasons concerned with content, but purely for directly formal reasons, nothing remains but dullness and indifference. Dutch painting is a great example of the positive aspect of this development. This painting sprang from the victories of the Dutch in their war of liberation against the feudal and autocratic Spanish kingdom, and from Van Goyen to Vermeer they laid the bases for the new painting of the new world. Rembrandt is the only painter who stands apart from this line of development. Why? Because Rembrandt turned to his own use, yet put aside, the great majority of the conquests achieved by this line of development, which directly created reality, and represented the most profound problem of the new man, the new vision of the world, on the basis of undetermined objectivity, this deepest problem being the manifestations of life of the new man which have developed into irreparable tragedy. Many artists and thinkers, then and later, felt and perceived the true insoluble problems of the new man, and of a world advancing towards capitalism and then establishing it. Neither Diderot, nor Rousseau, nor even Goethe can be properly understood without this knowledge. And yet: there is no other intellectual or artistic reflection of this epoch of great transition, which expresses it as it is expressed in the undetermined objectivity of Rembrandt's pictures, revealing as they do the fundamental and insoluble inner contradictions of the new man in a manner which also gives it contemporary validity. (There is one exception: the last part of *Gulliver*, with the opposition of wise horses and vile men.) If we wish to experience this problem in its true reality and depth, and if we are looking for a way to lead us out of these contradictions of humanity, we should look at Rembrandt's pictures today.

Without a comprehension of this situation we cannot fully understand the real greatness of Bartók. The Kossuth Symphony, even if it sprang from revolutionary sentiments, could still be welcomed by conservative Hungarian critics who saw in it the appearance of a new Hungarian musical genius. This appreciation was not without foundation; the specific substance of the Hungarian people, the essence of their life was already expressed in it, even if as yet in an immature form. It was still limited, it was only an inner generalization of the true Hungarian people, it was the first attempt of a people wanting to renew itself, the first attempt to express its intrinsic self, in music if in nothing else. If at the same time the young Bartók and his followers struggled against the pretension of gipsy music to represent essential Hungarian quality they fought for what Ady fought in his attacks on a fashionable minor poet of the period. They were perhaps more radical, and they generalized more on the basis of the maximal undetermined objectivity of music. So the enthusiastic welcome given by some conservative critics was already an error at the time.

*

The substance of Bartók's development can be expressed in a brief, and of course too generalized, form as follows. Although Hungarian folk music always remained the foundation of Bartók's compositions, he did not stop at this first and powerful impulse: he went further, towards a comprehension and artistic utilization of all folk music. Here the right wing ceased their praise; it is well known that he was even accused of high treason because he praised Rumanian folk music. Nor did he stop there; he included Czech, Slovak, Arab, Portuguese, indeed all folk music among the ever-broadening and deepening basic elements of the new music. For Bartók the central problem of renewing the world (i.e. music) was the true life of every people, and the insoluble contradiction of the distorting effects of capitalist pseudo-culture upon it; the irreconcilable contradiction between the natural life lived by the peasant and the distorted and alienated life of modern man provided him with the point of departure for solving the problem of human living today.

If the peasant is here mentioned as a central figure who is the authentic social basis for revolt, we must remember not to regard it only in a directly social or political context. Here too—with the help of the undetermined objectivity of music—the crux of the matter is the turning-point in world history, just as in the case of Rembrandt's bourgeois. Directly, in the literal sense of the term used here, we could say that neither of them "existed" in this artistically realized form, but at the same time both expressed a turning-point in world history in an artistically perfect way clear and understandable to all. If we wish to understand correctly the historical role of this peasant in its full significance, neither the real role played by the peasants in contemporary political and social life nor the personal political views of Bartók provide a clue. Bartók himself considered the peasants a natural force, and this is why he could, in both his criticism and by his positive influence, artistically transcend the artificial alienated human type created by contemporary capitalist development.

When Lenin said to Gorky of Tolstoy, "before this count there was no real peasant in our literature," he did not think, or at least he did not think exclusively, of the great political and social significance of peasant revolution which played a major role in his own activities; rather he thought (or at least, also thought) how the peasant created by Tolstoy became the criterion of the genuine popular substance of revolution. If this role of the peasant was not as immediately apparent in the works of Tolstoy with the same historical universality as later in the works of Bartók, the difference must not be ascribed to their different positions in the evolution of society nor even to the differences in their respective personalities but rather to the fact that the undetermined objectivity of music is capable of deeper and wider generalization, even in a universal historical sense, than the most exquisite literature.

The concrete methods which led to the domination of this plebeian type in the works of Bartók was also the result of inner development. The basis of the playful fairy-tale style of *The Wooden Prince* is undoubtedly the final victory of the people's forces over the distortions of alienation. Here the natural force which informs Bartók's oeuvre expresses itself in almost the literal sense of the term, because he appears to be saying that if we honestly take hold of ourselves, if we genuinely experience our own human self, then these threatening air-castles of alienation will fade into the nothingness they deserve. A few years later, in the music of the *Miraculous Mandarin*, the struggles of the contradictions of alienation are painted in quite another manner. In our average "civilized" world alienation has become a second nature to us, and must be borne as such. "Natural forces" like the Mandarin can only break in from "outside": against these "natural forces" the general alienation which is common to all men who have become estranged from their human selves is powerless. Bence Szabolcsi, in his excellent essay, has centred his analysis on Bartók's rage against alienation. But we must not forget that this rage is much more than a personal emotion: it is a passionate criticism of a whole world.

The Mandarin himself—in the sense of determined and determinable objectivity—is as far from being a peasant as the idyllic and unambigously victorious figures of *The Wooden Prince*. But I think that we are entitled to suppose that even on the level of the undetermined objectivity of music— in a contrasting manner, and with a constrasting outcome—both figures are the personifications of Bartók's peasant revolution against the "conquests" of capitalist civilization, which merely satisfy the wishes of the particular Ego through the market, but divest him of his original character, his human self.

This trend reached its peak in the *Cantata Profana*. Here the peasant of Bartók enters the scene—in the climate of musical undetermined objectivity of course—and, probably not accidentally, his original superiority and his later rage and passionate protest are replaced by a revolt against alienation, an open revolt full of horror and tension, when the youths who have turned into stags do not even wish to return to his pseudo-human and distorting environment. Bartók is here perhaps the only great and resolute representative of the social criticism which openly declares that what usually is called civilization and recognized, even if criticized, as a human mode of life, is in reality the negation of man's humanity. The peasant youths transformed into deer are not only right in not wishing to return but even—by maintaining a profound universal truth—they, as great revolutionaries, declare the human justification of this world invalid.

Some two hundred years after Swift's wise horses Bartók's deer were the first to raise their voice as radical revolutionaries against the dehumanizing effects of capitalist culture. And it was an odd accident of development (if it was only an accident) that the *Cantata Profana* was presented to the public at about the same time as Kafka's great novels which, similarly, also followed the hoofmarks of Swift's horses. It is impossible here to go into further detail on Kafka's significance and the connection of his negations with those of Bartók, but there is one aspect of them worth noting here: Kafka, like Swift, believed that the human situations they described and condemned were the unchangeable conditions of existence. And here two more points must be mentioned: it is one thing to prophesy some kind of development, as was done by Swift, and quite another to represent realistically an existing state of things, as was done by Kafka. A world-wide view of the general development of mankind is one thing, and the currents of our daily life which confront us and provoke our direct action are another. They are different because their relation to the everyday conduct of people is different. And secondly, it would be an error to believe that Kafka's world vision was consistently fatalist. He saw what the characters he created did not see: that from an objective point of view individual issues may exist, though those in the middle of them do not perceive them. But only individual issues. Bartók, on the contrary, condemned the whole world and system of this social reality, *a priori* to destruction.

But quite apart from the great difference between Bartók's and Kafka's vision of the world it needs only a slight comparison to show a decisive element in Bartók's work, if we consider it as it came into being in terms of the continuity of Hungarian development, that is in its division into basically different phases. The movement of the poor and dispossessed at the beginning of the last century represented by those prototypes of peasant heroes *(Ludas Matyi*—Mat the Goose-boy, *János Vitéz*—Gallant John and *Toldi)* was the ideological preparation for the Hungarian 1793 which never occurred. The literary movement of the time had consequently to try to renew popular forms in an appropriate style, bring them to life on the national level at least. When Ady and Bartók began their career, the position from a social point of view was quite different. And no devices of art or form could reestablish, in terms of valid art, the connection which had its roots in reality. So Ady, Bartók and Attila József had no choice, but to be modern artists in both the form and the content of their works.

Ady's development and influence is a clear demonstration of this. Everyone knows how Bartók, whose beginnings were influenced by Richard Strauss, broke with the continuation of the Wagner–Brahms tradition dominating Hungary at the time and became the great representative of the new music, in its formal aspect as well. But today, at a distance of several decades, we have a better view of the real image of the new epoch. Hanns Eisler, the disciple of Schönberg, a man who always remembered his master with gratitude, once characterized Schönberg's basic attitude towards life, which included of course the essential content of his art, in saying: "A long time before the discovery of bombers he expressed the feelings of people crowded in the shelters." If we translate this into a social language we find that Schönberg fundamentally condemned the new world that grew up with himself, but he believed it was the fate of mankind to be unable to change this situation; it was impossible to attempt any change. There was only one possibility: hide in the shelter and try to survive individually.

What else is this if not the new, modernized form of "power-protected intimacy"? It is new because society has a great deal changed. And it is new especially and above all because the ideology which grew out of the new situation expressed the belief that the ultimate forms of existence were the pseudo-lives attainable in manipulated capitalism: it thought that the final incarnation of man was that unlimited rule of particularism developed and supported by this manipulation. It therefore proclaimed the need to extinguish all ideologies together with the need to oppose every old art guided by and struggling with ideologies.

The right thing for every really up-to-date person was to despise ideals, especially those of the nineteenth century. Thomas Mann who by temperament never belonged to those who represented open revolutionary protest left this prejudice of his time far behind him in his last great novel. His hero was a musician who composed works very like those of Schönberg, and who accepted the ultimate consequences of this outlook (which, according to the author, was inspired in the last resort by the devil's hostility to man): he withdrew his Ninth Symphony. Here an honest-thinking great writer drew the consequences that followed from the dominating artistic trends of his epoch. Bartók's specific position in the evolution of his time could perhaps be most exactly determined by saying that he never withdrew a Ninth Symphony but sought a genuinely modern and musical form of expression which through contemporary music could fully and worthily be measured against the best of the music of the past. So here is no so-called historical continuity. On the contrary. He recognized that

Beethoven had exhausted all the possibilities of renewal for humanity following the great but unsuccessful revolution of his time, whose content remained a living actuality in the consciousness of the human race until its realization. This is the true continuity of human history, as against the attempts to describe today's manipulated and particular alienation as an achievement.

The way from folk music to Beethoven and Rembrandt: this is what distinguishes Bartók from his famous contemporaries, stuck fast in today's human degradation. It is not surprising, therefore, that many of the theoreticians of this specifically new music have criticized Bartók because of his compromise with the music of the past. It was also no accident that Adorno, whose musical theory postulated Schönberg's standpoint as the only one leading to salvation, saw something suspicious in Bartók's folklorist approach. The liberalist opponents of fascism who uncritically accepted the universal validity of this shelter-particularism, the "power-protected intimacy" of new capitalism, with any and every innovation of form, quite naturally shrank from the truly great innovator whose truly revolutionary attitude blew up the human foundation underlying the merely formal innovations.

This period of development which lasted over several decades, is now over. The open and patent crises of the ruling regimes have now to create new movements in all fields of political thinking. So it may well be argued that Bartók, as the great representative of the pre-1945 era, can now be viewed in historical perspective. But I think that this perspective reveals him as one of the truly great. He, like Rembrandt and Beethoven, joins the ranks of those whose works have expressed a major turning-point in the development of mankind in a perdurable form of art.

The Hungarian people, who have not yet resolved the great dilemma of "power-protected intimacy" and true human protest in their cultural life, have to reach a full understanding and carry further the works of Csokonai, Petőfi, Ady and Attila József, and base themselves, above all, on Bartók in order to find the truly progressive way to their national development. But Hungarian culture will only be able to appreciate Bartók at his true value when the answer is found to the question which history has repeatedly asked: What does it mean to be a Hungarian? This question must not be answered in the old way, tricking out the most odious historical compromises by representing them as qualities of the Hungarian people; Hungarian culture must have the courage and social and moral basis to say: Bartók has opened for us the historical way to true Hungarian culture.

BARTÓK

by

GYULA ILLYÉS

Call if they will "discordant chaos"
   what will soothe and assuage us;
   yes! let the curse
   of glass burst on the floor
and the shrieks of the rasp got stuck perverse
   between the teeth of saw
   instruct the throat and violin:
there should be no more peace, no more serenity within
   the gilded walls of concert halls,
   aloft the smart, secluded stalls
until the heart's dark prison falls!

Call if they will "discordant chaos"
   what will soothe and assuage us:
that the "folk" still has spirit
and life and vigour in it,
and speaks articulate! Like steel and stone
   when ground together groan
and gnash and curse and swear although this rings
on well-tuned vocal chords or piano strings,
if it cannot do else this way it brings
true testimony to harsh reality;
   for just these battle sighs
demand—this hell let loose, this chaos cries:
      let there be
         Harmony!

For just these wails cry out, if any,
—above the false, the pretty songs so many—
and plead to Fate for Harmony,
true Order, else the world must cease to be:
   the world must perish of its wrongs
if not again the "folk" sings mighty songs!
True Hungarian, spare and stern musician
(among your peers—"a man by fame preferred"),
was it not preordained by destiny
that you had sounded just this nation's soul
and through the shaft—as if a throat yet narrow—
of that deep mine sent up the shriek for help
to pierce the dome of cold rigidity
which has the stars for chandeliers?

Who now cheap comfort plays insults my woe:
   Mother's dead—it ill fits
to have for requiem the "hits"
   composed by Zerkovitz.
Where homelands are lost who dare bewail
   the loss on hurdy-gurdy?
Is there some hope left for the human race?
When minds struck dumb must face this last concern,
   you speak up firmly,
"aggressive," wild musician, great and stern,
   and reason: there's a case
   for us to live and hope.

   And have the right
—as diers of death and bearers of birth—
   to look bravely in the face
the lot we can't avoid upon this earth.
   For he who hides the troubles makes them worse.
   No more can they as once they tried
   to keep us blind and deaf when storms unleashed
would lay the land in ruins and rough-shod ride,
and then with "why were you idle" us to chide.

You honour and esteem us when you share
        the secrets trusted to your care:
the good and bad, virtue and sin—
you raise us by your revelation
treating us as if we equals had been.
        This—the consolation!
        How different, how fair
        human speech, and sterling,
gives us the strength to bear the most disturbing,
        bleakest moments of despair.

        Thanks to you,
thanks for the strength which helped us overcome
        the hells of torture.
Here the end: a new departure;
here the example: he who finds expression
for horror liberates from its oppression.
Here a great soul's response to existence,
        the artist's who did his penance
        and suffered in hell.

Because the evils that our lives befell
        were such words cannot tell.

    Picasso's double-nosed maids and six-footed
        horses galloping wild—
only they would have been able to put it
        into some noise and wailed or whined
    what we humans were made to stand,
what no one but those who suffered can understand;
for which no words exist and perhaps words never can,
only music, like yours, music magnificent, grand,
yours and that of the living Grand Old Man,
        only music, music divine,
full of the primeval fires of a mine,

full of the songs of things to come that dream
    of when the people reigns supreme;
  all prisons topple down to ground
    before its impetuous stream;
  for the promised bliss to be found
  on earth it prays, though it blaspheme
  the sacred, only to redeem;
  it heals though hurting it may seem
  and lifts its every good hearer
into a world above, better and clearer!

Work, good doctor, who feigns no lulling calm,
    but with your music sound
and feel the pain where we have come to harm,
    and then compound
  what strange and magic, beneficent balm
    by making the sound
  that would rush from our hearts into a dirge,
  a lament of pain but cannot upsurge
  —for us, mute of the heart's expressive urge—
on the vibrant strings of your nerves resound!

Translated by L. T. András

THE RESULTS AND PROBLEMS
OF BARTÓK RESEARCH IN HUNGARY

by

JÁNOS DEMÉNY

As the years pass, and the great composer increasingly takes his place among the classics of music, the stream of literature dealing with Béla Bartók's life and works grows ever broader. Bartók's art today belongs to all mankind, so that the study of his art cannot be confined to any particular geographic or cultural limits. Eloquent proofs of this fact are provided by the significant studies from the pens of Belgian, American and other musicologists which are appearing one after the other. On the other hand, it should obviously not require special proof that the natural centre of Bartók research is Hungary, where the great composer was born, grew up, taught and worked, where his fellow artists and friends still live, and where even today fresh, hitherto unknown documents concerning his life and work are coming to light.

Profound and intensive Bartók research is at present being done in Hungary, the results of which are being condensed in ever newer studies and compilations of documents. However, due mainly to the isolation of the Hungarian language, only a fragment of the Hungarian Bartók literature is known abroad. An occasional volume published in French or in German is all that has reached the world at large. This is why the editors of THE NEW HUNGARIAN QUARTERLY have felt it necessary to ask János Demény, the noted Bartók scholar, to give an account in our periodical of the Bartók literature of Hungary over the past fifteen years. His study, which we publish below, discusses the Hungarian Bartók literature in chronological order from 1945 to the present day and outlines the problems and results of Bartók research.

I

The first publication[1]*—a thin booklet—which contains five studies by Bartók from five different periods, appeared in a selection by Mrs. Lili Almár-Veszprémi. We may read here Bartók's autobiography of 1918—1921, a study on Hungarian folk music and one on Liszt's music written in 1911, a paper on Hungarian folk music and new Hungarian music read in the United States in 1928, and finally

*This and subsequent citation numbers refer to bibliography at end of article. See pp. 245-247.

an article written in 1937 on the problem of folk-song research and nation-alism. This was the first—somewhat sparse—bouquet of Bartók's studies.

The pamphlet was printed in a series embracing a ramified range of subjects. The editor of the series, Béla Hamvas, published Bartók's writings among studies by John C. Powys, André Gide and Paul Valéry, and he thus endeavoured also to give expression to the eminence of Bartók's spirit. It is worth noting that he was the only Hungarian literary critic who wrote a sharp criticism of Bartók from the standpoint of abstract art, in the yearbook of the Hungarian Aesthetics Society "Mouseion," published in 1946. According to him Bartók shrank back from the form-dissolving methods of Stravinsky, Picasso and Joyce, which had opened up newer depths, and, losing his composure, had written new classical music. "Bartók," he said, "had a very great theoretical knowledge of music, but he was only slightly informed on the modern situation. He was a blind artist, who lacked the ability and the perspective to judge his own works. The newer music not only can, but must go beyond Bartók. The attempt to place the classics under lock and key must be regarded as never having taken place, the lock must be opened anew for the sake of the great questions..." Later[a] he does admit that Bartók built a whole system of reverberations which recall the primeval world, and that this system represents the greatest value of his classical art.

In this same series there appeared from the pen of the present author—in a booklet of hardly fifty pages—the first study[2] which could lay claim to surveying Bartók's entire composing activity and which also evaluates Bartók's exceptional human greatness in a tone of unconditional homage. In my silent debate with the editor of the series—as I see it today—I defined too strongly those spiritual limits into which I eclectically placed Bartók's lifework: "It was he," I wrote, "who discovered the essence of music. Behind the age of classical antiquity he tore open the age of prehistory, the archaic world, and at the end of his lifetime, he created music equal in value to the hymns of the Veda and the wisdom of Lao-tze." The booklet, which was intended as a contribution to the comparative history of ideas, is inadequate on the musical discussion of Bartók's works. More-over, there are only allusions to three important compositions of Bartók's years in America. Finally, it does not portray the research scientist on folk music and the phenomenal pianist, not to speak of the lack of even the simplest biographical facts. It sees its task only in flaunting Bartók's exceptional greatness, at the prominence which was its due in the universal history of art. Mountain peaks without foothills. A criticism from Paris[b] stated with justification that the author of the work had, with loving admiration, turned Bartók into a god, but had forgotten to write of him—where, for example, he lived, what his room was like, who his friends were, with whom he corresponded, and—horribile dictu—how he worked.

The publisher was responsible for compressing the two booklets just discussed into the form of a single volume[3], he placed in front of the sparsely compiled Bartók articles, printed in loosely composed type, an introduction in densely baroque style with a crowded train of thoughts.

In that same year Béla Kiss wrote and published an attractive little Bartók biography.[4] In its well-balanced chapters, he turns from the decline of our culture and the romantic folk ideology to Bartók's point of departure, his discovery of the folk song, to the new Hungarian musical culture. Bartók's pedagogical significance, the example he sets in friendly relations between peoples, and in a few chapters (New Cultural Viewpoint, Towards the Primeval Melos, The Lonely Bartók) he constructs the actual—realistic—foundations of Bartók's view of the world. The book is a fine document edited by of the Hungarian national group in Rumania about the musical genius who in his youthful years spent happy hours collecting folk songs—the happiest hours of his life!—among the Székely-Hungarian and Transylvanian Rumanian peasants. The Bartók publications of that year include an unsuccessful attempt at fiction: a journalistically flavoured biographical novel by György Láng.[5]

2

The first selected volume of Bartók writings was compiled and published by András Szöllősy.[6] Bence Szabolcsi wrote the preface to the volume and also prepared the notes. The volume ends with an epilogue by Szöllősy, dated from Rome.

There are 28 studies by Bartók in the volume—some very extensive—in five, cleverly arranged chapters.

The first chapter contains the writings of Bartók about the Hungarian folk song, the old and the new Hungarian music. We hear the passionate voice of the young—then thirty-year-old—Bartók in the year of the formation of the New Hungarian Music Society, in 1911, directing his wrath against the "superficial Magyar gentry," who evinced an aversion and incomprehension towards the "newly (i. e. 3 or 4 years previously) discovered, valuable ancient Hungarian Transylvanian melodies, because they have never heard anything like them before. This truly Hungarian folk music they neither like, nor understand..."

Bartók writes: "The oddities built upon the accustomed majors and minors and chromaticism of the West Europeans are closer to the Hungarian 'critics' than the Asian 'frightfulness' of a simple ancient Székely melody..."

In the second chapter, Bartók's science, comparative folk-music research, is revealed to us. The origin of the first article here is also quite early, dating from 1912. "This title," writes Bartók, "designates an entirely young branch of science, the domain of which is where the limits of musicology and folklore touch. It can hardly be called more than a few years old. Its purpose is to determine—on the basis of reliable collections from related or neighbouring peoples or territories, or rather on the basis of their comparison—the original types of folk songs of the given peoples or territories, the relationship or mutual effect of their folk music. Thus there is a certain degree of similarity between it and comparative philology..." Bartók goes on to deplore the lack of usable collections and outlines the tasks confronting the research worker. About this time there were already some three thousand Hungarian melodies awaiting classification and publication. "Now we must undertake to search the huge Rumanian-populated 'virgin' territory," he writes," a large part of which has never been explored by a collector; we must become familiar with Ruthenian folk song; we must make up for the lack of scope of the Kuhac (Croatian) collection. And then all the material necessary for scientifically determining the Hungarian folk-song types and their characters will be together." In this chapter we have pioneering and masterful summaries of the characteristics of Hungarian, Rumanian, Slovak, Turkish and Bulgarian folk music, and, with the exception of the Bulgarian, they are the results of the research expeditions of Bartók.

The three articles of the third chapter—apart from the fascinating character of their subject matter—are a successful portrait of Bartók the humanist. His "Folk-song Research and Nationalism" (1937) and "Music and Racial Purity" (1944) implied a militant stand in the period of preparation for, and during the course of, the Second World War. His "Mechanical Music" (1937) painted a frightening picture of the mechanization of life—as presented by an artist who had still heard and could register in notes the rivalry between the former bagpipers of Hont, and the music-making of the peasants in the villages of Csík and on the farmsteads of Csongrád.

The articles of the fourth chapter refer to Bartók's musical antecedents. His article on "The Performance of Works Written for the Clavichord," which appeared early in 1912, testifies to his exceptional attraction to, and understanding of, pre-classical works. His sense of kinship and pianistic discernment already at that time made him feel at home in a sphere which, as regards the character of his compositions, he only reached fifteen years later! His two articles on Ferenc Liszt (1911,* 1936) were each a hidden self-confession, but even without divulging his innermost secrets they were an unconcealed reference to the identity of Liszt's and Bartók's artistic conceptions. A comparison of Liszt's late works with Bartók's early, so-called romantic period shows striking similarities, but, on the basis of a deeper understanding of Liszt's late works and Bartók's whole lifework, we are struck by the fact that many of Liszt's bold dreams were actually realized by Bartók. Without knowing the two relevant articles by Bartók, no real understanding of Bartók is possible. Once we are acquainted with them, the Hungarian musical heritage unfolds before us. It was in this sense that Aladár Tóth wrote his significant Liszt study while Bartók was still alive. And Bence Szabolcsi's recent book on Liszt's late works is also linked to this idea.

The documents of the fifth and last chapter present a startling picture of the chauvinistic controversies which flared up around Bartók. The Hungarian extremists accused Bartók of friendship with the Rumanians, and the Rumanian extremists accused him of Hungarian prejudice. They accused him because they hated each other: the dispute of the ruling circles of the two nations—particularly on account of the mixed population of Transylvania—was passionate and savage. Bartók's humanist voice was frail in this unfortunate hullabaloo of the Danube valley. Today it resounds beyond all others. The accusations which contradicted one another have shrunk to absurdity. Bartók's writings, exciting commentaries on his new and marvellous art, remain as immeasurable treasures.

András Szöllősy's first collection already well exemplifies that Bartók's articles are somehow similar to his music. As Bence Szabolcsi, in his preface to the volume, says of his literary style: "... it is pure and sober, steel-like and unflinching, but blazing with the fervour of discovery and the pure flame of conviction..."

In the year 1948 two Bartók biographies appeared, both of which gave a better picture of Bartók's lifework than any of the preceding attempts.

Antal Molnár's biography7, with recollections of the artist's life, consists of delicate psychological sketches, a profound background of cultural history and an ensemble of many minute personal experiences. In his youth Antal Molnár took part in the presentation of Bartók's first chamber works as the violist of the famous Waldbauer—Kerpely string quartet. Later, as a musicologist engaged in the explanation of the new Hungarian music, he reared

* The former appears on p. 121.

generations in the spirit of the new Hungarian musical art at the Budapest Academy of Music. Here are a few interesting reflections from his little book:

"Bartók is the embodiment of the new brotherhood; his will to identify himself with the spirit of the people is synonymous with his will to achieve a new musical style. The two main types of task: turning to the depths of the soul in order to find truth, and forming close bonds of brotherhood with the people, are united in a single revolutionary will in Bartók's art... If Schönberg—taking the Baroque revolution of around 1600 as an example— can correspond to *Peri*, then Bartók's pendant is rather *Monteverdi*. He too radically reappraises the elements of musical art, but at the same time establishes a complete stock of the new mode of expression... Bartók's faith is not Rousseau's faith in the given goodness of man. According to him man is neither good nor bad, but infinite and unknown. Infinite as the ways of truth and unknown as the deepest secret. Bartók does not yearn for the pipe-dream of the Nietzschean superman. According to him, man may at any moment become his own fulfilment, if he can face the undisguised depths of his inner self... His works are metapsychological, final reckonings, the bible of complete absolution... Since Monteverdi no revolutionary genius was born in whom such a great innovator was united with such a great conscience."

My own more recent attempt[8] I feel unsuited for comparison with Antal Molnár's work, but it is very well suited for comparison with my own earlier biographical sketch, written in 1946.

In the newer work I succeeded in drawing a more realistic picture of Bartók's lifework, supplemented by the hitherto unpublished works composed while he lived in America; a separate chapter is devoted to the folk-music research worker and another to the pianist. I believe there is a fairly good exposition here of how the discovery of Hungarian folk music repeated the example of Finnish literature a few generations earlier, of its spiritual rejuvenation on the basis of the collection and assembly of the runes of the Kalevala. Bartók's and his great friend Kodály's jointly undertaken work— transposed to the world of music—repeated this related miracle: the birth of a myth at the dawn of the 20th century.

The most significant volume, however, which appeared in 1948, was a collection of hitherto unknown letters of Bartók's[9]—more than 100 letters with nearly fifty, equally unknown, photographs and the photographic copies of many letters, scores and concert programs.

The publication of this collection was decided upon by the Hungarian Art Council at the end of 1947. The Council was headed by Zoltán Kodály.

The present writer was commissioned to compile and publish the material of this volume. Perhaps it is worth saying a few words about its preparation.

On this occasion the first assistance I received was from Bartók's oldest son Béla, who contributed a dozen letters which his father had sent him during the first years of his emigration in America (1940—1941). I could not count on any further material here, since the members of the family had been unable, despite a careful search, to find the boxes in which Bartók's mother kept his letters. She had listed them among their war losses.

The first witnesses to Bartók's early years during the course of my collecting were the half dozen letters which the young artist wrote (1904—1906) to a compatriot living in Vienna, a conservatoire piano teacher, Lajos Dietl. The conductor Jenő Kenessey had begun to purchase these letters from the aged and impoverished Vienna musician in the middle of the 30's. Their transmission was, however, not continued and the approximately half a hundred Dietl documents may be considered lost today.

A single letter can hardly be treated as a turning point in the collection, yet I had to regard as such the letter, so exceptionally rich in content, which Bartók wrote from Paris in the summer of 1905 to a girl of his age in Nagyszentmiklós. In this letter Bartók not only wrote Irmy Jurkovics about the artistic beauties and other sights of Paris, but he also touched upon musical conditions at home. In it we find his criticism of the motley society of the Hungarian capital, and his confidence in the vitality of the provinces and the creative strength of their culture. We read his first avowal of the value of Hungarian peasant music. At the same time we are struck by philosophical lines of melancholy—and behind these lines, since he addressed them to a girl, we may suspect a hidden passion. The music critic Viktor Papp must have obtained this letter from the family which was breaking up for good in the Second World War.

However interesting a few letters are, they cannot make up for the lack of material for an entire volume. The result of some months of collecting work was hardly two dozen letters. Coming to a standstill, I called on my patrons for advice on what should be done now. Hoping only to supplement the photographic material, I took the decisive step when I went to Bartók's still living younger sister, Elza. After half an hour's conversation the elderly lady, taking me into her confidence, greatly surprised me by bringing the suitcases containing her mother's bequest—the Bartók letters which had been explicitly declared lost—and permitted me to select from them, under her supervision.

An amazing treasure-chest was here revealed to me. Moving, sometimes lustily gay and at others tragically painful documents of Bartók's years at the Academy of Music and of his youthful struggles, as well as a great wealth of accounts about his concert tours in later years. Devoted as he was to his family and addressing his mother in a tone of liberated confidence, the letters of the youth clearly reveal the characteristic shown in the achievements of the artist: his genuine humanism. Already at an early age a wide intellectual horizon, a profound knowledge of human character, fervent patriotism and humanity, straightforwardness bordering on stubbornness, unwavering resoluteness, a style sometimes coarse to the point of awkwardness, at other times infinitely satirical, often irritable, but never rude, and finally a modest lyrical ardour hidden behind a cool intellect. Bartók is manifestly not a polished man and not a man of the world even in his letters! But he is a genuine man: a powerful character, with unbelievable energy and clear-sighted reason.

Of a young man enthused by Bartók's music it is difficult to conceive that, amidst so many fascinating documents, he should take the only "correct" course and leave these letters unread, lock their secrets (if such there are) in his heart and hand back his commission. These letters drew me towards them as into a whirlpool.

I therefore continued my work, or more precisely, I only really began it then.

The volume, consisting largely of family material, to which a few outstanding personalities (Mrs. Zoltán Kodály, Iván Engel, Gyula Kertész, Jenő Takács, Sándor Veress, Jenő Zádor) contributed one or two letters, had the effect of a revelation. Bartók's youthful declaration—"For my part, throughout my life in every respect, I shall always and in every way serve one aim: the welfare of the Hungarian nation and the Hungarian fatherland"—became a veritable creed. And Bartók's admirers read with a shock the sigh which the genius committed to paper a few weeks before he passed away, far from his country—"Yet I too would like to go home, and that for good..." This written evidence of Bartók's intention to return home, constituting the last line of the letter published at the end of the volume, is a resounding declaration even in the symbolic sense.

3

The most tangible evidence of the success of the first volume of correspondence was undoubtedly the fact that it very quickly and easily established the conditions for the appearance of a second volume. With its publication it veritably attracted to itself the raw material of a further collection of documents.

The volume, presented as a souvenir to participants of the First Bartók Festival in the autumn of 1948, was taken abroad in dozens of copies, and—acting on the advice of a number of people—I myself sent many copies to Hungarian devotees of Bartók living abroad, or, for that matter, to foreign admirers. In this volume, the adherents of the Hungarian master throughout the world could once again meet with that immortal man whose works they had so often played in his lifetime, the excitement of whose musical revolution they had experienced and of whom they were the first harbingers and had, in some cases, given the first performances of works dedicated to them. The volume called attention to the launching of Hungarian Bartók research and stimulated a number of people to contribute to the next volume photostat copies of unpublished letters written to them by Bartók.

The first larger consignment of material for the new volume[10] was sent by Mrs. Pál Kecskeméti née Erzsébet Láng (d. 1959), a harpsichordist, who had lived in New York since 1940. These letters, written in the last years of Bartók's life, are a testimonial to the way the great musician preserved his sense of humour even when he was suffering from his fatal illness. Off hand I cannot recall a series of letters which so radiantly reflects the pacified optimism of the Bartók of the Third Piano Concerto.

The Bartók postcards sent to Etelka Freund, a pianist living in Washington, are old documents; whether they bring news of the mountains of Transylvania, or Switzerland, or of the seaside in Southern France, or the excitement of a première in Berlin, all of them recall the youthful portrait of the Bartók of the Second Suite and the First Quartet.

Ottó Gombosi, a Hungarian musicologist who lived in the United States (d. 1959), happened to be in Switzerland in the spring of 1949 when the copies of the first volume of correspondence arrived there. As the result of his enthusiastic cooperation I was able to obtain the important material in the hands of Mrs. Oscar Müller-Widmann, an art patron in Basel, consisting of an extensive series of sombre Bartók letters written in the darkening years of the 1930's. From these letters there emerges the fragile figure of a humanist turning against the barbarism of German and Italian fascism. It was well known how intense Bartók's hatred of the Nazi poison was, but it was quite a different thing to read in these letters his ominous, gloomy pessimism that later became reality. These letters were written in German and thus represented the first set of documents from abroad, written in a foreign language.

On the very same day, József Szigeti, in the United States, posted the photographic copy of his own most esteemed Bartók letter. From Belgium

Denijs Dille, Bartók scholar, sent the photographic copy of a letter Bartók had written to him in French.

In the summer of 1949 Mrs. Wilhelmine Creel sent me particularly valuable material from Seattle; from March 1936 till June 1937 this outstanding pianist had been Bartók's pupil in Budapest. She sent not only her own rich collection, but also the complete correspondence which the heads of the University of Washington, Seattle, had carried on for years in order to persuade Bartók to become a professor at the University. These letters gave news of Bartók's serious illness and also of his difficult lot in America.

This tremendous English language material was supplemented by Yehudi Menuhin's and Douglas Moore's valuable contributions.

In transmitting Fritz Reiner's documents Ottó Gombosi was once again the benevolent collaborator. Géza Frid's material from Holland and André Gertler's from Belgium arrived in time to enrich the material of the volume. I must pay special acknowledgement to the important letter contributed by Max Rostal then living in London, a letter which Bartók had sent him in Berlin in the early thirties, containing the exact metronome changes for the correct performance of the First and Fourth String Quartets, and very many tempo indications. Artists performing Bartók's quartets may draw a great deal from it.

Much is revealed of Bartók's humanism and his philosophical world concept by the few very extensive letters which—also on Ottó Gombosi's initiative—Stefi Geyer, the violinist, sent from Zürich in July 1949. These letters date from the late summer and early autumn of 1907. The humorous "Gyergyókilyénfalva dialogue" is a parody of the many vexations of folk-song collecting. The aged peasant woman sings only city songs and church hymns, although the collector is interested in folk melodies. The next letter though pure philosophizing, is essentially none other than a profound confession, the bold undertaking of a free-thinking youth—a modern Perseus—to liberate his ideal—the Andromeda of the Greek myth—from the shackles of theology. The intellectual intention, however, was broken on the girl's unshakable faith, and in the following letter there appears Stefi Geyer's "Leitmotif", the first formulation of the signature of the ideal portrait, D, F-sharp, A, C, which returns again and again in many of Bartók's works.

Together with her letters Stefi Geyer also sent me the last two pages of the score of a violin concerto composed and dedicated to her in Bartók's early years and carrying Bartók's own annotations, with the understanding that she was not to make the whole composition public. Her death at the end of 1956 broke the ban, and the first performance of this composition—which had remained in manuscript form—took place in Basel on May 30, 1958, exactly half a century after it was born.

To this rich material from abroad, there was added, here in Hungary, the bequest of István Thomán, Bartók's piano teacher at the Academy of Music, from which I selected a few interesting items, as well as a few letters which I had preserved from the maternal legacy.

As a result of all this, more than two hundred letters awaited publication—twice as many as there were in the first volume.

However, a delay occurred because for a long time there was a controversy over Bartók in Hungary. Certain of his works were considered to be formalistic. The sharpness of the debate is shown by the fact that finally the Hungarian Communist Party had to close it with a positive evaluation of Bartók.

The manuscript consequently could only be taken to the printers at the beginning of 1951, and it was released with a theoretical preface by András Mihály.

I regret that the chary publisher induced me to blot out sections of a few letters which he considered awkward but which I did not regard as such. However, I particularly deplore the fact that I could not include the foreign language texts at least as an appendix, because this diminished the work's scientific value. (Of 202 texts, 33 in English, 24 in German and one in French had to be omitted.)

In other respects the volume met the critical requirements that were raised in connection with the first volume. My first volume necessarily served as a basis for the second one, and this, at the same time, complements the first with a profile of the globe-trotting Bartók, the fighting humanist. The tones of passionate love also ring from it and—together with the earlier volume—it will surely become a source for an authentically written Hungarian biography.

*

Hungarian Bartók research emerged strengthened from the difficult years of unclarified ideas. With the support of the Hungarian Academy of Sciences there began, in 1952, a systematic study of Bartók's life work and the collection and arrangement of the contemporary press material. The work went on at full speed in 1953.

The first results of this research appeared in 1954 in the Second, so-called Erkel-Bartók Volume[11] of "Studies in Musicology", edited by Bence Szabolcsi and Dénes Bartha. This was an outline of the first part of a projected great Bartók monograph, "The Student Years and Romantic Period of Béla Bartók," which elaborates the six years Bartók spent at the Budapest Academy of Music from the autumn of 1899 to the end of 1905, and the following two and a half years that constituted his romantic period under Liszt's influence. In the intellectual centre of this period was Bartók's legendary work that aroused exceptionally great attention: the "Kossuth symphony", the patriotic declaration of a Bartók fired by the ideals of Hungarian freedom.

The press material is not selected. That is, the majority of the articles are published in full. The reader is left to select from the texts what he finds most characteristic, what interests him most. It is gratifying that even thus, this work has not become dry. Endre Illés, the discriminating and fastidious critic, calls it "exciting, gripping reading" in his report designed to "recruit disciples, readers." According to him, "every item referring to Bartók immediately possesses some kind of violent characteristic: just like a bit of sodium picked up unsuspectingly, within seconds it begins to blaze in our fingers."

In this same year multifold preparations were made to ensure that Hungarian Bartók research should make an outstanding contribution to the tenth anniversary of the artist's death.

4

In the collecting of Bartók letters there was hardly any essential progress for years. Hardly more than a few dozen letters accumulated, but then I did not wish to tread any further on the already travelled paths. The Western sources still trickled, as though they could never run dry. Hans Priegnitz, the pianist sent documents from Western Germany, Storm Bull, a pianist of Norwegian origin and a former Bartók pupil—sent some from the United States. József Szigeti delighted me with fresh Bartók letters, Zoltán Székely's rich material was sent to me by Halsey Stevens, the American musicologist (author of a weighty book on Bartók). However, in these quiet years I turned my eyes towards South-East Europe, more specifically I was now seeking for the Rumanian and Slovak material. The librarian of the Slovenská Matica, Antal Ágoston Banik, sent me Bartók's letter offering his Slovak folk-song collection for publication, and I corresponded with Ion Busitia, Bartók's Rumanian friend of those times—the versatile schoolmaster of Belényes who supported the work of folk-music collecting in Bihar. These were the first heralds from Bartók's broader realm of the Hungarian-Rumanian-Slovak triple folk-music idiom.

At the beginning of 1954 there unexpectedly opened up the prospect of a new volume of correspondence[12], entirely as the result of the brotherhood stemming from this Hungarian-Rumanian-Slovak folk music, in other words, of scientific cooperation. Ladislav Burlas, a musicologist of Bratislava, and Viorel Cosma, a Bucharest scholar, almost simultaneously suggested the plan for a surprisingly extensive collection of Bartók's correspondence.

It turned out, in these same elevating days, that Professor László Rásonyi, who was the custodian of Bartók's correspondence during his folk-music collecting expedition to Anatolia and whom so many letters of mine had sought to locate in far away Turkey, was to be found in the Eastern Library of the Hungarian Academy of Sciences, and that I could see him at the cost of a few minutes' stroll. Rásonyi's documents became valuable material for the Hungarian collection of the planned volume.

The unforgettably wonderful journey I made to Rumania during the summer of that year was undertaken for the purpose of arranging the Bartók material found there and to seek new material for the volume. I was able to supplement this work in respect to Czechoslovakia during the visit of my Slovak colleague to Budapest that autumn.

Some 124 Rumanian, 72 Slovak and 92 Hungarian documents were thus compiled, to which the American material from the University of Washington in Seattle that had remained over from the earlier volume was added as an appendix. To complete the collection, the foreign language (French, German, English) texts were also included, as a result of which the book assumed imposing proportions. The reason why the Rumanian letters are first in this enumeration is that since they contain the most interesting newer data illuminating Bartók's personality, I agreed with my Rumanian friend when he asked that this material be placed at the head of the compilation.

The volume appeared. Further work, however, is still being obstructed by unfortunate circumstances.

The Third Volume of Correspondence, which is the work of Hungarian, Slovak and Rumanian research workers, placed Bartók, the folk-music scholar in the centre of interest. Sons of each of the three countries which had once been set against one another by the poison of nationalism made use of the new, peaceful atmosphere to cooperate in scientific research with the encouragement of official circles.

From the exceptional richness of the collection I have selected, by way of example, just one of the letters in the Rumanian material, which Bartók addressed to Octavian Beu early in the 1930's. A section of this letter throws Bartók's humanism into particularly sharp relief: "My true ideal ... of which I am perfectly aware since I found myself as a composer—is the brotherhood of peoples, a brotherhood despite all wars and all dissension. I am striving to serve this ideal—as far as my strength permits—in my music..."

The volume attracted great attention, not only in musical, but also in literary circles. As a matter of fact it affected the whole of Hungarian intellectual life.

The appearance of the Third Volume of Correspondence was soon followed by a new section of the great Bartók monograph, published in the Third Volume of "Studies in Musicology", the so-called "Liszt—Bartók" Volume.[13] The study entitled "The Years of the Unfolding of Béla Bartók's Art" follows Bartók between the years 1906 and 1914 on the steep path he blazed for himself to the wild heights towards which the aversion of leading strata of Hungarian society had driven him. Bartók entered into a fraternal community with the Hungarian, Slovak and Rumanian peasants, and a whole new world opened up before him. Bartók's later work, the train of thought of his "Cantata Profana", composed for tenor and baritone solo, choruses and orchestra, faithfully preserves every psychological moment, all the stormy passion of this drama. In this composition, in the language of the youths who have turned into deer, Bartók tells the story of his own transformation. The new biographical chapter follows the life of Bartók to the outbreak of the First World War—this dreadful shock, in which he had to experience the conversion of a large part of his dear villages into battlefields, brought about a certain break in his career, and represents an external caesura in the unfolding of his art as well. Not only was his "approaching" folk-song collecting expedition in Moldavia abandoned, but his next expedition to Kabyl could not be realized either: his aim of roaming more and more distant regions in order to collect folk-music had became utterly unreal. In the final pages of the new volume we find the symbolical scene describing how in the spring of 1914, in the Rumanian village of Alsóorosz in Transylvania, Bartók at the "last moment" came across the "hunter-colinda", a folk heritage, the text to the "Cantata Profana..."

In this year a new biographical sketch[14] also appeared in Russian, for the purpose of satisfying the interest in Bartók's life-work aroused by the Bartók celebrations arranged in about twenty large towns in the Soviet Union. In this work I made use of the latest results of Hungarian Bartók research; moreover, some recently unearthed material relating to Bartók's late years was first published here.

András Mihály's Bartók booklet[15] was a serious and noteworthy publication. It was prepared for popular information, under the professional supervision of Bence Szabolcsi.

Péter Csobádi's booklet[16] prepared for a similar purpose was a work of no great ambition. Bartók's life-work obviously interested the author only ad hoc.

The most controversial Bartók book of 1955 was undoubtedly Ernő Lendvai's significant work on Bartók's style[17], in which the author analyses Bartók's music in the mirror of the "Sonata for Two Pianos and Percussion" and his "Music for Strings, Percussion and Celesta."

The extensive work contains a subtle analysis of the two Bartók works from the point of view of the tone, harmony and form of these compositions. Ernő Lendvai revealed the characteristic features of Bartók's tonal world, and through the numerical ratios of a specific Bartók harmonics he pointed out an ancient law of form construction: the golden intersection. He modelled the Schönbergian dodecaphony into various systems of axes and defined Bartók's laws of chromaticism and diatonism. In Lendvai's view the "Sonata for Two Pianos and Percussion" is the culmination of that precipitous school of a hundred and fifty piano pieces, the "Microcosmos", the splendid artistic verification of his workshop studies; as a summary embracing the complete repertory of Bartók's technique, it is therefore eminently suited for the establishment of a Bartókian harmonics, the suggester of a new *Rameau-attitude*.

As was to be expected, there was an exceptionally violent controversy over Lendvai's book. The majority of the critics recognized its significance. Lendvai's work[17], they said, was a great event not only in the Hungarian but also the international history of Bartók literature. They correctly perceived that here it was not a question of revealing one or two elements of Bartók's style, not the explanation of a few rhythmic or melodic characteristics of folk music, but of the examination of the logic of Bartók's musical idiom through a most detailed analysis of style. They objected, however, to the fact that he referred to Bartók as a conscious magician, who "seated in an enchanted chair of five symmetrical parts, rests with one hand on the ruins of the City of Ur, and with the other turns crystal globes, listening to Cocytus with his inner ear, and the hyperspheres with the outer."[d]

5

Given the scope of this study we must, unfortunately, omit many valuable musical analyses which have appeared in the columns of Hungarian periodicals (Zenei Szemle, Új Zenei Szemle, Muzsika). Apart from Ernő Lendvai's work another ambitious study was János Kárpáti's interesting and useful analysis of Bartók's first two string quartets.[18] This work illuminates particularly the important role of Arab folk music which is deeply rooted in Bartók's music. Kárpáti convincingly points out that although Bartók did not borrow ready-made Arab melodic phrases, he nevertheless adopted more than one internal element of the melodic texture of Arab folk songs. Several other characteristics (the crowding of minor seconds, periodic scale episodes, the symmetrical circumscribing of certain melodic centres, etc.) indicate that the study of Arab folk music, particularly the research expedition to Algeria in the summer of 1913, represented for Bartók, in the form of a direct experience, that pristine music which enabled his modern music so triumphantly to resist the attracting influence of the Schönbergian dodecaphony.

János Kárpáti's work was prepared as a dissertation, and after writing it he went to North Africa and continued in Morocco the work begun by Bartók, the study of the folk music of the North African Arab nomads.

After Kárpáti's work we increasingly feel the absence of the two fundamental studies written by Bartók about Arab (Biskrian) folk music from Bartók's collected writings.

In 1956 a new selection of Bartók's writings, compiled by András Szöllősy, appeared.[19] The reason Szöllősy compiled and published Bartók's articles again was because the Bartók research pursued over a number of years had discovered the whereabouts of many new articles, and the requirements too had increased; thus there was need of a more complete and varied collection. Most of the writings accord with the material of the earlier volume published in 1948. Of the 28 articles to be found there 23 were also included in the new compilation, so that only five articles were omitted, mostly because he replaced them by a more recently discovered article dealing with the same subject matter.

The new volume comprises 47 writings of which 24 appeared for the first time in a compilation. Outstanding among the new material are Bartók's articles analysing his own works and his statements on contemporary composers, among them Richard Strauss, Schönberg and Ravel.

In this year a book in Hungarian by a Hungarian authoress appeared in the Rumanian People's Republic, entitled "Béla Bartók, the Folk-

BÉLA BARTÓK, WHILE COLLECTING FOLK MUSIC (1912)

TRANSCRIPTION OF AN UKRAINAN FOLK SONG
(FRAGMENT)

32 Park Avenue
Saranac Lake, N.Y.

Aug. 17, 1943

Dear Mrs. Creel,

I was very much surprised seeing the content of your letter, and at the same time deeply touched by your care. Only I have to tell you, you must not do this again; I know you are not a well to do person, and am very much worried by the thought of your privations incurred by such acts. Under this condition I accept this time your offer, and if you allow me to give you a Ms. of one of my works as a souvenir. I succeeded to bring over many of them, but since they are now kept somewhere in New York, I can send it only after my return, which probably will be in Oct.

The situation concerning my disease is practically unchanged. Further examinations, made in this place, remained unsuccessful: the doctors cannot find out what the trouble is; as one of them put it "it is a baffling case." But this is getting to be a rather annoying subject, so I leave it.

A LETTER OF BARTÓK'S . . .

What you are telling me about your language work is very interesting, at least to me. As you perhaps know it was (always) one of my hobbies to study languages. I read somewhere how terribly difficult the Japanese is. And what about the Korean? Is it related to the Chinese, or to the Japanese? I am sure I could not master any of these terrific language (I had even my difficulties with the Turkish which is said to be one of the easiest languages, having no irregular verbs, nouns!) But I think it is too much for you these three languages. I would have refused the Korean in your stead; you should be careful not only about other peoples' health, but about your own, too, and avoid to much strain.
I kill the time by reading much (there is a "Free library") and just finished Don Quixote in a 330 old translation "the which" did not give me particular difficulties.
We both send you our kindest regards.
  Yours, very sincerely
    Béla Bartók

... TO HIS PUPIL, WILHELMINE CREEL

Béla Bartók (1928)

Music Research Worker."[20] The writer of this work, relying to a great extent on the collected correspondence, presented the life of Bartók in a popular and extensive form. Its special value lies in making public a study by Bartók ("The Musical Dialect of the Rumanian People of Hunyad"), which is not contained in Szöllősy's volumes, as well as a few original recollections.

In November 1951 a worker at the Bucharest Folklore Institute called on Onisan Petru, an aged Rumanian peasant in Transylvania and recorded his recollections of Béla Bartók. This old man recalled the time when Bartók brought a few Rumanian peasants—men and women—to Budapest as his guests, in order to provide singing and dancing illustrations for his lecture at the Hungarian Academy of Sciences on Rumanian music in Transylvania. Although he was not with them, Onisan Petru painted a remarkably living picture of Bartók in his thirties, busily at work among the people.

Even earlier days were recalled when Rumanian and Hungarian ethnologists paid a visit to Kőrösfő in 1954. Here a Hungarian peasant, Ferenc Péntek, a small boy in 1907, now in his 60th year, recalled Bartók. His father, György Gyugyi Péntek, had been a skilled maker of carved-wood handicraft furniture, and the young Bartók had furnished his home in Rákospalota (Budapest) with peasant furniture ordered from him. "...He was a man of simple habits and tastes... Bartók did not laugh, when a joke was made; he was always serious. He never forced anybody (to sing), but only used good humour... He was very well liked—old and young, everyone liked him, because he knew how to talk to everyone in his own language..."

Ferenc Bónis's booklet,[21] to which Bence Szabolcsi contributed his finest comprehensive essay on Bartók as a preface, recalls Bartók's life in more than a hundred photographs. Here we meet Bartók's parents, teachers, friends, see his places of residence, and naturally encounter Bartók himself at the various stages of his career.

The most significant accomplishment of the year was the Bartók volume in French[22] published by Corvina Press, with the collaboration of Bence Szabolcsi. This book told the world for the first time about the state of Bartók research in Hungary, and in this respect it may be regarded as a pioneering work.

Zoltán Kodály wrote the preface to the volume, and Bence Szabolcsi, Ernő Lendvai, András Szöllősy and the writer of this study collaborated by contributing articles, musical analyses, a bibliography and a selection of letters and photographs. The book also contains articles by Bartók himself. Seven important writings of Bartók were on this occasion presented to the public abroad for the first time simultaneously. The book's eminence is heightened by the inclusion of three articles by Kodály dating from very different periods. Preceding the Kodály articles we find Bence Szabolcsi's study, and after them Lendvai's essay closes the chapter of writings on Bartók.

The writer of a review on the book, Jacques-Lonchampt,[e] considered that the confession to Stefi Geyer which is so full of the wisdom of life and so strikingly expressed Bartók's character should have been included among the letters. But at the time when the volume was compiled, the fact that the violinist was still living probably justified its omission.

In the following year (1957) this same work appeared in German.

In a published review of this volume Heinrich Lindlar[f] writes with appreciation of the studies and, speaking of Bartók's letters, mentions that in reading them the most diverse legends that have sprung up around Bartók's career inexorably dissolve in thin air.

Two further books on Bartók, both of them consisting of reminiscences, appeared in 1957.

Júlia Székely's book "Professor Bartók"[24] gives little of Bartók, but all the more of a student's admiration for her teacher at the Academy of Music. The authoress had been Bartók's pupil, a teacher who to this day frequently appears as a pianist. She has written a useful study on Bartók's teaching method. However, in asserting her literary talents, she unfortunately overdid herself in this book.

Károly Kristóf's book "Conversations with Béla Bartók" presents records of talks with the great musician. However, he published his information not in the contemporary text, but in a revised, improved version, and it is precisely this modernization that has deprived his articles of their authenticity, their historical flavour. Nevertheless, the author, being a true journalist, faithfully followed the events of the world in which Bartók moved, and in his book many facts that had become obscure since then have been revived and light has been thrown on many unknown events.

In 1958 Ferenc Bónis's attractive little book of photographs with Bence Szabolcsi's Bartók outline was published again.

The year 1958 was one of the most enduring as regards Bartók publications. József Ujfalussy compiled his Bartók Breviary from ten years of Bartók research. The small-size bibliophile volume embraces extensive material in its more than 500 pages. The author's selection is tasteful, sound and reliable. One cannot sufficiently praise the accuracy and sense of proportion with which he selected from the material that had been brought to light as a partial result of the scientific fact-finding work of Hungarian Bartók research. The breviary presents those documents (letters, articles), or at least the most important parts of the documents, which illuminate Bartók the man and artist, the composer, the pianist and folk-music research worker. It divides Bartók's life chronologically into four great chapters: his childhood, student years and the early stage of his career (1881—1906), the period of his unfolding as a man and artist (1906—1919), the years of growing world fame (1920—1940), and finally the story of his emigration (1940—1945). He has grouped his material skilfully within his main chapters too, but here—very properly—he does not cling to the rigid application of chronological presentation. The various indices and tables of the volume's appendix are also very good and offer a reassuring feeling of completeness.

A more recent chapter—the third—of biographical documentation, consisting of about 500 pages, takes up the major part of Volume Seven of "Studies in Musicology" which was published by the Hungarian Academy of Sciences in 1959. This second, concluding portion of "The Years of the Unfolding of Béla Bartók's Art" pursues Bartók's path through life from 1914 to 1926 inclusive. The subtitle chosen—"Béla Bartók's Appearance in European Musical Life"—indicates that it was in these years that Bartók found recognition among the widest circles of experts in progressive art. His name became the most honoured concept in the international community of new music; the first performance of each of his compositions was an international event. The first performances in Frankfurt of his two stage works composed to Béla Balázs's librettos laid the basis for his fame, just as did his appearances in Berlin, London, and Paris. With his chamber-music works—the first two quartets, two violin-piano sonatas (in the latter he played the piano part himself)— he finds himself in the centre of stormy interest just as in the case of his Dance Suite—with its orgiastic orchestration—which was included in the programs of several dozen excellent European orchestras. The Cologne scandal of the "Miraculous Mandarin" in November 1926 did not shake him, because he wisely knew that all this belonged to the Calvary of the innovating spirit. The year 1926 was important for another reason: it was in that year that the first precursors of the large-scale works of Bartók's late period, composed in the golden era of the 1930's, burst forth. Like the pieces appearing for the piano in his earlier period in 1908, they were again formulated on the piano. Most of them were introduced at the concert of his own works that took place in Budapest at the end of 1926.

For in those years Bartók still maintained contact with his Hungarian public by means of an occasional program of his works, which in the first half of the 1930's his adherents so painfully had to do without on account of the indifference of official circles. The material from Hungary—from Budapest and the provincial towns—documenting Bartók's recognition and reception is almost complete, thanks to the help of Denijs Dille, the Belgian Bartók scholar, who, with the aid of the dates on a concert schedule obtained through the family, directed Hungarian Bartók research to the dormant reviews of Bartók's concerts in Hungary's provincial cities. Of course in this volume—in contrast to the section preceding it—emphasis shifts in every respect from folk-music research at home to tours and first performances abroad. The material of the foreign reviews is not complete. Still it is surprisingly bulky. And this is mainly to the credit of those musicians abroad who, imbued with a feeling of international scientific solidarity, sent documents to Hungary.

The last book, the publication of which coincides with the writing of the present report, is the first volume of Bartók's letters to appear in a foreign language. This collection, containing two hundred letters, is being published in German. And although it was not prepared as a fourth volume to follow the three that have already appeared, it was compiled not only of the material already published but also contains 50 new letters. These latter have never yet appeared even in Hungarian and have thus been put—as though impatiently leaping over their mother tongue—into the centre of world musical interest. Among the items of interest in the volume the valuable letter material of the American pianist, Dorothy Parrish-Domonkos, should be mentioned. The artist was Bartók's pupil at the time when Wilhelmine Creel was also studying in Budapest. No less interesting are a few very important letters of A. Adnan Saygin, a Turkish composer, and Vinko Zganec, a Croatian folklorist. Bartók's exertions in connection with the production of his theatrical works on the Budapest stage appear in the form of separate material. And how much space was devoted to new material, apart from the volume's striving for completeness, is shown by the following weighty example: for the first time a few documents from the box in which Mrs. Béla Bartók, Ditta Pásztory, kept her letters, have been made public, and this in connection with Bartók's tour in the Soviet Union.

That all this material has so far not been accessible—and perhaps will not be so for some time—to the English-reading public, is not the fault of Hungarian Bartók research...

*

The next chapters of the story of Bartók research in Hungary are still unwritten. But research has not stopped, and in the forthcoming chapters it is to be hoped that we shall be able to report on undisturbed work and more results.

The major part of Bartók's legacy is as yet unpublished. Hungarian research workers have no access to most of it. It is not always the ocean that separates us from it. It is much more the ocean-like distance of the spirit in the understanding of common aims.

It is our duty to publish documents. And in doing so we must strive for completeness. We have no right to conceal anything from posterity.

Musical history has condemned the irreplaceable destruction carried out by Beethoven's faithful man Schindler. Schindler took reverence for the dead to mean zeal in the virtue of annihilation. Hundreds of the "conversation notebooks" were destroyed at his hand. In his sense of reverence he wiped out the major part of Beethoven's spiritual legacy and forever deprived us of the most direct human disclosures, the intellectual verification of his revolutionary music.

We are endeavouring to see that this tragedy of being compressed between Philistine boundaries should not be repeated with Bartók's legacy.

Bartók's spiritual legacy—his musical works, writings, letters—are in the first place a Hungarian heritage. For this reason the natural centre of Bartók research is Hungary. And the signs indicate that it will remain so for a long time. At the same time we are observing with pleasure the ever growing interest in Bartók's life-work the world over. Hungarian Bartók research is endeavouring to serve this interest and to satisfy it despite every obstacle.

BIBLIOGRAPHY

1. BARTÓK Béla: *Önéletrajz. Írások a zenéről.* [Autobiography. Writings on Music.] [Compil. by Mrs.] Lili *Almár-Veszprémi.* Budapest, 1946, Egyetemi ny. 32.

a) HAMVAS Béla: *Bartók:* = *Mouseion.* (A Magyar Esztétikai Társaság Évkönyve.) [Yearbook of the Hungarian Aesthetics Society.] 1946. pp. 23—27.

2. DEMÉNY János: *Bartók.* Budapest, 1946, Egyetemi ny. 41 p.

b) GERGELY Pál [*Paris*]: *Párisi levél a szerkesztőhöz.* [A Letter from Paris to the Editor.] = *Zenei Szemle,* 1948. V. [March] pp. 278—279.

3. BARTÓK Béla: *Önéletrajz. Írások a zenéről.* [Autobiography. Writings on Music.] [Intr. by] János *Demény.* Budapest, 1946, Egyetemi ny. 77 p.

4. KISS Béla: *Bartók Béla művészete.* [Béla Bartók's Art.] Cluj, 1946, Ifjú Erdély. 71 p.

5. Láng György: *Bartók élete és művei.* [Bartók's Life and Works.] Budapest, 1946, Grill K. 144 p.

6. Bartók Béla: *Válogatott zenei írásai.* [Béla Bartók's Selected Writings on Music.] [Compil. by] András Szőllősy, [Intr. by] Bence Szabolcsi. Budapest, 1948, Magyar Kórus. 111 p.

7. Molnár Antal: *Bartók művészete, emlékezésekkel a művész életére.* [Bartók's Art with Recollections of the Artist's Life.] Budapest, 1948, Rózsavölgyi és Társai. 96 p.

8. Demény János: *Bartók élete és művei.* [Bartók's Life and Works.] Budapest, 1948, Székesfőv. Irodalmi és Művészeti Int. 119 p. [Új Könyvtár 33]

9. Bartók Béla, (Levelek, fényképek, kéziratok, kották.) [Letters, Photographs, Manuscripts, Scores.] [Compil. by] János Demény. Budapest, 1948, Magyar Művészeti Tanács. 212 p.

10. Bartók Béla: *Levelei.* [Letters—collection of the last two years.] [Compil. by] János Demény. [Preface by] András Mihály. Budapest, 1951, Művelt Nép. 252 p.

11. Demény János: *Bartók Béla tanulóévei és romantikus korszaka.* [Béla Bartók's Student Years and Romantic Period.] 1899—1905. = *Zenetudományi Tanulmányok* 2. köt. [Studies in Musicology. 2. vol.] [Ed. by] Bence Szabolcsi [and] Dénes Bartha. Budapest, 1954, Akadémiai K. pp. 323—487.

c) Illés Endre: *Egy olvasó tűnődése. III.* [Reflections of a Reader.] = *Irodalmi Újság.* Jan. 22, 1955. p. 4.

12. Bartók Béla: *Levelei.* 3. köt. Magyar, román, szlovák dokumentumok. [Letters. 3. vol. Hungarian, Rumanian, Slovak Documents.] [Ed. by] János Demény. Budapest, 1955, Zeneműkiadó. 505 p.

1. Romániai levelek. [Letters in Rumania.] [Coll.] Viorel Cosma. 2. Csehszlovákiai levelek. [Letters in Czechoslovakia.] [Coll.] Ladislav Burlas. 3. Magyarországi levelek. [Letters in Hungary.] [Coll.] János Demény.

13. Demény János: *Bartók Béla művészi kibontakozásának évei* (1. r.) *Találkozás a népzenével 1906—1914.* [The Years of the Unfolding of Béla Bartók's Art. Part I; Meeting with Folk Music, 1906—1914.] = *Zenetudományi Tanulmányok* 3. köt. [Studies in Musicology. 3. vol.] [Ed. by] Bence Szabolcsi [and] Dénes Bartha. Budapest, 1955, Akadémiai K. pp. 286—459.

14. Béla Bartók: [Brief Outline of his Life and Work.] Budapest, 1955, Magyar—Szovjet Társaság—Kultúrkapcsolatok Int. 37 p.

15. Mihály András: *Bartók Béla.* Budapest, 1955, T. T. I. T. 41 p.

16. Csobádi Péter: *Bartók.* Budapest, 1955, Orsz. Béketanács. 62 p.

17. Lendvai Ernő: *Bartók stílusa a "Szonáta két zongorára és ütőhangszerekre" és a "Zene húros-, ütőhangszerekre és celestára" tükrében.* [Bartók's Style as Reflected in the "Sonata for Two Pianos and Percussion", and the "Music for Strings, Percussion and Celesta".] Budapest, 1955, Zeneműkiadó. 156 p.

d) Reviewed by József Ujfalussy = *Új Zenei Szemle* [New Musical Review.] Nov. 1955. p. 1—7.

18. Kárpáti János: *Bartók korai melódia világa az első és második vonósnégyes tükrében.* [Bartók's Early World of Melody as Reflected in his First and Second String Quartets.] Budapest, 1956, [Mimeographed.] 76 p.

19. Bartók Béla: *Válogatott írásai.* [Selected Writings.] [Compil. by] András Szőllősy. Budapest, 1956, Művelt Nép. 426 p.

20. Szegő Júlia: *Bartók Béla, a népdalkutató.* [Béla Bartók the Folk-Music Research Worker.] Bucuresti, 1956, Állami K. 335 p.

21. Bartók Béla *élete képekben.* [The Life of Béla Bartók in Pictures.] [Intr. by] Bence Szabolcsi. [Compil. by] Ferenc Bónis. Budapest, 1956, Zeneműkiadó. 36 p. 105 ills.

22. BARTÓK, *sa vie et son oeuvre*. Publ. sous la dir. de Bence *Szabolcsi*. Budapest, 1956, Corvina. 351 p.

23. BÉLA Bartók: *Weg und Werk — Schriften und Briefe*. Zusammengestellt von Bence *Szabolcsi*. Budapest, 1957, Corvina. 371 p.

e) JACQUES-Lonchampt: *Avec Béla Bartók sur les routes de Hongrie et du Monde. = Le Journal Musical Francais*. VI/58. (Apr. 8. 1957.) pp. 4—6.

f) LINDLAR Heinrich: *Zwei Quellenwerke aus Ungarn. = Melos. Zeitschrift für Neue Musik*. 25/7—8. (July-August 1958.) p. 239.

24. SZÉKELY Júlia: *Bartók tanár úr*. [Professor Bartók.] Pécs, 1957, Dunántúli Magvető. 144 p.

25. KRISTÓF Károly: *Beszélgetések Bartók Bélával*. [Conversations with Béla Bartók.] Budapest, 1957, Zeneműkiadó. 192 p.

26. BARTÓK Béla *élete képekben*. 2. bőv. kiad. [The Life of Béla Bartók in Pictures. 2. enl. ed.] [Intr. by] Bence *Szabolcsi*. [Compil. by] Ferenc *Bónis*. Budapest, 1958, Zeneműkiadó, 36 p. 119 ills.

27. BARTÓK Breviárium. Levelek, írások, dokumentumok. [Bartók Breviary, Letters, Writings, Documents.] [Compil. by] József *Ujfalussy*. Budapest, 1958, Zeneműkiadó. 556 p.

28. DEMÉNY János: *Bartók Béla művészi kibontakozásának évei* (2. r.) *Bartók Béla megjelenése az európai zeneéletben 1914—1926*. [The Years of the Unfolding of Béla Bartók's Art. Part II; Béla Bartók's Appearance in European Musical Life. 1914—1926.] = *Zenetudományi Tanulmányok* 7. köt. [Studies in Musicology. 7. vol.] [Ed. by] Bence *Szabolcsi* [and] Dénes *Bartha*. Budapest, 1959, Akadémiai K. pp. 6—425.

29. BARTÓK Béla: *Ausgewählte Briefe*. Gesammelt und hrsg. von János *Demény*. Budapest, 1960, Corvina. 292 p.

SOURCE NOTES

Bence SZABOLCSI. "Bartók's Principles of Composition," *The New Hungarian*   **1**
Quarterly XI/39 (Autumn 1970), 10-12.

> Original version: "Bartók Béla kompozíciós elvei, egy nyilatkozata tükrében
> [The Compositional Methods of Béla Bartók in the Light of an Interview],"
> *Új Zenei Szemle [New Musical Review]* VII/9 (Sep 1956), 14-15.

Bence SZABOLCSI. "Bartók's Miraculous Mandarin," *The New Hungarian*   **2**
Quarterly VI/20 (Winter 1965), 108-24.

> Original version: "A csodálatos Mandarin [The Miraculous Mandarin]," in:
> Bence SZABOLCSI & Dénes BARTHA, eds, *Zenetudományi Tanulmányok*
> *III. Liszt Ferenc és Bartók Béla emlékére [Studies in Musicology, Vol. III.*
> *In Commemoration of Ferenc Liszt and Béla Bartók]* (Budapest: Akadémiai
> Kiadó, 1955), 519-35.
>
>   This article has appeared several times subsequently in Hungarian, French,
> and German. For a list of these translations, see "Bence Szabolcsi's Works,"
> *Studia Musicologica* XI/1-4 (1969), 18.
>
>   After the appearance of this article in 1955, there was a wave of research
> into *The Miraculous Mandarin* by a number of scholars. In addition to
> Szabolcsi's analysis, the major studies include: György KROÓ, "Monothematika
> és Dramaturgia Bartók színpadi műveiben [Monothematicism and dramaturgy
> in Bartók's theatrical compositions]," *Magyar Zene* I/9 (1961), 33-50 (also in
> German; See: Bibliography, No. **162**); Ernő LENDVAI, "Der wunderbare
> Mandarin," *Studia Musicologica* I/3-4 (1961), 363-431; Gy. KROÓ, *Bartók Béla*
> *színpadi művei [Béla Bartók's theatrical compositions]* (Budapest: Zeneműkiadó
> Vállalat, 1962); Aurél Ott NIRSCHY, "Varianten zu Bartóks Pantomime 'Der
> wunderbare Mandarin'," *Studia Musicologica* II/1-4 (1962), 189-223; E. LENDVAI,
> "Bartók pantomimje és táncjátéka [The pantomime and ballet of Bartók]," in:
> Bence SZABOLCSI & Dénes BARTHA, eds, *Zenetudományi Tanulmányok X.*
> *Bartók Béla emlékére [Studies in Musicology, Vol. X. In Commemoration of Béla*
> *Bartók]* (Budapest: Akadémiai Kiadó, 1962); Jacques CHAILLEY, "Essai
> d'analyse du 'Mandarin Merveilleux'," (See: Bibliography, No. **46**); E. LENDVAI,
> *Bartók Dramaturgiája [Bartók's dramaturgy]* (See: Bibliography, No. **171**); John
> VINTON, "The Case of the 'Miraculous Mandarin'," (See: Bibliography, No. **293**).

Ernő LENDVAI. "Duality and Synthesis in the Music of Béla Bartók," *The*   **3**
New Hungarian Quarterly III/7 (July-Sep 1962), 91-114.

> This also appeared in: György KEPES, ed, *Module. Proportion, Symmetry,*
> *Rhythm* (NY: George Braziller, 1966), 174-93.

Bence SZABOLCSI. "Man and Nature in Bartók's World," *The New Hungarian*   **4**
Quarterly II/4 (Oct-Dec 1961), 90-102.

> This also appeared as: "Mensch und Natur in Bartóks Geisteswelt," *Österreichische*
> *Musikzeitschrift* XVI/12 (Dec 1961), 577-85; same title in *Studia Musicologica*
> V/1-4 (1963), 525-39; in Hungarian as "Ember és természet Bartók világában," in:

Bence SZABOLCSI & Dénes BARTHA, eds, *Zenetudományi Tanulmányok X. Bartók Béla emlékére [Studies in Musicology, Vol. X. In Commemoration of Béla Bartók]* (Budapest: Akadémiai Kiadó, 1962), 5-15.

5   István KECSKEMÉTI. "An Early Bartók-Liszt Encounter," *The New Hungarian Quarterly* IX/29 (Spring 1968), 206-10.

6   Ferenc BÓNIS. "Bartók and Wagner," *The New Hungarian Quarterly* X/34 (Summer 1969), 201-9.

7   János KÁRPÁTI. "Bartók, Schoenberg, Stravinsky," *The New Hungarian Quarterly* VII/24 (Winter 1966), 211-16.

8   Béla BALÁZS. "The Wooden Prince," *The New Hungarian Quarterly* IV/11 (July-Sep 1963), 36-45.

9   Menyhért LENGYEL. "The Miraculous Mandarin," *The New Hungarian Quarterly* IV/11 (July-Sep 1963), 30-35.

10   Bence SZABOLCSI. "Liszt and Bartók," *The New Hungarian Quarterly* II/1 (Jan 1961). 3-4.

Original version: "Liszt és Bartók," *Élet és Irodalom [Life and Literature]* IV/51-52 (1960), 9.

11   Béla BARTÓK. "Liszt's Music and Our Contemporary Public," *The New Hungarian Quarterly* II/1 (Jan 1961), 5-8.

Original version: "Liszt zenéje és a mai közönség," *Népművelés* XVII-XVIII (1911), 359-62; also in *Zeneközlöny* XVIII (1911), 556-60.

This essay also appeared as: "Bartók on Liszt: I. Liszt's Music and Today's Public," *The Monthly Musical Record* LXXVIII/899 (Sep 1948), 180-83; "Liszts Musik und das Publikum unserer Zeit," *Das Musikleben* IV/7-8 (July-Aug 1951), 211-12; "Liszts musik og vor tids publikum," *Dansk Musiktidsskrift* XXVI/10 (1951), 212-14; "La Musica di Liszt e il Pubblico d'oggi," *Nuova Rivista Musicale Italiana* IV/5 (Sep-Oct 1970), 913-16.

12   "Letters to Béla Bartók" *The New Hungarian Quarterly* XI/40 (Winter 1970), 37-48.

The letters are taken from Denijs DILLE, ed, *Documenta Bartókiana* III (1968). All but the final three letters of this article are properly identified in *NHQ* with respect to their placement in *Documenta Bartókiana* III. The latter three letters, not identified in *NHQ*, are given here with their respective authors, page numbers, and letter number in *Documenta Bartókiana* III:

Letter from Arthur Bliss   - p. 114, No. 64.
Letter from Cecil Gray   - p. 129, No. 79.
Letter from Yehudi Menuhin - p. 263, No. 175.

János LIEBNER. "Unpublished Bartók Documents," *The New Hungarian Quarterly* III/6 (Apr-June 1962), 221-24.   13

The section, "A Forgotten Work of Bartók's," also appeared as: "Une oeuvre oubliée de Bartók," *Schweizerische Musikzeitung* C/6 (Nov-Dec 1960), 357-59; "Ein verschollenes Werk von Béla Bartók," *Gesellschaft für Musikforschung. Bericht über den Internationalen Musikwissenschaftlichen Kongress Kassel 1962* (Kassel: Bärenreiter, 1963), 315-17; "Ein wiederentdecktes Werk Béla Bartók," *Beiträge zur Musikwissenschaft* VI/3 (1964), 243-44.

The score of the *Andante* is published in *Új Zenei Szemle [New Musical Review]* VI/10 (Oct 1955), 3-4.

The original version of the section, "Béla Bartók's Last American Radio Interviews," appeared as: "Bartók utolsó amerikai rádióinterjui [Bartók's last radio interviews in America]," *Új Zenei Szemle [New Musical Review]* VI/12 (Dec 1955), 26-28. Bartók's replies in this interview may be heard on Bartók Records, No. 903. For a complete listing of Bartók's voice on phonodiscs, see the discography compiled by László Somfai in: József UJFALUSSY, *Béla Bartók* (Budapest: Corvina Press, 1971; Boston: Crescendo, 1972), 446-47.

Péter RUFFY. "The Dispute Over Bartók's Will," *The New Hungarian Quarterly* VII/22 (Summer 1966), 204-9.   14

Béla BARTÓK, Jr. "Remembering My Father, Béla Bartók," *The New Hungarian Quarterly* VII/22 (Summer 1966), 201-3.   15

Lajos HERNÁDI. "Bartók—Pianist and Teacher," *The New Hungarian Quarterly* IX/30 (Summer 1968), 194-200.   16

Original version: "Bartók Béla a zongoraművész, a pedagogus, az ember [Béla Bartók the pianist, the teacher, the man]," *Új Zenei Szemle [New Musical Review]* IV/9 (Sep 1953), 1-7.

This article also appeared as: "Béla Bartók, le pianiste, le pedagogue, l'homme," *Revue Musicale* 224 (1955), 77-90; "Béla Bartók, Uchitel', pianist, chelovek," *Sovetskaya Muzyka* XXXI/12 (Dec 1967), 123-28; "Béla Bartók—Pianist and Teacher," *American Music Teacher* XXII/3 (Jan 1973), 28-31.

Gerald ABRAHAM. "Bartók and England," *The New Hungarian Quarterly* II/4 (Oct-Dec 1961), 82-89.   17

This article was reprinted as: "Bartók and England," *Studia Musicologica* V/1-4 (1963), 339-46.

Miklós SZINAI, "Documents: Béla Bartók and the Permanent Committee on Literature and Art of the League of Nations," *The New Hungarian Quarterly* V/15 (Autumn 1964), 143-46.   18

Yolan HATVANY. "An Evening with Thomas Mann and Béla Bartók in Budapest," *The New Hungarian Quarterly* VI/19 (Autumn 1965), 72-75.   19

This was Bartók's last meeting with Thomas Mann.

20   Pál RÉZ. "Thomas Mann and Bartók," *The New Hungarian Quarterly*
     II/3 (July-Sep 1961), 89-91.

     This is an excerpt from the article, "Thomas Mann and Hungary—His
     Correspondence with Hungarian Friends," *ibid.*, 84-99.

21   Magda VÁMOS. "A 1932 Interview with Bartók," *The New Hungarian
     Quarterly* XIV/50 (Summer 1973), 141-51.

22   Iván VITÁNYI. "Bartók and the Public," *The New Hungarian Quarterly*
     II/2 (Apr-June 1961), 175-79.

23   István LÁNG. "Bartók's Heritage: A Composer's View," *The New Hungarian
     Quarterly* XI/39 (Autumn 1970), 13-16.

24   László NAGY. "Bartók and the Beasts of Prey," *The New Hungarian Quarterly*
     VII/23 (Autumn 1966), 134.

25   György LUKÁCS. "Béla Bartók (On the 25th Anniversary of his Death)," *The
     New Hungarian Quarterly* XII/41 (Spring 1971), 42-55.

26   Gyula ILLYÉS. "Bartók," *The New Hungarian Quarterly* IV/11 (July-Sep
     1963), 20-23.

27   János DEMÉNY. "The Results and Problems of Bartók Research in Hungary,"
     The New Hungarian Quarterly II/1 (Jan 1961), 9-31.

     This article also appeared as: "Ergebnisse und Probleme der Bartók-Forschung
     in Ungarn," *Beiträge zur Musikwissenschaft* III/4 (1961), 49-61.

BIOGRAPHIES OF AUTHORS

ABRAHAM, GERALD (b. 1904). The eminent English musicologist whose primary interests have been in Eastern European music, and nineteenth-century music. At an early age he became interested in philology and later mastered Russian and the languages of other Eastern European countries. From 1916 to 1920 he studied the piano, but apart from that, was entirely self-taught in music. During the period 1935-1947, he worked as a Musical Advisor at the BBC in London. From 1947 to 1962 he was Professor of Music at the University of Liverpool, and from 1962 until 1967 worked again at the BBC as Assistant Controller of Music. At present, he is President of the Royal Musical Association.

Abraham is Secretary of the Editorial Board of *The New Oxford History of Music*, of which he edited Volumes III and IV. He also conceived and was general director of the phonodisc series, *The History of Music in Sound*, intended as a companion to *The New Oxford History of Music*.

In addition to his numerous books and articles on Russian music and musicians, Abraham has edited collections of articles dealing with specific composers, including Tchaikovsky (1945), Schubert (1946), Sibelius (1947), Grieg (1948), Schumann (1952), and Handel (1954). *Slavonic and Romantic Music* (1968) is an anthology of Abraham's articles drawn from various (mostly British) journals covering the period 1922-1966. Included in this collection is an article on Bartók's string quartets. More recently, Abraham completed and orchestrated Schubert's fragmentary third movement from the "Unfinished" Symphony (Oxford University Press, 1971), and published his most recent book, *The Tradition of Western Music* (University of California Press, 1974).

BALÁZS, BÉLA (1884-1949). Author and film critic. Balázs was born in Szeged (in southern Hungary) and studied in Budapest. In his youth he was influenced mainly by the French symbolists. During the First World War he came under the spell of Socialism and in 1919, was one of the leaders of the Hungarian Soviet Republic. After the crushing of the revolution Balázs was forced to emigrate and live successively in Vienna, Berlin, and finally Moscow where he stayed until 1945. While there, he lectured at the Moscow Film Academy. After 1945 he returned to Hungary and taught at the Budapest Academy of Dramatic Art.

His voluminous *oeuvre* consists of tales characterized by rich fantasy, novels, short stories, and plays, two of which, *Bluebeard's Castle* and *The Wooden Prince*, served as libretti for Bartók. Balázs' professional and personal contact with Bartók, Kodály, and other musicians, renders him a position of special significance in the development of twentieth-century Hungarian music. In 1947, he wrote the drama, *Dance Suite*, in memory of Béla Bartók.

Balázs was a pioneer in film making and script writing. In addition to his two books on film technique, he was an important motion picture critic.

BARTÓK, BÉLA, Jr. (b. 1910). The composer's first son, born to Bartók and Márta Ziegler, is a retired engineer and Chief Counsellor of the Hungarian State Railways. Mr. Bartók also lectures at the Budapest Technical University, and in recent years, has been a touring lecturer on the subject of his father, often in the company of the pianist, György Sándor, one of Bartók's most famous students and Professor of Music at the University of Michigan. Mr. Bartók has also written a number of articles containing remembrances of his father. In addition, he is a prominent spokesman for Unitarianism in Hungary.

BÓNIS, FERENC (b. 1932). A musicologist who has headed a department at the Budapest Bartók Archives and is presently Professor of Musicology at the Ferenc Liszt Academy of Music. In addition, Bónis heads the music department for the young at the Hungarian Radio and Television. He studied composition with Endre Szervánszky at the Academy of Music as well as musicology with Zoltán Kodály, Bence Szabolcsi, and Dénes Bartha. Bónis is a specialist in Hungarian music history and has written books or articles on Liszt, Ferenc Erkel, Mihály Mosonyi, Bartók, Kodály, and others. In the field of Bartók research, he has been most closely associated with Bartók iconography (See: Bibliography, Nos. **30, 31, 32, 38 & 39**).

Since 1959 Bónis has been the editor of the series, *Magyar Zenetudomány [Hungarian Musicology]*, and from 1968, the editor of *Magyar Zenetörténeti Tanulmányok [Studies in Hungarian Musical History]*. He is the author of *A Vietórisz kódex táncai [Dances of the Codex Vietoris]* (1958), *Die Ungarischen Tänze in der Handschriften Apponyi* (1964), *Beethoven und die Ungarische Musik* (1970), *Bartók und der Verbunkos* (1970), and the general editor of a *festschrift* for Bence Szabolcsi (See: Bibliography, No. **36**).

DEMÉNY, JÁNOS (b. 1915). An eminent Bartók scholar and library official of the Hungarian government. Dr. Demény studied law at the University of Budapest (Dr. jur., 1939) and music at the Fodor Music School. He has edited seven volumes of Bartók's letters (in Hungarian, 1948, 1951, 1955, 1960, as well as volumes of selected letters translated into German, Italian, and English), published several biographies of Bartók, and since the Second World War, has been compiling and preparing material for a documentary biography of Bartók. Some of this material has been published in the yearbooks of the *Zenetudományi Tanulmányok [Studies in Musicology]*, edited by Bence Szabolcsi & Dénes Bartha (See: Volumes II [1954], III [1955], VII [1959], & X [1962]).

HATVANY, YOLAN. Mrs. Hatvany is the widow of the well-known Hungarian writer, Baron Lajos Hatvany (1880-1961), a Kossuth Prize winner and member of the Hungarian Academy of Sciences. His financial backing was important in the founding of the progressive literary review, *Nyugat [West]* in 1908.

HERNÁDI, LAJOS (b. 1906). Pianist. Hernádi studied with Bartók at the Ferenc Liszt Academy of Music from 1924 to 1927, and with Artur Schnabel in Berlin in 1928. The following year he returned to Budapest to work with Ernő Dohnányi. In 1933,

Hernádi was awarded the Liszt Prize by the city of Budapest, and since 1945, has been Professor of Piano at the Academy of Music. He has taught a number of the most talented pianists of the present generation, including Tamás Vásáry, Péter Frankl, and Gábor Gabos.

Professor Hernádi's concert tours began in Berlin in 1929 and since then he has performed in all of the European musical capitals. He has also recorded many of the works of Liszt and Bartók, and has written a number of articles and essays on the technique of piano playing. In addition, he has sat on the juries of many leading international piano competitions including those at Warsaw, Moscow, Bolzano, Munich, and Paris. Professor Hernádi's first visit to the United States was in August, 1971, when he lectured at the Southern Vermont Art Center in Manchester.

ILLYÉS, GYULA (b. 1902). Poet, essayist, dramatist, translator, critic—a leading and influential personality in modern Hungarian literature. Illyés was closely connected with the Communist movement in 1919 and, having joined the army of the Hungarian Soviet Republic, was forced to flee to Vienna in 1920, and later to Paris. During his six years in Paris, he was associated with members of the literary avant-garde such as Eluard, Breton, Crevel, and Desmos. In 1926, Illyés returned to Hungary and published his first book of poems. Soon after, he abandoned the avant-garde movement and turned to writing about the social conditions of the downtrodden. Indeed, he had come from a family of agricultural laborers, and his most famous work, *The People of the Puszta* (1937), is a literary sociography describing living conditions of the agricultural laborers near the author's birthplace. Since the 1930's, Illyés has continued to write on sociological and political problems, and has been an important figure in left-wing politics and literature up to the present time.

Illyés has written much autobiographical fiction and has authored a biography of Hungary's greatest poet, Sándor Petőfi. Since 1945 he has written several plays dealing with problems brought about through various decisive phases of Hungarian history. Volumes of his poetry have been published in several languages, including English. He has compiled a Hungarian anthology of French literature, and has translated poetry from almost every European nation as well as Chinese and American poetry. Winner of two Kossuth Prizes, Illyés has received many literary awards, and at present is Vice-President of P.E.N. International.

KÁRPÁTI, JÁNOS (b. 1932). Distinguished musicologist. He studied violin and musicology at the Ferenc Liszt Academy of Music, and has worked as a musical adviser for the Hungarian Radio and Television. Since 1961, he has headed the library at the Academy of Music. During 1957-1958, Kárpáti did research on the folk music of Morocco as a continuation of Bartók's efforts in North Africa. Kárpáti's extensive study of Bartók's quartets has revealed him to be one of the most important Bartók theorists.

KECSKEMÉTI, ISTVÁN (b. 1920). A musicologist who, since 1966, has been Director of the Music Division of the National Széchenyi Library in Budapest. Kecskeméti studied musicology, piano, organ, and composition at the Ferenc Liszt Academy of Music. He is the author of numerous articles in Hungarian and Western European journals, including many on the autograph manuscripts of Johann Joseph Fux, Franz Xaver Süssmayr, Schubert, and Liszt. He has also done a considerable amount of Mozart research. Kecskeméti is the editor of the *Te Deum* in the *Johann Joseph Fux Sämtliche Werke* (Kassel & Graz: Bärenreiter, 1963).

LÁNG, ISTVÁN (b. 1933). Composer. He studied composition at the Ferenc Liszt Academy of Music with János Viski and later with Ferenc Szabó. Since 1966 Láng has been Musical Director of the Hungarian State Puppet Theater. He is the composer of many stage works as well as orchestral and chamber works, and has been a winner of the 1961 Ludwigshafen Composer Competition and of the Erkel Prize in 1968.

LENDVAI, ERNŐ (b. 1925). Musicologist and prominent Bartók theorist. Born in Kaposvár (in southwestern Hungary), Lendvai studied at the Ferenc Liszt Academy of Music with G. Faragó. He was director of the state music schools at Szombathely, Győr, and Szeged from 1949 to 1956. In 1955, he was appointed Professor of Music at the Academy of Music, and from 1960 to 1965 served as Musical Director of the Hungarian Radio and Television. In addition to his numerous books and articles on Bartók, Lendvai is the author of *Tonality and Modality* (1968), a book on Verdi's *Aida* (1966), as well as researcher on the relationship of performers and the works they perform (most notably Toscanini's interpretation of Beethoven).

LENGYEL, MENYHÉRT (1880-1974). Noted writer and dramatist. Lengyel was born in Balmazújváros, and started his career as a journalist. He soon began to write for the theater, however, and by 1929 was appointed director of a Budapest avant-garde theater. In 1931, he emigrated to England, and in 1937, to the United States. It was during these years abroad that he wrote several plays which were adapted for motion pictures, including *The Blue Angel* (1932, with Marlene Dietrich) and *Ninotchka* (1940, with Greta Garbo). His most important plays include *A hálás utókar [Grateful Posterity]*, *Róza néni [Aunt Rose]*, *Sancho Panza királysága [The Kingdom of Sancho Panza]*, and his most famous work, *Taifun [Typhoon]*. Some five years before his death in Budapest, Lengyel left the United States to return to his native Hungary.

LIEBNER, JÁNOS (b. 1923). Violoncellist and music critic. After studying in Budapest, Liebner finished his studies at the Paris Conservatoire where his cello teachers included Pierre Fournier and Maurice Marechal. Liebner has been soloist with the Hungarian State Opera Orchestra, the Budapest Philharmonic, the Hungarian Radio Symphony Orchestra, and is cellist with the Hungarian String Trio. He also plays and is an authority on the *viola da gamba* and the *baryton (viola di bordone)*, the latter an eighteenth-century stringed instrument (now obsolete) found primarily in South Germany. (Joseph Haydn wrote nearly two hundred works for this instrument, mostly in a trio combination with viola and cello written especially for Prince Esterházy, a noted baryton player.) Liebner is a frequent contributor to music journals. A book on Mozart's dramaturgy *(Mozart a színpadon)* was translated into English as *Mozart on the Stage* (London: Calder & Boyars; NY: Praeger, 1972).

LUKÁCS, GYÖRGY (1885-1971). The foremost Marxist philosopher of the twentieth century. Born into an ennobled Jewish family in Budapest, Lukács first came to public attention with a collection of essays on art and philosophy, *Die Seele und die Formen* (1911). He participated in the Communist revolution in Hungary in 1918-1919, and became Minister of Education when Béla Kun's Communist regime took control. When Kun's regime collapsed, however, Lukács fled to Vienna and soon after in 1923, published his best-known work, *History and Class Consciousness*, a study which reinterpreted cultural values from a Marxist viewpoint and at the same time criticized Communism as it had developed in Russia. During these years he came to prefer a less dogmatic and militant view of Marxism as it was currently practiced, and shifted toward a humanitarian socialism based on respect for the individual.

When Hitler came to power, Lukács went to the Soviet Union and lived there through World War II. Following the war he returned to Hungary and became a member of Parliament, President of the Hungarian Academy of Sciences, and Professor of Aesthetics and Philosophy at the University of Budapest. Although purportedly conforming to Stalinist dogmatism during the war years and after, Lukács came to be regarded as a proponent of a Marxist-humanist alternative, which, prior to the Hungarian revolution of 1956, brought him frequent clashes with the Hungarian Communist Party because of his unorthodox views. At the time of the revolution, Lukács was Minister of Culture for the Imre Nagy regime. When Soviet troops stormed into Budapest, Lukács was forced to seek refuge in the Yugoslav embassy. After the revolution, he was deported to Rumania and held under house detention for four months. Thereafter, he was allowed to return to Budapest to resume teaching and publishing, but lost his post and membership in the Communist Party. However, in 1967, he was reinstated into the Party and looked upon with tolerance by the Kádár regime.

An issue of *The New Hungarian Quarterly* (XIII/47 [Autumn 1972]) has been published as a memorial to Lukács, and some of his writings appear there for the first time in English. It is interesting to note that his last public appearance was on March 24, 1971, at the International Bartók Musicological Conference in Budapest.

NAGY, LÁSZLÓ (b. 1925). An outstanding poet of great influence in modern Hungary. Nagy studied at the Budapest Academy of Art, but afterwards began to devote his greater energies to poetry. At present, he is Art Editor of the literary weekly, *Élet és Irodalom [Life and Literature]* in Budapest. He has published nine volumes of poetry and numerous translations of Balkan folk poetry. His overriding interest in peasant culture, which has influenced his own poetry, is attributed to Bartók and his revolutionary approach to the study of folk peoples. A volume of his poems translated into English was published in 1973 by Oxford University Press under the title, *Love of the Scorching Wind*.

RÉZ, PÁL (b. 1930). Literary historian, critic, and translator. Réz finished his studies at Eötvös University in Budapest, majoring in French and Hungarian literature. Since 1951, he has worked in the publishing field, and is currently a reader for Szépirodalmi Könyvkiadó (fiction and poetry publishers) in Budapest. Réz has translated many French, German, and Rumanian novels into Hungarian, has written studies on the history of literature, and is the author of a monograph on Marcel Proust (Budapest: Gondolat, 1961).

RUFFY, PÉTER (b. 1914). Journalist, and frequent contributor to the Budapest daily, *Magyar Nemzet*. For a period, he was a reporter in Paris. His main journalistic interests lie in the cultural fields, and his reports have brought him the Ferenc Rózsa Award, a prize of high distinction in Hungary. His publications include several books on travel, a novel, and a collection of his journalism.

SZABOLCSI, BENCE (1889-1973). A venerable and distinguished musicologist whose work left an indelible mark on Hungarian musical history. Szabolcsi studied law at the University of Budapest and composition at the Ferenc Liszt Academy of Music with Zoltán Kodály and Albert Siklós. He subsequently received his doctorate in musicology in 1923 at the University of Leipzig under Hermann Abert with the dissertation, *Benedetti und Saracini: Beiträge zur Geschichte der Monodie*. In 1926 he joined the staff of the periodical, *Zenei Szemle [Musical Review]*, and in 1929 became a member of that periodical's editorial board. The journal suspended publication during the Second World War, and resumed publication in 1947. Szabolcsi continued his duties with the journal at that time, and returned to the editorial board in 1950.

In 1946, Szabolcsi joined the faculty of the Ferenc Liszt Academy of Music and in the following year, was promoted to Professor of Musicology and made a member of the board of governors of the Academy. In 1948, Professor Szabolcsi became a member of the Hungarian Academy of Sciences, and in 1961, became director of the Budapest Bartók Archives, a division of the Hungarian Academy of Sciences. In addition, he was editor, from the second half of 1967 until his death, of the respected journal, *Studia Musicologica*, was a member of the editorial board of *The New Hungarian Quarterly* from its inception in 1960, and was on the staff of editors preparing the *Corpus Musicae Popularis Hungaricae* which was originally begun by Bartók and Kodály.

Szabolcsi's unique contribution to musicological research is revealed in a bibliography of his works up to 1968 (not including reviews in periodicals or newspapers) in *Bence Szabolcsi Septuagenario*, a special issue of *Studia Musicologica* (XI/1-4 [1969]) edited by his colleague, Professor Dénes Bartha. Szabolcsi's first major work was the two volume *Zenei Lexikon [Dictionary of Music]*, done in collaboration with Aladár Tóth in 1930. A second edition appeared in 1935, and a revised, third edition was published in 1965 under the editorship of Dénes Bartha. His numerous books include: *A zene története [A History of Music]* (1940); *A magyar zenetörténet kézikönyve* (1947; translated into English as *A Concise History of Hungarian Music*, 1964); a monograph on Beethoven (1948); *Liszt Ferenc estéje* (1956; translated into English as *The Twilight of Ferenc Liszt*, 1959); and the two volume *A magyar zene századai [Centuries of Hungarian Music]* (1959-1961). This latter work has been called Szabolcsi's *magnum opus* by his colleague and former student, Ferenc Bónis. Szabolcsi's work on Vivaldi, including the discovery of presumed lost works of this composer, is well known. With Bartha, Szabolcsi was co-editor of *Zenetudományi Tanulmányok [Studies in Musicology]* from 1952 to 1962. Much of contemporary Hungarian Bartók research has emanated from the volumes of this series.

SZINAI, MIKLÓS (b. 1918). Archivist at the Hungarian National Archives in Budapest. His historical research has been addressed mainly toward Hungarian history between 1919 and 1944. His most recent book, done in collaboration with László Szücs, was *Bethlen István titkos iratai [The Secret Papers of István Bethlen]*, published in 1972. An earlier collaboration of these authors resulted in *Horthy Miklós titkos iratai [The Secret Papers of Miklós Horthy]*, first published in 1963 with an English language edition appearing in 1965. The book is now in its fourth edition.

VÁMOS, MAGDA. Journalist, formerly on the staff of the Budapest daily, *Magyar Nemzet*. Although her main area of interest is music criticism, she has also written translations and biographies, including a biography of Ármin Vámbéry (1832-1913), the Hungarian Orientalist-Ethnologist (*Resid Efendi; Vámbéry Ármin élete*, Budapest: Móra Ferenc Könyvkiadó, 1966), and a book on Abraham Lincoln, done in collaboration with Endre Sós (Budapest: Magvető Könyvkiadó, 1964).

VITÁNYI, IVÁN (b. 1925). Writer and journalist. Vitányi attended the English-language college at Sárospatak. He has worked on the staff of the periodical, *Muzsika*, and since 1960, has been on the staff of *Valóság*, a monthly devoted to philosophy, sociology, and anthropology. He has written numerous essays in various musical and sociological reviews, and his books include *A tánc [The Dance]* (Budapest: Gondolat, 1963), and *A zene lélektana [The Psychology of Music]* (Budapest: Gondolat, 1969). An example of his profound interest in relating the arts to the social sciences is found in the article, "Psycho-Sociological Experiments with Music in Hungary" (*Studia Musicologica* XIII/1-4 [1971], 95-121), written in collaboration with M. Sági.

BIBLIOGRAPHY

The present selective bibliography is intended as a guide to the most significant books and articles written on Bartók during the period 1963-1973. The second edition of Halsey Stevens' *The Life and Music of Béla Bartók* (NY: Oxford University Press, 1964) contains the most complete Bartók bibliography up to the time of its publication. Reviews of books, music, recordings, and concerts have not been included in the present bibliography. Articles from important anthologies have been cited individually. These include selected studies from *Documenta Bartókiana* (See: DILLE, No. **70**), all essays from the *International Musicological Conference in Commemoration of Béla Bartók 1971* (See: UJFALUSSY, No. **287**), and relevant articles from the Szabolcsi Festschrift (See: BÓNIS, No. **36**). English translations are given for titles in languages other than French, German, and Italian. American doctoral dissertations are identified with the appropriate UM and DA numbers. UM stands for University Microfilms, Inc., Ann Arbor, Michigan, from whom microfilms and xerographic reproductions of dissertations may be purchased. DA refers to the volumes of *Dissertation Abstracts*, also published by University Microfilms, Inc., where six-hundred-word abstracts of the dissertation appear. *Dissertation Abstracts* is available in most college and university as well as large public libraries.

The organization of the bibliography is purely alphabetical by author, with appropriate cross references added. All items by one person are placed in chronological order so that the reader may see how a given author produced work on Bartók. Separate entries are included for subsequent translations of a given book or article.

Not included in this bibliography, but of special interest, is the project undertaken by the Hungarian State Recording Company, *Hungaroton* (formerly *Qualiton*), to record on phonodisc the complete works of Bartók. The project, begun in 1966, has maintained generally high standards of performance and of recording technique. The record jacket notes are scholarly, all of them written by leading Hungarian Bartók authorities.

ABRAHAM, Gerald. "Bartók and England," *Studia Musicologica* V/1-4 (1963), 339-46.   **1**

ACKERE, Jules van. *Vioolconcerto 1937/38 en Concerto voor orkest 1943 van Béla Bartók [Violin Concerto 1937/38 and Concerto for Orchestra 1943 by Béla Bartók].* Antwerp: Nederlandsch boekhandel, 1963. [*Leren luisteren,* 9.]   **2**

AHRENDT, Christine. See: WALSH, No. **302**.

ALEXANDRU, Tiberiu. "Béla Bartók et la musique populaire roumaine," *Muzica* XXI/12 (Dec 1971), 43-46.   **3**

BARACZKA, István. "Egy ismeretlen Bartók-levél [An unknown Bartók letter]," *Budapest* V/2 (Feb 1967), 11.   **4**

BARTHA, Dénes. "La Musique de Bartók," in: Edith WEBER, ed, *La Résonance dans les échelles musicales* (Paris: Centre National de la Recherche Scientifique, 1963), 279-90.   **5**

6   BARTÓK, Béla. *Slovenské L'udové Piesne [Slovakian folk songs]*. Bratislava: Vydavatel'stvo Slovenskej Akadémie Vied, 1959-70. 2 vols.

7   BARTÓK, Béla. "The Second Piano Concerto," *Tempo* No. 65 (Summer 1963), 5-7.

8   BARTÓK, Béla. *Bartók Béla kézírása [Béla Bartók's handwriting]*, Bence Szabolcsi & Benjámin Rajeczky, eds. Budapest: Zeneműkiadó Vállalat, 1964.

     Revised edition from the 1961 original.

9   BARTÓK, Béla. "Ein Brief an Kodály," *Documenta Bartókiana* I (1964), 16-18.

10   BARTÓK, Béla. *Ethnomusikologische Schriften, Faksimile-Nachdrucke*, Denijs Dille, ed. Budapest: Editio Musica; Mainz: B. Schott's Söhne. 4 vols.

     I.   Das ungarische Volkslied, 1965.
     II. Volksmusik der Rumänen von Maramureş, 1966.
     III. Rumänische Volkslieder aus dem Komitat Bihar, 1967.
     IV. Melodien der rumänischen Colinde (Weihnachtslieder), 1968.

11   BARTÓK, Béla. "Vier unbekannte Briefe," *Österreichische Musikzeitschrift* XX/9 (Sep 1965), 449-60.

     Edited, with commentary by Denijs Dille.

12   BARTÓK, Béla. *Bartók Béla összegyűjtött írásai I [Collected writings of Béla Bartók I]*, András Szőllősy, ed. Budapest: Zeneműkiadó Vállalat, 1966.

13   BARTÓK, Béla. *Rumanian Folk Music*, Benjamin Suchoff, ed. The Hague: Martinus Nijhoff. 5 vols.

     I.   Instrumental Melodies, 1967.
     II. Vocal Melodies, 1967.
     III. Texts, 1967.
     IV. Rumanian Carols and Christmas Songs (Colinde), 1975.
     V.   Folk Music of Maramureş County [projected; to be published]

14   BARTÓK, Béla. *Béla Bartók. Lettere scelte*, János Demény, ed, Italian translation by Paolo Ruziscka. Milan: Il Saggiatore di Alberto Mondadori Editore, 1969.

15   BARTÓK, Béla. *A Complete Catalogue of His Published Works.* London: Boosey & Hawkes, 1970.

     Includes all works published by Boosey & Hawkes (London & NY), Universal Edition (Vienna & London), and Zeneműkiadó Vállalat-Editio Musica (Budapest).

BARTÓK, Béla. *Bartóks Briefe in die Slowakei*, Vladimir Čížik, ed. Bratislava: **16**
Slovenské Národné Múzeum, 1971.

BARTÓK, Béla. *Béla Bartók Letters*, János Demény, ed, English translation by **17**
Péter Balabán and István Farkas, translation revised by Elisabeth West
and Colin Mason. London: Faber & Faber; NY: St. Martin's Press, 1971.

BARTÓK, Béla. "Két Bartók-levél Reményi Józsefhez [Two letters of Béla **18**
Bartók to József Reményi]," *Muzsika* XIV/5 (May 1971), 1-4.
Edited, with commentary by János Demény.

BARTÓK, Béla. "Revolution and Evolution in Art," *Tempo* No. 103 (1972), 4-7. **19**
Lecture of February 1943 delivered at Harvard University. The first of eight
projected lectures, only four of which were given. (Also included in *Béla Bartók
Essays*. See: BARTÓK, No. **21**.)

BARTÓK, Béla. *Musiksprachen—Aufsätze und Vorträge*, Bence Szabolcsi, ed, **20**
German translation by Jörg Buschmann & Mirza Schüching, with a
foreward & comments by Christian Kaden. Leipzig: Philipp Reclam, 1972.

BARTÓK, Béla. *Béla Bartók Essays*, edited & compiled by Benjamin Suchoff. **21**
London: Faber & Faber, [in progress].

BARTÓK, Béla, Jr. "Mein Vater Béla Bartók—sein Weg für die moderne **22**
Musik," *Universitas* [Stuttgart] XX/3 (Mar 1965), 291-97.

BARTÓK, Ditta Pasztory. "26 September 1945: zum 20. Todestag von Béla **23**
Bartók," *Österreichische Musikzeitschrift* XX/9 (Sep 1965), 445-49.

BÁTOR, Victor. *The Béla Bartók Archives; History and Catalogue*. NY: Bartók **24**
Archives, 1963.

BENKŐ, András. *Bartók Béla Romániai Hangversenyei (1922-1936) [Béla* **25**
Bartók's Rumanian concert programs (1922-1936)]. Bucharest:
Kriterion, 1970.

BERGER, Gregor. *Béla Bartók*. Wolfenbüttel: Möseler, 1963. (*Beiträge zur* **26**
Schulmusik, 13.)

BIGGS, George B., Jr. *The Return Effect in Selected Twentieth-Century Works* **27**
for Orchestra as Determined by Factors other than Theme and Key.
Ph.D. Dissertation: Indiana University, 1968. 164 pp. UM:69-4729.
DA: XXIX/9 (Mar 1969), 3166-7-A.

28   BODNÁR, György. "Bartók et le mouvement 'Nyugat'," *Studia Musicologica*
        V/1-4 (1963), 347-54.

29   BÓNIS, Ferenc. "Quotations in Bartók's Music," *Studia Musicologica* V/1-4
        (1963), 355-82.

30   BÓNIS, Ferenc. *Béla Bartóks Leben in Bildern.* Budapest: Corvina Press;
        London: Boosey & Hawkes, 1964.

31   BÓNIS, Ferenc, & Bence SZABOLCSI, eds. *Bartók par l'image.* Budapest:
        Corvina Press, 1964.

32   BÓNIS, Ferenc, & Bence SZABOLCSI, eds. *Béla Bartók: His Life in Pictures.*
        Budapest: Corvina Press; NY: Boosey & Hawkes, 1964.

33   BÓNIS, Ferenc. "Gemeinsame musikalische und wissenschaftliche Werke von
        Béla Bartók und Zoltán Kodály," *Documenta Bartókiana* I (1964), 11-12.

34   BÓNIS, Ferenc. "Zoltán Kodálys Schriften uber Béla Bartók," *Documenta
        Bartókiana* I (1964), 13-15.

35   BÓNIS, Ferenc. "Zitate in Bartóks Musik," *Österreichische Musikzeitschrift*
        XX/9 (Sep 1965), 467-82.

        BÓNIS, Ferenc. (1968)   See: SZABOLCSI, No. **265**.

36   BÓNIS, Ferenc, ed. *Magyar Zenetörténeti Tanulmányok: Szabolcsi Bence 70.
        születésnapjára [Studies in Hungarian musical history dedicated to Bence
        Szabolcsi on his 70th birthday].* Budapest: Zeneműkiadó Vállalat, 1969.

        Szabolcsi Festschrift. Contains articles on Bartók by Denijs DILLE [See: No. **86**],
        György KROÓ [See: No. **163**], László SOMFAI [See: No. **241**], Margit TÓTH
        [See: No **278**], & József UJFALUSSY [See: No. **283**].

37   BÓNIS, Ferenc. "Bartók und der Verbunkos," in: József UJFALUSSY & János
        BREUER, eds, *International Musicological Conference in Commemoration
        of Béla Bartók 1971* (Budapest: Editio Musica, 1972), 145-53.

38   BÓNIS, Ferenc. *Béla Bartók: His Life in Pictures and Documents.* Budapest:
        Editio Musica, 1972.

39   BÓNIS, Ferenc. *Bartók Béla élete képekben és dokumentumokban [Béla Bartók:
        his life in pictures and documents].* Budapest: Zeneműkiado Vallalat, 1972.

BRATUZ, Damiana. *The Folk Element in the Piano Music of Béla Bartók.* Doctoral **40**
Document (D. Mus., piano, Part One): Indiana University, 1967. 215 pp.

BREUER, János. "Egy Bartók-dallam nyomában [The tracing of a Bartók **41**
melody]," *Muzsika* XIV/8 (Aug 1971), 26-29 (I. Szerkezet [Structure]);
XIV/9 (Sep 1971), 37-39 (II. Dramaturgiája [Dramaturgy]); XIV/10
(Oct 1971), 25-27 (III. Interpretáció [Interpretation]); XIV/11 (Nov 1971),
31-32 (IV. Tradició [Tradition]).
Discusses a melody from the *Concerto for Orchestra.*

BREUER, János. "On Three Posthumous Editions of Works by Bartók," *Studia* **42**
Musicologica XIII/1-4 (1971), 357-62.

BREUER, János, co-editor. (1972) See: UJFALUSSY, No. **287**.

BREUER, János. "Die zeitgenössische ungarische Musik auf dem Pfade Bartóks," **43**
in: József UJFALUSSY & János BREUER, eds, *International Musicological*
Conference in Commemoration of Béla Bartók 1971 (Budapest: Editio Musica,
1972), 163-67.

BURLAS, Ladislav. "Neuerertum und Tradition in Bartóks Formenwelt," *Studia* **44**
Musicologica V/1-4 (1963), 383-91.

BURLAS, Ladislav. "The Influence of Slovakian Folk Music on Bartók's Musical **45**
Idiom," in: József UJFALUSSY & János BREUER, eds, *International*
Musicological Conference in Commemoration of Béla Bartók 1971 (Budapest:
Editio Musica, 1972), 181-87.

BUSH, Alan. See: LENDVAI, No. **181**.

CHAILLEY, Jacques. "Essai d'analyse du 'Mandarin Merveilleux'," *Studia* **46**
Musicologica V/1-4 (1963), 11-39.

CHAO FENG. "Bartók and Chinese Music Culture," *Studia Musicologica* V/1-4 **47**
(1963), 393-401.

CHIRA, I., D. SMÂNTÂNESCU, *et al. Contribuţii la cunoaşterea legăturilor lui* **48**
Béla Bartók cu viaţa noastră muzicală. Volum editat cu prilejul comemorăii
unui sfert de veac de la moartea [Contributions to the knowledge of the
relation between Béla Bartók and our musical life. A volume published on
the commemoration of the anniversary of his death]. Oradea: Comitetul de
cultură şi educaţie socialistă al judeţulŭi Bihor, 1971.
A collection of essays on Bartók's ethnomusicological activities in Rumania.

49   CHITTUM, Donald. "The Synthesis of Materials and Devices in Non-Serial Counterpoint," *The Music Review* XXXI/2 (May 1970), 123–35.
Refers to Bartók's *Music for Strings, Percussion, and Celesta.*

50   CITRON, Pierre. *Bartók.* Paris: Éditions du Seuil, 1963. (*Collection "Solfèges,"* 24.)

51   ČÍŽIK, Vladimír. "Neuverejnené listy Bélu Bartóka z korešpondencie Alexandra Albrechta [The unpublished letters by Béla Bartók from the correspondence of Alexander Albrecht]," *Slovenska Hudba* XIII/6–7 (1969), 214–20.

ČÍŽIK, Vladimír, ed. (1971) See: BARTÓK, No. **16.**

52   CLEGG, David. "Das englische Programm der Kossuth-Symphonie," *Documenta Bartókiana* I(1964), 70–74.

53   CLEGG, David. "Remarks to the Article, 'Quotations in Bartók's Music' by F. Bónis," *Studia Musicologica* VI/3–4 (1964), 380–81. See also: BÓNIS, No. **29.**

54   COSMA, Viorel. "Bartók şi începuturile culegerilor de folclor românesc. Pe marginea unor documente inedite [Bartók and the first collection of Rumanian folklore. Marginal notes concerning several unpublished documents]," *Studii şi cercetări de istoria artei. Teatru, Muzică, Cinematografie* XVIII/2 (1971), 239–51.

55   CROSS, Anthony. "Debussy and Bartók," *The Musical Times* CVIII [No. 1488] (Feb 1967), 125–27.

56   DALTON, David. *Genesis and Synthesis of the Bartók Viola Concerto.* Doctoral Document (D. Mus., viola, Part One): Indiana University, 1970. 77 pp.

57   DAWSON, George C. *Bartók's Development as Orchestrator.* Ph.D. Dissertation: University of Southern California, 1970. 2 vols.: 397, 523 pp. UM: 70–19, 112. DA: XXXI/4 (Oct 1970), 1831-A.

58   DEMÉNY, János. "Béla Bartóks Stellung in der Musikgeschichte des 20. Jahrhunderts," *Studia Musicologica* V/1–4 (1963), 403–14.

59   DEMÉNY, János. "Zeitgenössische Kritiken über die Erstaufführungen der Kossuth-Symphonie von Béla Bartók (Budapest, 13 Jan. 1904—Manchester, 19. Febr. 1904)," *Documenta Bartókiana* I (1964), 30–66.

DEMÉNY, János. "Das Konzert vom 12. Februar 1911 (Pressestimmen),"   **60**
    Documenta Bartókiana II (1965), 77–90.

DEMÉNY, János. "A Bartók-kultusz tévedései [Errors of the Bartok cult],"   **61**
    Kortárs XI/4 (Apr 1967), 637–43.

DEMÉNY, János. "A szecesszió zenében [Seccession in music]," *Filológiai*   **62**
    Közlöny XIII/1–2 (1967), 221–26.

    Discusses Bartók in relation to Busoni, Debussy, Delius, Reger, & R. Strauss.

DEMÉNY, János. *Bartók Béla a zongoraművész [Béla Bartók the pianist].*   **63**
    Budapest: Zeneműkiadó Vállalat, 1968.

DEMÉNY, János. (1968) See: SZABOLCSI, No. **265**.

DEMÉNY, János, ed. (1969) See: BARTÓK, No. **14**.

DEMÉNY, János. "Ady-tanulmánykötet Bartók könyvtárában [A volume of   **64**
    Ady's essays in Bartók's library]," *Muzsika* XIV/3 (Mar 1971), 9–11.

DEMÉNY, János, ed. (May 1971) See: BARTÓK, No. **18**.

DEMÉNY, János. "Ady-Gedichtbände in Bartóks Bibliothek," in: József   **65**
    UJFALUSSY & János BREUER, eds, *International Musicological*
    Conference in Commemoration of Béla Bartók 1971 (Budapest: Editio
    Musica, 1972), 111–20.

DEMÉNY, János, ed. (1971) See: BARTÓK, No. **17**.

DEMÉNY, János. "Bartókiána a Thália Színházban [Bartókiana in the Thalia   **66**
    Theater]," *Muzsika* XV/1 (Jan 1972), 22–25.

DERI, Otto. "Béla Bartók: A Portrait of His Personality Drawn from His   **67**
    Letters," *Current Musicology* No. 13 (1972), 90–103.

    Edited with an introduction by Neal Zaslaw.

DEZSÉNYI, Béla. "Bartók és a nemzeti könyvtár zenei gyűjteménye [Bartók   **68**
    and the music collection of the national library]," *Muzsika* XIV/3
    (Mar 1971), 15–17.

DILLE, Denijs. "Les problèmes des recherches sur Bartók," *Studia Musicologica*   **69**
    V/1–4 (1963), 415–23.

70   DILLE, Denijs, ed. *Documenta Bartókiana.* Budapest: Akadémiai Kiadó; Mainz: B. Schott's Söhne. Vol. I (1964), Vol. II (1965), Vol. III (1968), Vol. IV (1970).

71   DILLE, Denijs. "Bemerkungen zum Programm der symphonischen Dichtung 'Kossuth' und zur Aufführung dieser Komposition," *Documenta Bartókiana* I (1964), 75-103.

72   DILLE, Denijs. "Béla Bartók und Wien," *Österreichische Musikzeitschrift* XIX/11 (Nov 1964), 510-18.

73   DILLE, Denijs. "Az ifjú Bartók három kamaraműve [Three chamber works of the young Bartók]," *Muzsika* VII/12 (Dec 1964), 16-17.

DILLE, Denijs, ed. (1965-)   See: BARTÓK, No. 10.

74   DILLE, Denijs. "A Bartók-archivum munkájáról [The Budapest Bartók Archives]," *Magyar Zene* VI/1 (1965), 140f.

75   DILLE, Denijs. "Budapestškii Archiv Bartóka [The Budapest Bartók Archives]," *Sovetskaya Muzyka* XXIX/2 (Feb 1965), 109-10.

76   DILLE, Denijs. "Die Beziehung zwischen Bartók und Schönberg," *Documenta Bartókiana* II (1965), 53-61.

DILLE, Denijs, ed. (1965)   See: BARTÓK, No. 11.

77   DILLE, Denijs. "Dokumente über Bartóks Beziehung zu Busoni," *Documenta Bartókiana* II (1965), 62-76.

78   DILLE, Denijs. "Angaben zum Violinkonzert 1907, den Deux portraits, dem Quartett Op. 7 und den Zwei rumänischen Tänzen," *Documenta Bartókiana* II (1965), 91-102.

79   DILLE, Denijs. "Le vingtième anniversaire de la mort de Bartók," *Studia Musicologica* VIII/1-4 (1966), 3-10.

80   DILLE, Denijs. "Bartók—seine Persönlichkeit und sein Werk in Kunst und Wissenschaft," *Universitas* [Stuttgart] XXII/2 (Feb 1967), 171-77.

81   DILLE, Denijs. "Ein unbekanntes Bartók-Manuskript," *Österreichische Musikzeitschrift* XXII/5 (May 1967), 283-84.

82   DILLE, Denijs. "Béla Bartók und sein Lebenswerk für die moderne Musik," *Universitas* [Stuttgart] XXIII/2 (Feb 1968), 125-30.

DILLE, Denijs. "Bartókov hudobný prejav a folklór [Bartók's musical language   83
and folklore]," *Slovenská Hudba* XII/5 (June 1968), 216-21.

DILLE, Denijs. "Bartók, lecteur de Nietzsche et de La Rochefoucauld," *Studia*   84
Musicologica X/3-4 (1968), 209-28.

DILLE, Denijs. "Bartókov pobyt v Grlici a jeho objavenie l'udovej piesne   85
[Bartók's stay in Grlica and his discovery of folk songs]," *Slovenská Hudba*
XIII/3 (1969), 116-21.

DILLE, Denijs. "Bartók és Kodály első találkozása [The first meeting of Bartók   86
and Kodály]," in: Ferenc BÓNIS, ed, *Magyar Zenetörténeti Tanulmányok*
. . . [Szabolcsi Festschrift], 317-22. See: BÓNIS, No. **36**.

DILLE, Denijs. "L'Allegro Barbaro de Bartók," *Studia Musicologica* XII/1-4   87
(1970), 3-9.

DILLE, Denijs. "Gerlice puszta: Mai bis November 1904," *Documenta*   88
Bartókiana IV (1970), 15-40.

DILLE, Denijs. "Bartók und das Historisches Konzert vom 12. Januar 1918,"   89
Documenta Bartókiana IV (1970), 43-69.

DILLE, Denijs. "Bartók und die Volksmusik," *Documenta Bartókiana* IV (1970),   90
70-128.

DILLE, Denijs. "Bartóks Text zur 'Cantata Profana'," *Documenta Bartókiana*   91
IV (1970), 190-93.

DILLE, Denijs. "Bartók defenseur de Kodály," *Studia Musicologica* XIII/1-4   92
(1971), 347-53.

DILLE, Denijs. "Bartóks Jeugdwerken [Bartók's early works]," *Vlaams*   93
muziektijdschrift XIII (1971).

DJOUDJEFF, Stoyan. "Bartók—promoteur de l'ethnomusicologie balkanique   94
et sud-est européenne," in: József UJFALUSSY & János BREUER, eds,
International Musicological Conference in Commemoration of Béla Bartók
1971 (Budapest: Editio Musica, 1972), 189-95.

Documenta Bartókiana. See: DILLE, No. **70**.

DOFLEIN, Erich. "Bartók und die Musikpädagogik," *Kontakte* (1964), 12-16.   95

96   DONAHUE, Robert L. *A Comparative Analysis of Phrase Structure in Selected Movements of the String Quartets of Béla Bartók and Walter Piston.* D.M.A. Dissertation (Part Two): Cornell University, 1964. 161 pp. UM: 64-8732. DA: XXVIII/8 (Feb 1968), 3207-8-A.

97   DOWNEY, John W. *La Musique populaire dans l'oeuvre de Béla Bartók.* Paris: Centre de Documentation Universitaire, 1966. (*Publications de l'Institut de Musicologie de l'Université de Paris*, 5.)

98   ELLSWORTH, Ray. "The Shadow of Genius: Béla Bartók and Tibor Serly," *The American Record Guide* XXXII/1 (Sep 1965), 26-33.

99   ELSCHEK, Oskár. "Bartóks Beziehung zur Volksmusik und Volksmusikforschung," in: József UJFALUSSY & János BREUER, eds, *International Musicological Conference in Commemoration of Béla Bartók 1971* (Budapest: Editio Musica, 1972), 197-207.

100   FÁBIÁN, Imre. "Debussy und die Meister der ungarischen Musik," *Österreichische Musikzeitschrift* XVIII/1 (Jan 1963), 23-28.

101   FÁBIÁN, Imre. "Béla Bartók und die Wiener Schule," *Österreichische Musikzeitschrift* XIX/5-6 (May-June 1964), 255-57f.

102   FÁBIÁN, Imre. "Bartók im Wandel der Zeiturteile," *Österreichische Musikzeitschrift* XXVI/3 (Mar 1971), 127-34.

103   FÁBIÁN, Imre. "Bartók und die Zeitgenossen," *Melos* XXXVIII/11 (Nov 1971), 465-68.

104   FASSETT, Agatha. *Béla Bartók: The American Years.* NY: Dover, 1970. (Reprint of the original edition, whose title was: *The Naked Face of Genius: Béla Bartók's American Years.* Boston: Houghton Mifflin, 1958.)

105   FEUER, Mária. *Kinek kell a modern zene? [Who wants modern music?]. Zeneélet.* Budapest: Zeneműkiadó Vállalat, 1970.

      Discusses the audience appreciation of Bartók and other contemporary Hungarian composers.

106   FLEURET, Maurice. "Lorsque Béla Bartók découvrait Paris...," *Musica-Disques* No. 109 (1963), 4-10.

FLEURET, Maurice. "Bartók e a juventude," *Arte Musical* XXXIII/25-26   107
    (1967), 44-52.

FODOR, Ilona. "A fából faragott királyfi: elidegenedés és művészi teremtmény   108
    [*The Wooden Prince:* alienation and artistic achievement]," *Valóság* X/4
    (1967), 22-33.

FODOR, Ilona. "Bartók magyarság-élményének gyökerei [Origins of Bartók's   109
    patriotism]," *Kortárs* XIV/9 (Sep 1970), 1370-78.

FRENCH, Gilbert G. "Continuity and Discontinuity in Bartók's *Concerto for*   110
    Orchestra," *The Music Review* XXVIII/2 (May 1967), 122-34.

FUCHSS, Werner. "Béla Bartók und die Schweiz: eine Wanderausstellung,"   111
    Schweizerische Musikzeitung CX/5 (Sep-Oct 1970), 312-14.

GÁL, István. "Babits és Bartók [Babits and Bartók]," *Kortárs* XII/5 (May   112
    1968), 798-808.

GÁL, Zsuzsa. *Bartók Béla.* Budapest: Zeneműkiadó Vállalat, 1970.   113
    For young readers.

GENTILUCCI, Armando. "Appunti su Bartók e l'espressionismo," *Musica*   114
    d'oggi VIII/8-10 (1965), 243-44.

GERVERS, Hilda. "Béla Bartók's *Öt Dal (Five Songs), Op. 15,*" *The Music*   115
    Review XXX/4 (Nov 1969), 291-99.

GOLÉA, Antoine. "Bartók, humaniste et musicien," *Musica-Disques* No. 141   116
    (1965), 15-21.

GORCZYCKA, Monika. "Neue Merkmale der Klangtechnik in Bartóks   117
    Streichquartetten," *Studia Musicologica* V/1-4 (1963), 425-33.

GOW, David. "Tonality and Structure in Bartók's first two String Quartets,"   118
    The Music Review XXXIV/3-4 (Aug-Nov 1973), 259-71.

GROTH, Clause R., Jr. *A Study of the Technical and Interpretative Problems*   119
    Inherent in Bartók's Violin Sonatas. D.M.A. Dissertation: University
    of Oregon, 1971. 147 pp. UM: 72-8536-A. DA: XXXII/9 (Mar 1972),
    5266-A.

120 GUERRY, Jack E. *Bartók's Concertos for Solo Piano: A Stylistic and Formal Analysis*. Ph.D. Dissertation: University of Michigan, 1964. 216 pp. UM: 65-684. DA: XXV/9 (Mar 1965), 5319-20-A.

121 HÄNDEL, G. "Hommage à Robert Schumann. Ein Beitrag zum Thema: Bartók und Schumann," *Studia Musicologica* V/1-4 (1963), 173-77.

122 HALL, Anne Carothers. *Texture in Violin Concertos of Stravinsky, Berg, Schoenberg, and Bartók*. Ph.D. Dissertation: University of Michigan, 1971. 367 pp. UM: 72-14,884. DA: XXXII/11 (May 1972), 6476-A.

123 HARANGOZÓ, Gyula. "Erinnerungen an Béla Bartók," *Österreichische Musikzeitschrift* XXII/5 (May 1967), 258-61.

124 HARTZELL, Lawrence W. *Contrapuntal-Harmonic Factors in Selected Works of Béla Bartók*. Ph.D. Dissertation: University of Kansas, 1970. 225 pp. UM: 70-25,343. DA: XXXI/6 (Dec 1970), 2957-A.

125 HELM, Everett B. "Bartók on Stage: Fresh Light on a Long Undervalued Dramatic Trilogy," *High Fidelity* XIV/11 (Nov 1964), 74f.

126 HELM, Everett B. "Bartóks Kindheit und Jugend," *Melos* XXXII/5 (May 1965), 145-54.

127 HELM, Everett B. "Béla Bartók und die Volksmusik—zur 20. Wiederkehr von Bartóks Todestag," *Neue Zeitschrift für Musik* CXXVI/9 (Sep 1965), 330-33.

128 HELM, Everett B. *Béla Bartók in Selbstzeugnissen und Bilddokumenten*. Reinbek bei Hamburg: Rowohlt, 1965. [*Rowohlts Monographien*, 107.]

129 HELM, Everett B. *Bartók*. London: Faber & Faber, 1971; NY: Thomas Y. Crowell, 1972.

   Abridged version of the German edition, No. 128.

130 HERNÁDI, Lajos. "Béla Bartók—Pianist and Teacher," *American Music Teacher* XXII/3 (Jan 1973), 28-31.

   Similar to an article in the present volume (see pp. 152-58).

131 HIRASHIMA, Naeko. "Barutoko no Ongaku no Tokushitsu nikansuru ichi Kosatsu [A consideration of the character of Béla Bartók's music]," *Ongakugaku* XV/1 (1969), 53-65.

HORN, Herbert A. *Idiomatic Writing in the Piano Music of Béla Bartók.*   132
   D.M.A. Dissertation: University of Southern California, 1963. 237 pp.
   UM: 64-3811. DA: XXIV/12 (June 1964), 5451-2-A.

HUNDT, Theodor. *Bartóks Satztechnik in den Klavierwerken.* Regensburg: 133
   Gustav Bosse, 1971. (*Kölner Beiträge zur Musikforschung,* 63.)

JAGAMAS, Ioan. "Despre sisteme tonale în 'Mikrokosmos' de Béla Bartók,"   134
   Lucrări de muzicologie II (1966), 99-122.
   Summaries in French, German, and Russian.

JÁRDÁNYI, Pál. "Bartók und die Ordnung der Volkslieder," *Studia*   135
   Musicologica V/1-4 (1963), 435-39.

JÁRDÁNYI, Pál. "Die Volksmusik in Bartóks Kunst," in: Ludwig FINSCHER   136
   & Christoph-Hellmut MAHLING, eds, *Festschrift Walter Wiora* (Kassel:
   Bärenreiter, 1967), 466-70.

JEMNITZ, Sándor. "Persönliches über Béla Bartók," in: Erich MARCKHL, ed,   137
   Festschrift aus Anlass der Erhebung des Steiermärkischen Landeskonser-
   vatoriums zur Akademie für Musik und darstellende Kunst in Graz (Graz:
   Leykam, 1963), 83-92.

KAPST, Erich. *Die "polymodal-Chromatik" Béla Bartóks - Ein Beitrag zur*   138
   stilkritischen Analyse. Ph.D. Dissertation: Karl Marx University (Leipzig),
   1969. 2 vols. 413 pp.

KAPST, Erich. "Stilkriterien der polymodal-chromatischen Gestaltungsweise im   139
   Werk Béla Bartóks," *Beiträge zur Musikwissenschaft* XII/1 (1970), 1-28.

KAPST, Erich. "Bartóks Anmerkungen zum 'Mikrokosmos'," *Musik und*   140
   Gesellschaft XX/9 (Sep 1970), 585-95.

KAPST, Erich. "Zum Tonalitätsbegriff bei Bartók," in: József UJFALUSSY   141
   & János BREUER, eds, *International Musicological Conference in*
   Commemoration of Béla Bartók 1971 (Budapest: Editio Musica, 1972),
   31-40.

KÁRPÁTI, János. "Bartók és Schönberg [Bartók and Schönberg]," *Magyar*   142
   Zene IV/6 (Dec 1963), 563-85; V/1 (Feb 1964), 15-30, 130-42.

143 KÁRPÁTI, János. "Bartók Béla és a kelet [Béla Bartók and the East]," *Magyar Zene* V/6 (Dec 1964), 581-93.

144 KÁRPÁTI, János. "Béla Bartók and the East (Contribution to the History of the Influence of Eastern Elements on European Music)," *Studia Musicologica* VI/3-4 (1964), 179-94.

145 KÁRPÁTI, János. *Bartók vonósnégyesei [Bartók's string quartets]*. Budapest: Zeneműkiadó Vállalat, 1967.

146 KÁRPÁTI, János. "Les gammes populaires et le système chromatique dans l'oeuvre de Béla Bartók," *Studia Musicologica* XI/1-4 (1969), 227-40.

147 KÁRPÁTI, János. "Le désaccordage dans la technique de composition de Bartók," in: József UJFALUSSY & János BREUER, eds, *International Musicological Conference in Commemoration of Béla Bartók 1971* (Budapest: Editio Musica, 1972), 41-51.

148 KARTMAN, Myron H. *Analysis and Performance Problems in the Second, Fourth, and Sixth String Quartets by Béla Bartók.* Mus.A.D. Dissertation: Boston University, 1970. 253 pp. UM: 71-13,418. DA: XXXII/3 (Sep 1971), 1552-A.

149 KECSKEMÉTI, István. "Bartók Béla Keszthelyen. Egy emlékkiállítás tanulsága iból [Béla Bartók in Keszthely. The lesson of a commemorative exhibition]," *Magyar Zene* IX/3 (Sep 1968), 301-8.

150 KERÉNYI, György, & Benjámin RAJECZKY. "Über Bartóks Volksliedaufzeichnungen," *Studia Musicologica* V/1-4 (1963), 441-48.

151 KESZI, Imre. "A vitatott Bartók [Bartók the debated]," *Új Irás* XI/3 (Mar 1971), 75-83.

152 KHOLUPOVA, V. "Ritmi i forma [Rhythm and form]," *Sovetskaya Muzyka* XXX/3 (Mar 1966), 26-31.

153 KLIMO, Štefan. "Bartókove klavírne koncerty [Bartók's piano concertos]," *Slovenská Hudba* XV/3-4 (1971), 103-9.

154 KNEIF, Tibor. "Zur Entstehung und Kompositionstechnik von Bartóks Konzert für Orchester," *Die Musikforschung* XXVI/1 (Jan-Mar 1973), 36-51.

155 KÖHLER, Hans-Joachim. *Béla Bartóks pädagogisches Klavierwerk "Mikrokosmos" als Weg zum Hören neuer Musik.* Ph.D. Dissertation: Leipzig, 1966. 312 pp.

KOLNEDER, Walter. "Béla Bartók—seine Musik und seine Persönlichkeit,"   **156**
   Universitas [Stuttgart] XXIV/4 (Apr 1969), 417-24.

KÖRTVÉLYES, Géza. *A modern táncművészet útján [Concerning the art*   **157**
   of modern dance]. Budapest: Zeneműkiadó Vállalat, 1970.
   Includes a discussion of a performance of *The Miraculous Mandarin.*

KOVÁCS, Zoltán. "'Heiliger Dankgesang in der lydischen Tonart' und 'Adagio   **158**
   religioso'," in: József UJFALUSSY & János BREUER, eds, *International
   Musicological Conference in Commemoration of Béla Bartók 1971*
   (Budapest: Editio Musica, 1972), 25-30.

KOZAK, Hanna Barbara. *Koncerty fortepianowe Béli Bartóka [Piano concertos*   **159**
   of Béla Bartók]. M.A. Thesis: University of Warsaw, 1969.

KRAMER, Jonathan. "The Fibonacci Series in Twentieth-Century Music,"   **160**
   Journal of Music Theory XVII/1 (Spring 1973), 110-48.
   Includes a discussion of Lendvai's theories on Bartók's music.

KRONES, Hartmut. "Stilkundliche Betrachtungen auf soziologischer Basis,   **161**
   insbesondere dargestellt am Beispiel Béla Bartók," in: József UJFALUSSY
   & János BREUER, eds, *International Musicological Conference in Commemoration of Béla Bartók 1971* (Budapest: Editio Musica, 1972), 83-88.

KROÓ, György. "Monothematik und Dramaturgie in Bartóks Bühnenwerken,"   **162**
   Studia Musicologica V/1-4 (1963), 449-67.

KROÓ, György. "Adatok 'A kékszakállú herceg vára' keletkezéstörténetéhez   **163**
   [On the genesis of *Bluebeard's Castle*]," in: Ferenc BÓNIS, ed, *Magyar
   Zenetörténeti Tanulmányok . . .* [Szabolcsi Festschrift], 333-58. See:
   BÓNIS, No. **36**.

KROÓ, György. "Neostvareni Bartokovi planovi [Bartók's unrealized plans],"   **164**
   Zvuk No. 100 (1969), 546-57.

KROÓ, György. "Bartók Concert in New York on July 2, 1944," *Studia*   **165**
   Musicologica XI/1-4 (1969), 253-57.

KROÓ, György. "Unrealized Plans and Ideas for Projects by Bartók," *Studia*   **166**
   Musicologica XII/1-4 (1970), 11-27.

KROÓ, György. *Bartók Kalauz [A Guide to Bartók].* Budapest: Zeneműkiadó   **166a**
   Vállalat, 1971. (English translation published in 1974 by Corvina, Budapest.)

167   KROÓ, György. "On the Origin of the Wooden Prince," in: József UJFALUSSY
      & János BREUER, eds, *International Musicological Conference in Commemo-
      ration of Béla Bartók 1971* (Budapest: Editio Musica, 1972), 97-101.

168   KUCKERTZ, Josef. *Gestaltvariation in den von Bartók gesammelten
      rumänischen Colinden.* Regensburg: Gustav Bosse, 1963. (*Kölner
      Beiträge zur Musikforschung,* 23.)

169   LAMMERS, Joseph E. *Patterns of Change Under Identity in Shorter Piano
      Works by Béla Bartók.* Ph.D. Dissertation: Florida State University, 1971.
      237 pp. UM: 72-13,528. DA: XXXII/11 (May 1972), 6478-79-A.

170   LÁSZLÓ, Ferenc, ed. *Bartók-Könyv 1970-1971 [Bartók volume 1970-1971].*
      Bucharest: Kriterion Könyvkiadó, 1971.

      A collection of essays, poems, remembrances, etc., by Rumanian and Hungarian
      authors, published as part of the 1970-1971 Rumanian Bartók Commemoration.

171   LENDVAI, Ernő. *Bartók dramaturgiája [Bartók's dramaturgy].* Budapest:
      Zeneműkiadó Vállalat, 1964.

172   LENDVAI Ernő. "Bartók und der Goldene Schnitt," *Österreichische
      Musikzeitschrift* XXI/11 (Nov 1966), 607-14.

173   LENDVAI, Ernő. "Bartók vonósnégyesei [Bartók's string quartets]," *Muzsika*
      X/9 (Sep 1967), 25-28; X/10 (Oct 1967), 39-42; X/11 (Nov 1967),
      35-38; X/12 (Dec 1967), 26-30; XI/1 (Jan 1968), 34-37; XI/2 (Feb
      1968), 16-19.

174   LENDVAI, Ernő. "Bartók húros ütőhangszeres zenéjének néhány értelmezési
      problémájáról [On some analytical problems in Bartók's *Music for
      Strings, Percussion, and Celesta*]," *Muzsika* XI/7 (July 1968), 24-28.

175   LENDVAI, Ernő. "Bartók négy zenekari darabjáról [On Bartók's *Four Pieces
      for Orchestra*]," *Muzsika* XII/7 (July 1969), 13-18.

176   LENDVAI, Ernő. "Bartók Divertimentójáról [On Bartók's *Divertimento*],"
      Muzsika XII/9 (Sep 1969), 27-30.

177   LENDVAI, Ernő. "Bartók Hegedűversenyéről [Bartók's *Violin Concerto*],"
      Muzsika XII/10 (Oct 1969), 28-32; XII/11 (Nov 1969), 20-22.

178   LENDVAI, Ernő. "Bartók—Két Kép [Bartók—*Two Pictures*]," *Muzsika*
      XII/12 (Dec 1969), 35-37.

LENDVAI, Ernő. "Über die Formkonzeption Bartóks," *Studia Musicologica* XI/1-4 (1969), 271-80.   **179**

LENDVAI, Ernő. "Bartók—Két Portré [Bartók—*Two Portraits*]," *Muzsika* XIII/2 (Feb 1970), 24-26.   **180**

LENDVAI, Ernő. *Béla Bartók: An Analysis of his Music.* London: Kahn & Averill, 1971.   **181**
Introduction by Alan Bush.

LESZNAI, Lajos. "Realistische Ausdrucksmittel in der Musik Béla Bartóks," *Studia Musicologica* V/1-4 (1963), 469-79.   **182**

LESZNAI, Lajos. *Bartók*, English translation by Percy Young. London: J. M. Dent, 1973. (*Master Musicians Series.*)   **183**

LIEBNER, János. "Ein verschollenes Werk von Béla Bartók," *Gesellschaft für Musikforschung; Bericht über den Internationalen Musikwissenschaftlichen Kongress Kassel 1962* (Kassel: Bärenreiter, 1963), 315-17.   **184**

LIEBNER, János. "Ein wiederentdecktes Werk Béla Bartók," *Beiträge zur Musikwissenschaft* VI/3 (1964), 243-44.   **185**

LITTLE, Jean. *Architectonic Levels of Rhythmic Organization in Selected Twentieth-Century Music.* Ph.D. Dissertation: Indiana University, 1971. 419 pp. UM: 72-6802. DA: XXXII/8 (Feb 1972), 4651-A.   **186**
Includes a discussion of Bartók's *Violin Concerto* (1937/38).

LOEB van ZUILENBURG, Paul E. O. F. *A Study of Béla Bartók's "Mikrokosmos" with Respect to Formal Analysis, Compositional Techniques, Piano-Technical and Piano-Pedagogical Aspects.* Ph.D. Dissertation: University of Witswatersrand (Johannesburg), 1969. 934 pp.   **187**

LOSSAU, Günter. "Bartóks Pantomime 'Der wunderbare Mandarin'," *Melos* XXXIII/6 (June 1966), 173-77.   **188**

LOWMAN, Edward A. "Some Striking Proportions in the Music of Béla Bartók," *Fibonacci Quarterly* IX/5 (Dec 1971), 527-28, 536-37.   **189**

LUKÁCS, György. "Bartók und die ungarische Kultur," in: József UJFALUSSY & János BREUER, eds, *International Musicological Conference in Commemoration of Béla Bartók 1971* (Budapest: Editio Musica, 1972), 11-12.   **190**

LÜKŐ, Gábor. "Bartók tudományos öröksége [Bartók's scientific legacy]," *Kortárs* XIV/9 (Sep 1970), 1378-83.   **191**

192 MARI, Pierrette. *Bartók*. Paris: Hachette, 1970.

193 MARKOWSKI, Liesel. "Béla Bartók—ein grosser Humanist und Demokrat," *Musik und Gesellschaft* XX/9 (Sep 1970), 577-85.

194 MARÓTHY, János. "Új szovjet Bartók-kutatások [New Soviet Bartók investigation]," *Muzsika* XIV/1 (Jan 1971), 41-43.

195 MARTYNOV, Ivan I. *Béla Bartók*. Moscow: Sovetsky kompozitur, 1968.

   A revised edition of the original 1956 publication.

196 MARTYNOV, Ivan I. "Quelques pensées sur Bartók," in: József UJFALUSSY & János BREUER, eds, *International Musicological Conference in Commemoration of Béla Bartók 1971* (Budapest: Editio Musica, 1972), 107-10.

197 MASON, Colin. "Bartók's Scherzo for Piano and Orchestra," *Tempo* No. 65 (Summer 1963), 10-13.

198 MEYER, John A. "Bartók and Popularity," *Studies in Music* [Australia] III (1969), 70-73.

199 MEYER, John A. "Beethoven and Bartók—A Structural Parallel," *The Music Review* XXXI/4 (Nov 1970), 315-21.

200 MEYER, Peter. *Béla Bartók's Ady-Lieder, Op. 16*. Winterthur: P. G. Keller, 1965.

   Originally a Ph.D. Dissertation: University of Zürich, 1965. 95 pp.

201 MIHÁLY, András. "Metrika Bartók IV. vonósnégyesének II. tételében [Metrics in the second movement of Bartók's *String Quartet No. 4*]," *Muzsika* X/9 (Sep 1967), 18-24; X/10 (Oct 1967), 34-38; X/12 (Dec 1967), 35-43.

202 MILA, Massimo. "La Natura e il mistero nell'arte di Béla Bartók," *Chigiana* XXII [New Series 2] (1965), 147-68.

   A revised and expanded version of an article of the same title in *La Rassegna Musicale* XXI/2 (Apr 1951), 95-105.

203 MILA, Massimo, & Fred K. PRIEBERG. "Bartók—Webern 25 Years Later: Their Place in Today's Music," *The World of Music* XXI/3 (1970), 32-48.

MOLNÁR, Antal. "Die Bedeutung der neuen Osteuropäischen Musik," in: 204
József UJFALUSSY & János BREUER, eds, *International Musicological Conference in Commemoration of Béla Bartók 1971* (Budapest: Editio Musica, 1972), 159-61.

MONELLE, Raymond. "Notes on Bartók's Fourth Quartet," *The Music 205 Review* XXIX/2 (May 1968), 123-29.

MONELLE, Raymond. "Bartók's Imagination in the Later Quartets," *The 206 Music Review* XXXI/1 (Feb 1970), 70-81.

MORGAN, Robert P. "Bartók's Extraordinary Quartets," *High Fidelity* XX/9 207 (Sep 1970), 58-61.

MÓZI, Alexander. "Po stopách Bélu Bartóka v Drážovciach [Following traces 208 of Béla Bartók in Drážovce]," *Slovenská Hudba* XV/3-4 (1971), 110-17.

NEST'EV, Izrail'. "Béla Bartók v Rossii [Béla Bartók in Russia]," *Studia 209 Musicologica* V/1-4 (1963), 481-90.

NEST'EV, Izrail'. "Mirovozzrenie i estetika [World outlook and aesthetics]," 210 *Sovetskaya Muzyka* XXIX/4 (Apr 1965), 97-105.

NEST'EV, Izrail'. "Iz nablyudenii nad stilem [Observations on style]," 211 *Sovetskaya Muzyka* XXIX/7 (July 1965), 115-23.

NEST'EV, Izrail'. *Béla Bartók, zhizn' i tvorchestvo [Béla Bartók, life and 212 works]*. Moscow: Muzyka, 1969.

NEST'EV, Izrail'. "Prokofiev and Bartók: Some Parallels," in: József 213 UJFALUSSY & János BREUER, eds, *International Musicological Conference in Commemoration of Béla Bartók 1971* (Budapest: Editio Musica, 1972), 137-43.

NICOLA, Ioan R. "Colinda vînătorilor metamorfozati în cerbi [The Christmas 214 carol of the hunters transformed into stags]," *Lucrări di muzicologie* IV (1968), 59-86.

NORDWALL, Ove. "Béla Bartók och den moderna musiken [Béla Bartók and 215 modern music]," *Nutida Musik* VII/2 (1964), 1.

NORDWALL, Ove. "The Original Version of Bartók's Sonata for Solo Violin," 216 *Tempo* No. 74 (Autumn 1965), 2-4.

217   NORDWALL, Ove. "Béla Bartók and Modern Music," *Studia Musicologica* IX/3-4 (1967), 265-80.

218   OGDON, John. "Bartók's Mikrokosmos," *Tempo* No. 65 (Summer 1963), 2-4.

219   OLSVAI, Imre. "West Hungarian (Trans-Danubian) Characteristic Features in Bartók's Works ," *Studia Musicologica* XI/1-4 (1969), 253-57.

220   ORBÁN, László. "Bartók's Message Has Never Been More Topical Than Today," in: József UJFALUSSY & János BREUER, eds, *International Musicologicaι Conference in Commemoration of Béla Bartók 1971* (Budapest: Editio Musica, 1972), 9-10.

OVÁRY, Zoltán. See: ROGERS, No. **227**.

221   PÁLOVÁ-VRBONÁ, Zuzana. *Béla Bartók 1881-1945. Zivet a dilo [Béla Bartók 1881-1945. Life and works]*. Prague: Státni Hudební Vydavatelství, 1963. (*Hudební profily*, 9.)

222   PERLE, George. *The String Quartets of Béla Bartók*. NY: Dover, 1967.

A pamphlet accompanying the Dover phonodiscs HCR 5272-5274 and HCR-ST 7272-7274 containing the six quartets as performed by the Tatrai Quartet.

223   PETERSEN, Peter. *Die Tonalität im Instrumentalschaffen von Béla Bartók*. Hamburg: Verlag der Musikalienhandlung, 1971.

224   PETROV, Stojan. "Béla Bartók o bolgarskaya musikal'naya kultura [Béla Bartók and the Bulgarian music culture] ," *Studia Musicologica* V/1-4 (1963), 491-99.

225   PFROGNER, Hermann. "Hat Diatonik Zukunft?," *Musica* XVII/4 (July-Aug 1963), 146-55.

Refers to Bartók's harmony as derived from folk sources.

PRIEBERG, Fred K. See: MILA, No. **203**.

226   PÜTZ, Werner. *Studien zum Streichquartettschaffen bei Hindemith, Bartók, Schönberg, und Webern*. Regensburg: Gustav Bosse, 1968. (*Kölner Beiträge zur Musikforschung*, 36.)

281

RAJECZKY, Benjámin. (1963) See: KERÉNYI, No. 150.

RAJECZKY, Benjámin, & Bence SZABOLCSI, eds. (1964) See: BARTÓK,
No. 8.

ROGERS, Michael, & Zoltán OVÁRY. "Béla Bartók in the U.S.S.R. in 1929,"   227
MLA Notes XXIX/3 (Mar 1973), 416-25.

RUDZIŃSKI, Witold. *Warsztat kompozitorski Béla Bartóka [Béla Bartók's*   228
compositional style]. Krakow: Polskie Wydawnictwo Muzyczne, 1964.

SÁNDOR, György. "Béla Bartók—Budapest and Afterwards," *High Fidelity/*   229
Musical America XX/9 (Sep 1970), MA-13.

SANNEMÜLLER, Gerd. "Béla Bartóks Suite Opus 14: Stil- und Werkanalyse,"   230
Schweizerische Musikzeitung CV/1 (Jan-Feb 1965), 10-20.

SAYGUN, Ahmed Adnan. "Quelques réflexions sur certaines affinités des   231
musiques folkloriques turque et hongroise," *Studia Musicologica* V/1-4
(1963), 515-24.

SCHOLLUM, Robert. "Stilkundliche Bemerkungen zu Werken Bartóks und   232
der 2 Wiener Schule," in: József UJFALUSSY & János BREUER, eds,
*International Musicological Conference in Commemoration of Béla
Bartók 1971* (Budapest: Editio Musica, 1972), 77-82.

SCHRODER, Charles F. *Final Period of Mozart, Beethoven, and Bartók.*   233
Ph.D. Dissertation: University of Iowa, 1965. 520 pp. UM: 65-11,656.
DA: XXVI/6 (Dec 1965), 3397-A.

SCHWINGER, Wolfram. "Béla Bartóks Streichquartette," *Musica* XXVII/1-6   234
(Jan-Dec 1973), 13-18; 133-37; 245-52; 350-55; 445-51; 569-74.

Sesja Bartókowska [The Bartók session]. Zeszyta Naukowe. Pánstwowa   235
Wyzsza Szkola Muzyczna w Warszawie 2. Warszawa: Pánstwowa Wyzsza
Szkola Muzyczna, 1967.

Papers given at a Bartók conference at the State College of Music in Warsaw in
December, 1966.

SIDOTI, Raymond Benjamin. *The Violin Sonatas of Béla Bartók: An Epitome*   236
of the Composer's Development. D.M.A. Dissertation: Ohio State University,
1972. 55 pp. UM: 72-26,963. DA: XXXIII/4 (Oct 1972), 1773-A.

237 SKARBOWSKI, Jerzy. "O problemach interpretacyjnych utworów Béla
     Bartóka [The problem of interpretation in the works of Béla Bartók],"
     Ruch Muzyczny XII/7 (Apr 1968), 5-7.

     SMÂNTÂNESCU, D. See: CHIRA, No. **48**.

238 SOMFAI, László. "Nichtvertonte Libretti im Nachlass und andere
     Bühnenpläne Bartóks," *Documenta Bartókiana* II (1965), 28-52.

     SOMFAI, László. (1968) See: SZABOLCSI, No. **265**.

239 SOMFAI, László. "Bartók als Interpret," *Beiträge 1968-69* (Kassel: Bärenreiter,
     1969), 41-45.

240 SOMFAI, László. "'Per finire': Some Aspects of the Finale in Bartók's Cyclic
     Form," *Studia Musicologica* XI/1-4 (1969), 391-408.

241 SOMFAI, László. "Bartók egynemű kórusainak szövegforrásáról [On the sources
     of Bartók's male and female choruses]," in: Ferenc BÓNIS, ed, *Magyar
     Zenetörténeti Tanulmányok . . .* [Szabolcsi Festschrift], 359-76.
     See: BÓNIS, No. **36**.

242 SOMFAI, László. "Eine Erklärung Bartóks aus dem Jahre 1938," *Documenta
     Bartókiana* IV (1970), 148-64.

243 SOMFAI, László. "Bartók 2. Hegedűrapszódiájának rutén epizódja [A
     Ruthenian episode in Bartók's *Second Rhapsody for Violin*]," *Muzsika*
     XIV/3 (Mar 1971), 1-3.

244 SOMFAI, László. "Bartók 5. vonósnégyese: A zeneszerző kiadatlan formai
     analízise [Bartók's *Fifth Quartet:* The composer's unpublished formal
     analysis]," *Muzsika* XIV/12 (Dec 1971), 26-28.

245 SOMFAI, László. "A Characteristic Culmination Point in Bartók's Instrumental
     Forms," in: József UJFALUSSY & János BREUER, eds, *International
     Musicological Conference in Commemoration of Béla Bartók 1971*
     (Budapest: Editio Musica, 1972), 53-64.

246 SPINOSA, Frank. *Beethoven and Bartók: A Comparative Study of Motivic
     Techniques in the late Beethoven Quartets and the Six String Quartets
     of Béla Bartók.* D.M.A. Dissertation: University of Illinois, 1969. 214 pp.
     UM: 70-13,499. DA: XXXI/2 (Aug 1970), 791-A.

STEFANI, Gino. "Tritono e forma-arco nel 'Quinto Quartetto' di Bartók," 247
Nuova Rivista Musicale Italiana V/5 (Sep-Oct 1971), 847-60.

STEVENS, Halsey. *The Life and Music of Béla Bartók*, [2nd ed]. NY: 248
Oxford University Press, 1964. (Originally issued in 1953.)

STEVENS, Halsey. "Some 'Unknown' Works of Bartók," *The Musical* 249
Quarterly LII/1 (Jan 1966), 37-55.

STEVENS, Halsey. "The Sources of Bartók's Rhapsody for Violoncello and 250
Piano," in: József UJFALUSSY & János BREUER, eds, *International*
Musicological Conference in Commemoration of Béla Bartók 1971
(Budapest: Editio Musica, 1972), 65-76.

STUCKENSCHMIDT, Hans Heinz. "Béla Bartók und sein schöpferisches Werk 251
für die moderne Musik," *Universitas* [Stuttgart] XXVI/10 (Oct 1971),
1031-38.

SUCHOFF, Benjamin. "Some Observations on Bartók's Third Piano Concerto," 252
Tempo No. 65 (Summer 1963), 8-10.

SUCHOFF, Benjamin, ed. (1967-) See: BARTÓK, No. **13**.

SUCHOFF, Benjamin. "Computer Applications to Bartók's Serbo-Croatian 253
Material," *Tempo* No. 80 (Spring 1967), 15-19.

SUCHOFF, Benjamin. "Structure and Concept in Bartók's Sixth Quartet," 254
Tempo No. 83 (Winter 1967-68), 2-11.

SUCHOFF, Benjamin. "Computerized Folk Song Research and the Problems 255
of Variants," *Computers and the Humanities* II/4 (1968), 155-58.

SUCHOFF, Benjamin. "Some Problems in Computer-Oriented Bartókian 256
Ethnomusicology," *Ethnomusicology* XIII/3 (Sep 1969), 489-97.

SUCHOFF, Benjamin. "Aplicarea calculatoarelor electronice la 257
etnomuzicologia bartokiană [The use of the computer in Bartókian
ethnomusicology]," *Muzica* XX/11 (Nov 1970), 10-14.

SUCHOFF, Benjamin. "The Computer and Bartók Research in America," 258
Journal of Research in Music Education XIX/1 (Spring 1971), 3-16.

SUCHOFF, Benjamin. "Bartók's Rumanian Folk Music Publication," 259
Ethnomusicology XV/2 (May 1971), 220-30.

260 SUCHOFF, Benjamin. *Guide to Bartók's Mikrokosmos*, [revised ed]. London: Boosey & Hawkes, 1971. (Originally issued in 1956.)

261 SUCHOFF, Benjamin. "Béla Bartók: Man of Letters," in: József UJFALUSSY & János BREUER, eds, *International Musicological Conference in Commemoration of Béla Bartók 1971* (Budapest: Editio Musica, 1972), 89-96. (Article also in *Tempo* No. 102 [1972], 10-16.)

262 SUCHOFF, Benjamin. "The Musical Present as History to Be: Sources and Documents (Béla Bartók)," *Proceedings of the American Society of University Composers, April, 1970* No. 5 (1972), 124-28.
     Indicates the current status of the New York Bartók Archives.

263 SUCHOFF, Benjamin. "Bartók and Serbo-Croatian Folk Music," *The Musical Quarterly* LVIII/4 (Oct 1972), 557-71.

     SUCHOFF, Benjamin, ed & comp. (in progress) See: BARTÓK, No. **21**.

264 SZABOLCSI, Bence. "Mensch und Natur in Bartóks Geisteswelt," *Studia Musicologica* V/1-4 (1963), 525-39.

     SZABOLCSI, Bence, & Benjámin RAJECZKY, eds. (1964) See: BARTÓK, No. **8**.

     SZABOLCSI, Bence, & Ferenc BÓNIS, eds. (1964) See: BÓNIS, Nos. **31** & **32**.

265 SZABOLCSI, Bence. *Béla Bartók*, [2nd ed]. Leipzig: Philipp Reclam, 1968. (Auswahl und Erläuterungen der Abbildungen: Ferenc BÓNIS; Auswahl der Briefe Bartóks: János DEMÉNY; Zusammenstellung des Schallplattenverzeichnises: László SOMFAI). (Originally issued in 1961.)

266 SZABOLCSI, Bence, ed. *Bartók: sa vie et son oeuvre*, [2nd ed]. Budapest: Corvina Press; Paris: Boosey & Hawkes, 1968. (Originally issued in 1956.)

267 SZABOLCSI, Bence. "Über metrische Melodien in Beethovens und Bartóks Musik," in: Heinz WEGENER, ed, *Musa—Mens—Musici. Im Gedenken an Walther Vetter* (Leipzig: VEB Deutscher Verlag für Musik, 1969), 255-58.

268 SZABOLCSI, Bence. "Bartók and World Literature," in: József UJFALUSSY & János BREUER, eds, *International Musicological Conference in Commemoration of Béla Bartók 1971* (Budapest: Editio Musica, 1972), 103-6.

SZABOLCSI, Bence, ed. *Bartók: Weg und Werk–Schriften und Briefe*,   269
[2nd ed]. Kassel: Bärenreiter; München: Deutscher Taschenbuch-
Verlag, 1972. (Originally issued in 1957.)

SZABOLCSI, Bence, ed. (1972) See: BARTÓK, No. 20.

SZEGŐ, Júlia. *Bartók Béla élete [The life of Béla Bartók]*. Bucharest: 270
Editura Tineretului, 1964.

SZÉKELY, Júlia. *Elindultam szép hazámból. Bartók Béla élete [I left my*   271
country. The life of Béla Bartók]. Budapest: Móra Ferenc Könyvkiadó, 1965.

SZELÉNYI, István. "Előfutár, vagy valóraváltó? Stiluskritikai kisérlet Liszt   272
alkotókorszakaival kapcsolatban [Forerunner or accomplisher? A style-
critical analysis of various creative periods of Liszt]," *Magyar Zene* VIII/3
(June 1967), 231-41.
Discusses Liszt's influence on selected works by Bartók.

SZELÉNYI, István. "Bartók und Modalität," in: József UJFALUSSY & János   273
BREUER, eds, *International Musicological Conference in Commemoration
of Béla Bartók 1971* (Budapest: Editio Musica, 1972), 169-80.

SZEPLAKI, Joseph. See: WALSH, No. 302.

SZIGETI, József. Beszélő húrok [Speaking strings]. Budapest: Zeneműkiadó   274
Vállalat, 1965.
Contains remembrances of Bartók.

SZŐLLŐSY, András, ed. See: BARTÓK, No. 12.

TAWASTSTJERNA, Erik. "Sibelius und Bartók: einige Parallelen," in: József   275
UJFALUSSY & János BREUER, eds, *International Musicological
Conference in Commemoration of Béla Bartók 1971* (Budapest: Editio
Musica, 1972), 121-35.

THOMASON, Leta N. *Structural Significance of the Motive in the String   276
Quartets of Béla Bartók*. Ph.D. Dissertation: Michigan State University,
1965. 395 pp. UM: 66-6876. DA: XXVII/3 (Sep 1966), 793-4-A.

THOMPSON, Kenneth L. "First Performance?" *The Musical Times* CIX/[No.   277
1508] (Oct 1968), 914-15.
Discusses the *Concerto for Two Pianos and Percussion*.

278   TÓTH, Margit. "Egy népi énekes dallamainak változása Bartók óta [Variations in a folk singer's melodies since Bartók]," in: Ferenc BÓNIS, ed, *Magyar Zenetörténeti Tanulmányok* . . . [Szabolcsi Festschrift], 377-90. See: BÓNIS, No. **36**.

279   TRAIMER, Roswitha. *Béla Bartóks Kompositionstechnik, dargestellt an seinen sechs Streichquartetten*, [3rd ed]. Regensburg: Gustav Bosse, 1964. (*Forschungsbeiträge zur Musikwissenschaft*, 3.) (Originally issued in 1956.)

280   TRAVIS, Roy. "Tonal Coherence in the First Movement of Bartók's Fourth String Quartet," *Music Forum* II (1970), 298-371.

281   UJFALUSSY, József. "Einige inhaltliche Fragen der Brückensymmetrie in Bartóks Werken," *Studia Musicologica* V/1-4 (1963), 541-47.

282   UJFALUSSY, József, ed. "Béla Bartók Kinderjahre: aus den Tagebuchblättern seiner Mutter . . .," *Österreichische Musikzeitschrift* XX/9 (Sep 1965), 461-66.

       Taken from his *Bartók breviárium* (Budapest: Zeneműkiadó Vállalat, 1958).

283   UJFALUSSY, József. "Az Allegro Barbaro harmóniai alapgondolata és Bartók hangsorai [Basic harmonic ideas of the *Allegro Barbaro* and Bartók's Scales]," in: Ferenc BÓNIS, ed, *Magyar Zenetörténeti Tanulmányok* . . . [Szabolcsi Festschrift], 323-32. See: BÓNIS, No. **36**.

284   UJFALUSSY, József. *Bartók Béla*, [2nd ed]. Budapest: Gondolat, 1970. 2 vols. (Originally issued in 1965.)

285   UJFALUSSY, József. "Is Bartók's Concerto for Violin Really His Second?," *Studia Musicologica* XIII/1-4 (1971), 355-56.

286   UJFALUSSY, József. "Gemeinsame Stilschicht in Bartóks und Kodálys Kunst," in: József UJFALUSSY & János BREUER, eds, *International Musicological Conference in Commemoration of Béla Bartók 1971* (Budapest: Editio Musica, 1972), 155-57.

287   UJFALUSSY, József, & János BREUER, eds. *International Musicological Conference in Commemoration of Béla Bartók 1971*. Budapest: Editio Musica, 1972.

       Contains papers by the following: Ferenc BÓNIS [See: No. **37**], János BREUER [See: No. **43**], Ladislav BURLAS [See: No. **45**], János DEMÉNY [See: No. **65**],

Stoyan DJOUDJEFF [See: No. **94**], Oskár ELSCHEK [See: No. **99**], Erich KAPST [See: No. **141**], János KÁRPÁTI [See: No. **147**], Zoltán KOVÁCS [See: No. **158**], Hartmut KRONES [See: No. **161**], György KROÓ [See: No. **167**], György LUKÁCS [See: No. **190**], Ivan I. MARTYNOV [See: No. **196**], Antal MOLNÁR [See: No. **204**], Izrail' NEST'EV [See: No. **213**], László ORBÁN [See: No. **220**], Robert SCHOLLUM [See: No. **232**], László SOMFAI [See: No. **245**], Halsey STEVENS [See: No. **250**], Benjamin SUCHOFF [See: No. **261**], Bence SZABOLCSI [See: No. **268**], István SZELÉNYI [See: No. **273**], Erik TAWASTSTJERNA [See: No. **275**], József UJFALUSSY [See: No. **286**], Jaroslav VOLEK [See: No. **299**], and Dénes ZOLTAI [See: No. **315**].

UJFALUSSY, József. *Béla Bartók*, English translation by Ruth Pataki, **288**
translation revised by Elisabeth West. Budapest: Corvina Press, 1971;
Boston: Crescendo, 1972.

VANCEA, Zeno. "Einige Beiträge über das erste Manuskript der Colinda- **289**
Sammlung von Béla Bartók und über seine einschlägigen Briefe an
Constantin Brăiloiu," *Studia Musicologica* V/1-4 (1963), 549-56.

VANCEA, Zeno. "Béla Bartók. Un Mare Muzician al Veacului Nostra [Béla **290**
Bartók. A great musician of our century]," *Muzica* XX/11 (Nov 1970),
1-3.

VARGYAS, Lajos. "Bartók's Melodies in the Style of Folk Songs," *Journal of* **291**
the International Folk Music Council XVI (1964), 30-34.

VICOL, Adrian. "Premise teoretice la o tipologie muzicală a colinelor **292**
românesti [Theoretical premises for a musical typology of the Rumanian
colinde]," *Revista de etnografie şi folclor* XV/1 (1970), 63-71.

A critique of Bartók's classification system of Rumanian colinde, and suggestions
for a new classification.

VINTON, John. "The Case of the 'Miraculous Mandarin'," *The Musical* **293**
Quarterly L/1 (Jan 1964), 1-17.

VINTON, John. "New Light on Bartók's Sixth Quartet," *The Music Review* **294**
XXV/3 (Aug 1964), 224-38.

VINTON, John. "Towards a Chronology of the 'Mikrokosmos'," *Studia* **295**
Musicologica VIII/1-4 (1966), 41-69.

VINTON, John. "Bartók on His Music," *Journal of the American Musicological* **296**
Society XIX/2 (Summer 1966), 232-43.

297   VINTON, John. "Hints to the Printers from Bartók," *Music and Letters* XLIX/3 (July 1968), 224-30.

298   VOLEK, Jaroslav. "Über einige interessante Beziehung zwischen thematischer Arbeit und Instrumentation in Bartóks Werk 'Concerto für Orchester'," *Studia Musicologica* V/1-4 (1963), 557-86.

299   VOLEK, Jaroslav. "Bartók—Determination of a Period," in: József UJFALUSSY & János BREUER, eds, *International Musicological Conference in Commemoration of Béla Bartók 1971* (Budapest: Editio Musica, 1972), 19-24.

300   VOLLY, István. "Bartók és Serly [Bartók and Serly]," *Muzsika* VII/1 (Jan 1964), 15-18.

301   WALDBAUER, Iván. "Bartók's First Piano Concerto: A Publication History," *The Musical Quarterly* LI/2 (Apr 1965), 336-44.

302   WALSH, Connie, & Joseph SZEPLAKI. *Bibliography on Béla Bartók, Available in the Ohio University Main and Music Library, Athens, Ohio.* Athens: Ohio University, [c.1970].

    Mimeograph item available from the Ohio University Music Librarian. Includes "Bartók the Teacher," a personal experience by Christine Ahrendt.

WEBER, Edith. See: BARTHA, No. 5.

WEGENER, Heinz. See: SZABOLCSI, No. 267.

303   WEISS, Günter. *Die frühe Schaffensentwicklung Béla Bartóks im Lichte westlicher und östlicher Traditionen.* Ph.D. Dissertation: Universität Erlangen-Nürnberg, 1971.

304   WEISSMANN, John (János) S. "On Some Problems of Bartók Research in Connection with Bartók's Biography," *Studia Musicologica* V/1-4 (1963), 587-96.

305   WESOLOWSKI, Franciszek, ed. *Sesja Bartókowska [The Bartók session].* Państwowa Wyzsza Szkola Muzyczna w Lodzi. Zeszyt Naukowy 1. Lodz: Państwowa Wyzsza Szkola Muzyczna, 1969.

    Papers given at a Bartók conference at the State College of Music in Lodz, Poland in May, 1966.

306   WHITALL, Arnold. "Bartók's Second String Quartet," *The Music Review* XXXII/3 (Aug 1971), 265-70.

WINROW, Barbara. "Allegretto con indifferenza: A Study of the 'Barrel   307
Organ' Episode in Bartók's Fifth Quartet," *The Music Review* XXXII/2
(May 1971), 102-6.

WINTER, Barbara. "Bartók w Polsce [Bartók in Poland in the years 1927-   308
1939]," *Ruch Muzyczny* IX/18 (1965), 10-11.

WOLFF, Helmuth Christian. "Zum Kompositionsstil Béla Bartóks," *Beiträge*   309
zur Musikwissenschaft VII/3-4 (1965), 218-24.

WÖRNER, Karl H. "Die sieben Schlüssel. Bartóks operneinakter, 'Herzog   310
Blaubarts Burg'," in: Karl H. WÖRNER, *Die Musik der Geistesgeschichte;*
Studien zur Situation der Jahre um 1910 (Bonn: H. Bouvier, 1970), 119-
30. (*Abhandlungen zur Kunst-, Musik-, und Literaturwissenschaft,* 92.)

ZASLAW, Neal, ed.   See: DERI, No. 67.

ZIEGLER, Márta. "Bartóks Reise nach Biskra," *Documenta Bartókiana* II   311
(1965), 9-17.

ZIEGLER, Márta. "Über Béla Bartók," *Documenta Bartókiana* IV (1970),   312
173-79.

ZIELIŃSKI, Tadeusz A. *Bartók.* Krakow: Polskie Wydawnictwo Muzyczne,   313
1969.

ZIELIŃSKI, Tadeusz A. *Bartók.* German translation by Bruno Heinrich.   313a
Zürich & Freiburg: Atlantis, 1973.

ZOLTAI, Dénes. "Bartók nem alkuszik [Bartók does not compromise],"   314
Világosság XI/11 (Nov 1970), 663-68.

ZOLTAI, Dénes. "Bartók in Sicht der Frankfurter Schule," in: József   315
UJFALUSSY & János BREUER, eds, *International Musicological*
Conference in Commemoration of Béla Bartók 1971 (Budapest:
Editio Musica, 1972), 13-17.

GENERAL INDEX

294

INDEX OF BARTÓK'S MUSIC REFERRED TO IN THIS VOLUME